Hot Topics
for MRCGP
and
General Practitioners
2nd Edition

PASTEST
Dedicated to your success

Hot Topics
for MRCGP
and
General Practitioners
2nd Edition

PASTEST

Hot Topics
for MRCGP
and
General Practitioners
2nd Edition

Louise R Newson
BSc (Hons) MBChB (Hons) MRCP MRCGP
General Practitioner
West Midlands

Ash M Patel
MBChB MRCGP DRCOG DFFP
General Practitioner
Cheshire

PASTEST
Dedicated to your success

© 2002 PASTEST Ltd
Egerton Court
Parkgate Estate
Knutsford
Cheshire
Telephone: 01565 752000

First edition published in 2001 by PasTest Ltd
Second edition first published in 2002 by PasTest Ltd

ISBN 1 901198 82 0

A catalogue record for this book is available from the British Library.

The information contained within this book was obtained by the authors from reliable sources. However, while every effort has been made to ensure its accuracy, no responsibilty for loss, damage or injury occasioned to any person acting or refraining from action as a result of information contained herein can be accepted by the publishers or authors.

PasTest Revision Books and Intensive Courses

PasTest has been established in the field of postgraduate medical education since 1972, providing revision books and intensive study courses for doctors preparing for their professional examinations.
Books and courses are available for the following specialties:
MRCGP, MRCP Part 1 and Part 2, MRCPCH Part 1 and Part 2, MRCS, MRCOG, DRCOG, MRCPsych, DCH, FRCA and PLAB.

For further details contact:
PasTest, Freepost, Knutsford, Cheshire WA16 7BR
Tel: 01565 752000   Fax: 01565 650264
Email: enquiries@pastest.co.uk   Web site: www.pastest.co.uk

Typeset by Breeze Ltd, Manchester.
Printed and bound in the UK by Bell and Bain Ltd, Glasgow.

CONTENTS

Contents

Contents

Specialist GPs
Nurse practitioners
Outreach clinics
Practice formulary
Computer-generated repeat prescriptions
Post 'Shipman', what are the long-term effects?

General Medical Council
Complaints
Confidentiality
Consent
Medical negligence
Guidelines

Advance directives
End-of-life decisions

Refugees
Recent advances in ethics

Non-attendance
Telephone consultations
Consultation models

FOREWORD

A comprehensive and up to date awareness of the current evidence is essential for success in the MRCGP examination. Time is always at a premium and this excellent book provides a superb overview that highlights the key points, saving the reader time for that extra bit of revision! The authors have tried to be as topical as possible, with a second edition quickly following the first.

The content is not only useful to examination candidates but will also be valuable to trainers, course organisers and other doctors who want a succinct review of the main areas of general practice.

John Sandars MSc FRCGP MRCP
Examiner MRCGP Examination

ACKNOWLEDGEMENTS

We would like to thank our families, especially Paul and Priti, for all their patience, support and tolerance over the past months.

We would also like to thank John Sandars for all his advice and encouragement in developing both editions of this book.

Finally, we thank the PasTest Publishing Department, as without their help and guidance, we would have never been able to create this book.

INTRODUCTION

Following the success of the first edition of the book, we have updated and revised it to produce this edition. We have also added some new chapters on important and topical subjects.

The MRCGP exam seems like a long way off at the beginning of the Registrar year, but unfortunately it soon comes round! The amount of information required to work as a General Practitioner and to pass the exam can appear to be completely daunting and overwhelming.

When we were both preparing for the MRCGP exam in Summer 2000 we were disappointed to find a relative paucity of books and courses to help with 'hot topic' revision. Numerous laborious hours were spent trawling through and summarising back issues of the BMJ and BJGP by ourselves and with other members of our VTS group, hoping it would help with our revision but we found it quite a fruitless exercise. It is also sometimes difficult to prioritise and become familiar with the more important, well-researched papers on a topic.

This book has been designed to help you improve your breadth and depth of knowledge of various important clinical and non-clinical subjects. Medicine is a dynamic specialty and information is constantly being updated and theories altered as more research is performed and attitudes of both doctors and patients change.

It is impossible to predict topics for future exams successfully and for that reason the subjects covered in this book will be as relevant as possible to present and future general practice. This book is not meant to be a comprehensive revision course for the exam; it is written to provide some guidance and ideas upon which to base your revision. It will also hopefully save you some time by reducing the need for reading and summarising all the journals.

Each of the hot topics are presented as a broad overview with reference to recent literature. References, useful reading material and relevant web sites are also included for each topic.

The reviews of various key 'hot topics' will be important for both the exam and also future careers in General Practice. The book will also be very useful for established GPs who would like a review of the current literature on a wide variety of topics.

WHY BOTHER WITH HOT TOPICS?

There are questions in Paper 1 (the written paper) specifically designed to test candidates' knowledge and interpretation of general practice literature. Candidates are expected to be familiar with items in the medical literature which have influenced current thinking in general practice. Paper 2 (the MCQs) has questions based on articles and reviews printed over the last eighteen months. The viva also concentrates on topics that require an awareness of the recent literature.

In addition, good GPs use evidence-based medicine as a starting point and are able to apply it to meet the needs and circumstances of an individual patient, and as a joint decision with the patient. A 'patient-centred' approach is a highly desirable quality for the MRCGP exam and for future practice.

MYTHS ABOUT HOT TOPICS FOR THE EXAM

You need to know everything
Although the amount of information you are expected to know may feel insurmountable, it is important to remember that it is impossible to know everything, the examiners certainly don't! There is no shame and indeed much credit in knowing your own and your professional limitations. Too much pride or arrogance can actually be off-putting to the examiners.

You need to be able to quote papers to pass the exam
Candidates are not expected to be able to quote individual references of articles. It is more important, for example, to know that there are many papers with different results regarding the treatment of sore throats with antibiotics rather than to know only one paper and its design faults in detail.

If you know a key paper was printed recently in the BMJ, for example, then it is worth stating. However, it is worse to misquote a reference or quote a reference in the wrong context than to not quote at all! The college states that inaccurate or incomplete references will not be penalised but misleading ones will.

Hot Topics are the most important part of revision for the exam
There has recently been more emphasis placed on candidates' awareness of current issues for the exam, especially as evidence-based medicine is becoming a very important part of clinical practice.

However, the examiners are actually more interested in ensuring that candidates are broad-minded, patient-centred and can consider problems in general practice from many different perspectives and be able to think about social, ethical, political and cultural factors. It is the application of any knowledge obtained rather than the knowledge itself which is important for both the exam and working in general practice.

Although 3½ hours seems a long time for the written paper, the exam passes quickly with very little spare time. If candidates spend too much time on hot topics or current literature in their answers this may be detrimental because it leaves less time to spend on other very relevant issues. For example, when considering an answer about the optimal management of a newly diagnosed diabetic patient, the impact this diagnosis may have on both the patient and their family is equally as important as discussing various trials regarding target glycosylated haemoglobin levels.

USEFUL READING MATERIAL FOR 'HOT TOPICS' REVISION

There are a large number of revision books for the exam and a huge number of books about general practice. Your trainer and VTS scheme will be able to advise you about these.

It is generally advised that candidates should be up-to-date with the past eighteen months of the literature. However, it is worth bearing in mind that there are many older studies which still influence General Practice. The main journals to read are the *British Medical Journal* and the *British Journal of General Practice*, as exam questions are usually set from these and also they are the journals that examiners usually read! *Drugs and Therapeutics Bulletin* is a useful journal as it provides unbiased reviews. The new Clinical Evidence book, produced every six months by the BMJ is a useful reference source for evidence-based medicine.

The free weekly newspapers *GP*, *Pulse* and *Doctor* have very useful relevant discussion material, both clinical and non-clinical. *Update* also produces some very relevant articles and includes Self-Assessment exercises every month, which consist of MCQs, Modified Essay Questions, Short Answer Questions and a Critical Reading Exercise. These can be very useful to discuss with your trainer or in your study groups.

It is preferable to try to read some journals on a regular basis rather than trying to cram everything in the month before the exam. This not only makes last minute revision less stressful but it also means that some of the knowledge can be used during your clinical practice.

KEY POINTS

Do not panic!
You do not have to know everything
Try to read journals regularly
Use evidence-based medicine in your practice

USEFUL JOURNALS/PUBLICATIONS

British Medical Journal (BMJ)
British Journal of General Practice (BJGP)
Evidence-based Medicine
GP/Doctor/Pulse
Update
Drugs and Therapeutics Bulletin

CHAPTER 1: CHRONIC DISEASES

HYPERTENSION

Hypertension has been defined by the World Health Organisation (in 1993) as the blood pressure above which intervention has been shown to reduce risk. Hypertension is a very common but poorly managed condition. 50% of hypertensives are undetected, 50% of those detected are not treated and 50% of those treated are not adequately controlled! Up to 20% of the adult population in the Western world are hypertensive.

Hypertension treatment decreases the risk of fatal and non-fatal stroke, cardiac events and death. It may also actually improve quality of life. People at a greater cardiovascular risk when they start treatment, such as elderly patients with other risk factors, derive the most absolute benefit from drug treatment.

How much should BP be lowered by?
A very large, randomised controlled trial, the Hypertension Optimal Treatment Trial (HOT), looked at outcomes in terms of major cardiovascular disease (CVD) events (*Lancet 1998;351:1755–62*). The British Hypertension Society (BHS) guidelines (see later) are based on this study. This study showed that the lowest incidence of CVD events occurred at a mean diastolic blood pressure of 82.6 mmHg and the lowest CVD mortality at 86.5 mmHg. An even lower diastolic blood pressure was found to be beneficial in diabetics (optimal 80 mmHg).

The HOT study is the only study that has set out to evaluate optimal target BP levels and they reported an optimal pressure of 139/83 mmHg. This study also showed a 15% reduction in major CVD events and a 36% reduction in non-fatal myocardial infarction (MI) for patients on aspirin. The benefit of aspirin for primary prevention had been controversial before this study.

What is the best drug regime to treat hypertension?
It is still unclear whether the benefits of specific antihypertensive drugs come from their direct effects on raised blood pressure or from various other multiple indirect actions.

The LIFE (Lorsartan Intervention For Endpoint reduction in hypertension) study (*Lancet 2002;359:1004*) demonstrated less cardiovascular

1

morbidity and mortality, fewer strokes, fewer new diabetics and less left ventricular hypertrophy (LVH) in patients treated with losartan compared with atenolol, despite BP being lowered by the same amount. Taken together with the HOPE (Heart Outcomes Prevention Evaluation) study data, LIFE supports a move away from beta-blockers as first-choice agents in the treatment of hypertension.

Several large, multicentre trials have established the value of angiotensin-II receptor blockers (ARBs) in renoprotection in type 2 diabetes (*NEJM 2001;345:851, 861, 870*). It therefore seems logical that the treatment of patients with type 2 diabetes, hypertension and nephropathy should begin with ARBs with angiotensin-converting enzyme inhibitors (ACEI) as an alternative. For those diabetic patients without nephropathy, aggressive control of blood pressure is warranted, although the trials do not indicate the use of any particular class of drug.

It is generally accepted that best practice is to choose therapeutic agents likely to do more good than harm, given each patient's social circumstances, preferences, coexisting medical conditions and risk factors. This is also likely to improve compliance.

What is the evidence for treating hypertension in the elderly?
In the past decade, several landmark trials have helped to firmly establish the value and importance of treating hypertension in the elderly. The STOP-2 (Swedish Trial in Old Patients-2) study compared treatment with beta-blockers or thiazide diuretics with ACE inhibitors or calcium-channel blockers in patients aged 70–84 years (*Lancet 1999;354:1751*). The findings were that blood pressure was decreased similarly in all treatment groups and that old and new drugs were similar in preventing cardiovascular mortality or major events.

🐢 British Hypertension Society (BHS) Guidelines
(BMJ 1999;319:630)

These are evidence-based guidelines, written largely by professors, which aim to present the best currently available evidence on hypertension management. They recommend starting treatment on the basis of risk rather than blood pressure for patients with borderline hypertension.

Important points
- All adults should have their BP checked every 5 years, or every year if it's borderline
- All patients should receive non-pharmacological advice
- Initiate treatment if SBP >160 or DBP >100 mmHg
- Consider treatment in borderline patients if target organ damage/diabetes/10-year coronary risk >15%
- Choice of drug should be tailored to patient, e.g. ACEI for LVF, β-blockers for ischaemic heart disease (IHD)
- Aspirin should be considered if 10-year CVD risk >15%
- Statins should be considered if 10-year CVD risk >30%
- Drug treatment is of proven value until age 80 years; over this, the decision to treat should be based on biological age

NB.
10-year coronary heart disease risk is estimated by using the risk chart issued by the Joint British Societies in their recommendations for coronary heart disease prevention (*Heart 1998;119:329–35*).

Good points of guidelines
They are clear, concise and based on good evidence. They aim to address the incomplete detection, treatment and control of hypertension prevalent across all sections of the community. The emphasis on the assessment and reduction of cardiovascular risk rather than just the maintenance of an optimal blood pressure is to be welcomed.

Problems with these guidelines
Some of the treatment recommendations are based on consensus rather than evidence.

The resource implications are huge for GPs as the guidelines will result in a far greater proportion of patients needing treatment, monitoring and close follow-up.

It has been estimated that an average GP will have 272 patients under 75 years of age who would be eligible for treatment, which could mean a potential extra 4 hours of work a week to devote to their ongoing management!

There is no reference to patient preferences. Why choose a 10-year risk threshold of 15%? This means that over 10 years, 19 out of 20 patients taking treatment will derive no benefit from it.

What are the risk tables?
They are based on the Framingham data, which came from a 10-year follow-up of 5,000 patients. The risk equations from the Framingham data have been shown to be reasonably accurate when applied to other populations in northern Europe and the USA – but they have been criticised for not including other cardiovascular risk factors (such as family history, sedentary lifestyle and obesity). There are three main tables: The New Zealand, Sheffield and Joint British Societies. These take absolute rather than relative risk into consideration, which is far more relevant to individual patients.

How do the different risk tables compare?
Both the Joint British Societies chart and the Sheffield table are compatible with UK guidelines. However, a study in primary care found that although the Sheffield table correctly identified slightly more people who were at high risk compared with the Joint British Societies chart, it also falsely labelled more low-risk people as being at high risk. Overall, this study concluded that the Joint British Societies chart has the best balance of accuracy (*Heart 2001;85:37–43*).

How easy is it to measure cardiovascular risk for patients?
Accurate estimation of cardiovascular risk without the use of explicit risk charts or computer-based clinical decision support systems is not easy. Health professionals find it difficult to assimilate multiple risk factors into an accurate assessment of cardiovascular risk (*BMJ 2000;320:686–90*).

What are the disadvantages of using the risk tables?
They can only be used for primary prevention. They do not apply to people with familial hyperlipidaemia as these patients are high risk. Ethnic minorities are not mentioned. Sections of the ethnic community, particularly Afro-Caribbeans and South Asians, are at greatly increased risk of end-organ damage owing to hypertension. They also exhibit an increased incidence of concomitant cardiovascular risk factors such as

diabetes and obesity. They also underestimate the risk if there is a strong family history of coronary heart disease at a younger age. In addition, no allowances are made for heaviness of smoking or socioeconomic status in the risk calculations.

A recent BMJ article (*BMJ 2002;324:459–64*) showed that many GP patient records do not contain adequate information to allow the risk of coronary heart disease (CHD) to be calculated (mainly low-density lipoprotein (LDL) levels). Subjective estimations of risks often lead to an underestimation of risk.

How can risk information clearly be given to patients?
Results of a study from a surgery in London has shown that patient decisions regarding medication are strongly affected by the way information is explained to them (*BJGP 2001;51:276–9*). A questionnaire was sent to patients asking their likelihood of accepting treatment for a chronic condition on the basis of relative-risk reduction, absolute-risk reduction, number needed to treat and personal probability of benefit. The results varied from 44% stating they would accept treatment with a personal probability of benefit model, to 92% stating they would accept treatment using a relative-risk reduction model. This could therefore mean that the presentation of a risk statistic in 'everyday language' to ensure full comprehension may result in a proportion of patients refusing beneficial treatment.

What should we use to measure blood pressure?
GPs should not make decisions about treating patients with hypertension based solely on high readings of blood pressure taken by doctors, according to a recent study (*BMJ 2002;325:254–7*). This study concluded that measurements taken by the patient or a nurse helped to counteract the negative 'white coat' effect, as measurements taken by a GP were considerably higher.

Accurate measurement of blood pressure in patients is of paramount importance. For example, consistently underestimating the diastolic pressure by 5 mmHg could result in almost two-thirds of hypertensive individuals being denied potentially life-saving and certainly morbidity-preventing treatment (*Can Med Assoc J 1999;161:277–8*). Consistently overestimating it by 5 mmHg could more than double the number of individuals diagnosed as hypertensive (half of whom would be inappropriately labelled and treated).

In Sweden and The Netherlands the use of mercury is no longer permitted in hospitals. In the United Kingdom the move to ban mercury has not been received with enthusiasm because we do not have an accurate alternative to the mercury sphygmomanometer (*BMJ 2000;320:815*). However, aneroid devices can be extremely inaccurate and automated devices vary enormously.

Another problem is one highlighted in a survey of 1,500 sphygmomanometers, which revealed that 20% were 'appreciably inaccurate' and 2% were 'very seriously inaccurate' (*J Hum Hypertens 2001;15:587–91*). None of the 240 general practices surveyed had arrangements for regular checks and calibrations of their sphygmomanometers.

Are patients being overtreated?
An old study by Fry in 1979 demonstrated that 1 in 3 patients with hypertension became normotensive with time. This has been confirmed in a study that found 20% of well-controlled hypertensives could have their medication controlled without problems (*BJGP 1999;49:977–80*).

One recent study has managed to identify simple long term predictors of maintenance of normal blood pressure after withdrawal of anti-hypertensive medication (*BMJ 2002; 325:815–7*). Patients who were younger (65–74 years) had relatively low on-treatment systolic pressures and minimal drug treatment were more likely to respond well to a trial of withdrawal of treatment.

The overall conclusion regarding treatment choice is that it is the level of blood pressure that counts, not the drug used to treat it. It is sensible to prescribe the medication most likely to suit the patient's past medical history and, properly and more importantly, to choose a medication that is less likely to cause side-effects so improving compliance.

 USEFUL WEBSITES

www.hyp.ac.uk/bhs – British Hypertension Society (Includes copies of CVD risk charts)
www.bmj.com – British Medical Journal
www.bhf.org.uk – British Heart Foundation

ROUTINE INVESTIGATIONS FOR HYPERTENSION

❖ Urine dipstix for blood/protein
❖ Urea and creatinine
❖ Blood glucose
❖ Serum total:LDL cholesterol ratio
❖ 12 lead ECG

☐ **SUMMARY POINTS FOR HYPERTENSION**

❖ Hypertension is underdiagnosed
❖ BHS guidelines have huge resource implications
❖ Familiarise yourself with risk tables
❖ Risk is very difficult to explain to patients
❖ Consider statins and aspirin
❖ BP targets are lower for diabetics
❖ Some patients are actually overtreated

CORONARY HEART DISEASE

The prevention of coronary heart disease (CHD) is one of the most important tasks for general practice. CHD remains the principal cause of death in the UK and one-fifth of these deaths occur below retirement age. The main risk factors are smoking, hypertension, hyper-cholesterolaemia, diabetes and obesity.

The medical priority is to focus on those who are at highest risk of CHD. The first priority is secondary prevention for patients with established CHD. The second priority is primary prevention for people at high risk of developing CHD: i.e. those with an absolute CHD risk ≥15% over 10 years, as calculated using the Joint British Society's coronary risk-prediction charts. The charts use information on age, gender, lipid profile and blood pressure to calculate a patient's risk. It is suggested (see below) that the people at a higher cardiovascular risk should start drug therapy, but this is probably overambitious given the current financial state of the NHS!

Risk factors for CHD

Healthcare professionals tend to overemphasise the benefits of medication (e.g. statins) and neglect lifestyle factors (e.g. smoking, diet). Improvements in risk factors and treatment have been shown to be associated with reductions in CHD in a large epidemiological study conducted by the World Health Organisation. This study, MONICA, monitored 100,000 men and women aged 35–64 years from 21 countries over 10 years (*Lancet 2000;355:668–9*). However, the results were not as remarkable as had been anticipated. The most effective intervention was stopping smoking, which results in a 50% risk reduction over 2 years.

What are the benefits of lowering cholesterol?

There is overwhelming evidence that statins are highly beneficial in both the primary and secondary prevention of CHD. These are discussed on pages 38–43.

There is no longer any doubt that treatment benefits those who are at substantial coronary risk. An updated meta-analysis (*BMJ 2000;321:98–6*) shows that drugs which lower lipid concentrations prevent nearly one-third of myocardial infarctions and coronary deaths. However, many people who could substantially benefit from statins are not receiving them, perhaps due to a lack of understanding by physicians or to poor organisation (*BMJ 2000;321:971–2*). A recent study has found that patients with established CHD were much less likely to be on statins if they were older, smoked or had a history of angina (*Heart 2002;88:15–19*).

Data has shown that less than one-third of patients with a history of cardiovascular disease and only 3% of people with a ≥30% 10-year risk of CHD are currently receiving lipid lowering drugs, which is clearly very inadequate (*BMJ 2000;321:1322–5*). In addition, target cholesterol concentrations are achieved in less than 50% of patients receiving treatment. Treating all patients with a 10-year CHD risk of 15% would, in effect, mean statin treatment for about one-quarter of the UK's adult population – which is clearly not achievable with current NHS funding!

A more realistic approach is to ensure that all those with an absolute risk of CHD above 30% over 10 years receive optimal statin therapy, with appropriate monitoring of lipid concentrations and advice on non-drug measures.

Certain groups of people need to be given special consideration. These include:
• Patients with diabetes mellitus (risk of developing and dying from CHD is 2–5 times higher than non-diabetics)
• Patients of South Asian descent (typically have a 40% greater risk of developing CHD)
• Patients with familial hypercholesterolaemia (particularly high risk of dying from CHD)

The NNT (number needed to treat) with statins for secondary prevention of death over 5 years is 16: i.e. 16 patients have to take a statin for 5 years to prevent one death. NNT for primary prevention is 69.

In addition, a study has shown that patients taking statins may also reduce their risk of developing Alzheimer's disease! (*Arch Neurol 2000;57:1439–43*). This study reported that patients receiving lovastatin or pravastatin (but not simvastatin) had a 70% lower prevalence of Alzheimer's disease than a control group.

Are risk tables used in general practice?
Various risk tables are available for general use. A recent article (*BMJ 2002;324:459–64*) showed that many GP patient records do not contain adequate information to allow the risk of CHD to be calculated (mainly

LDL levels). Subjective estimations of risks often lead to an underestimation of risk by UK doctors, whereas Canadian doctors tend to overestimate their patients' risks. No allowances are made for heaviness of smoking or socioeconomic status in the risk calculations.

In addition, a simple new scoring system for calculating a patient's risk of death from CVD is now available which can help clinicians decide whether to start patients on antihypertensive treatment (*BMJ 2001;323:75–81*).

Is there an association between 'normal' glucose levels and coronary heart disease?
Although diabetes is a strong risk factor for coronary heart disease, the association between glycaemia in the 'normal' range and coronary heart disease has previously been controversial. However, one study has shown that glycosylated haemoglobin levels are positively correlated with the risk of future coronary heart disease independent of body mass index (BMI), cholesterol level, age, sex, blood pressure or smoking history (*BMJ 2001;322:15–18*).

This study looked at 4,662 men aged between 45 and 79 years and found that the HbA1C concentration significantly predicted all-cause mortality, even below the threshold commonly accepted for a diagnosis of diabetes. This implies that glucose control for coronary heart disease should begin in patients with impaired glucose tolerance. There is, however, still no trial to confirm that improved glycaemic control will reduce the risk of coronary heart disease in people without diabetes. It is possible that glucose is merely a marker for other risk factors rather than a causal risk factor for cardiovascular disease.

Should patients receive ramipril?
It is well established that treating hypertension reduces the risk of CHD. However, in the HOPE study (Heart Outcomes Prevention Evaluation), patients at high risk of cardiovascular events were given the ACE inhibitor ramipril (*NEJM 2000;342:145–53*). This resulted in a 22% reduction in the combined endpoint of cardiovascular death, non-fatal myocardial infarction and stroke. These benefits were similar in normotensive and hypertensive patients. From this it could therefore be argued that all patients at a high risk of CHD should receive ramipril!

Is there any evidence to support cardiac rehabilitation?
Meta-analyses of randomised trials have shown that cardiac

rehabilitation after myocardial infarction reduces mortality by 20–24%. Clinical guidelines for cardiac rehabilitation have been published by the Royal College of Physicians (www.rcplondon.ac.uk), but currently less than half of the patients receive any form of rehabilitation. Disadvantaged social groups include women, the elderly and ethnic minorities.

Is exercise beneficial?
Physical inactivity roughly doubles the risk of coronary heart disease and is also a major risk factor for stroke. Regular exercise has numerous benefits, including reducing hypertension and CHD. Short bouts of exercise can be just as effective at protecting the heart as longer workouts; however, getting the heart rate up is a key factor as light activity offers no cardiac benefit (*Circulation 2000;102:975–80, 981–7*).

Why are patients not more motivated in reducing their risk of CHD?
One of the biggest barriers for implementing evidence-based practice may be convincing patients that they need to take part in lifelong measures for the prevention of coronary heart disease. In one study, 30% of patients declined to participate in a nurse-led prevention programme (*BMJ 1998;316:1434–7*). Patients often perceive a 'heart attack' to be an acute, self-limiting condition rather than the onset of a high-risk chronic disease.

A very interesting qualitative study looked at identifying factors influencing the use of health services by people with angina (*BMJ 2001;323:214–17*). It found that fear, denial and low expectations in patients from lower socioeconomic classes are important barriers to accessing health services. This may also account for some of the regional and socioeconomic differences in the incidence and prevalence of CHD in the UK.

Summary
In summary therefore, it is important that GP teams are able to identify all people with established CHD and all people who are at significant risk of CHD but who have not yet developed symptoms. Both groups of people should then be offered the appropriate advice and treatment to reduce their risks in the future. It is very likely that secondary-prevention clinics will be organised at a primary care group level, which will facilitate the delivery of various aspects of the National Service Framework for Coronary Heart Disease and improve standards of care across the country.

USEFUL WEBSITES

www.bcs.com – British Cardiac Society
www.pccs.org.uk – Primary Care Cardiovascular Society
www.hyp.ac.uk/bhs – British Hypertension Society (Includes copies of CVD risk charts)
www.cardiacrehabilitation.org.uk – Information regarding rehabilitation
www.riskscore.org.uk – New scoring system for assessing cardiovascular disease risk

---

ALWAYS CONSIDER:

❖ Smoking status
❖ Weight
❖ Exercise
❖ Blood pressure
❖ Aspirin
❖ Statins

SUMMARY POINTS OF CORONARY HEART DISEASE

❖ Doctors often neglect lifestyle factors
❖ Statin treatment is still inadequate
❖ Risk tables are not being used properly
❖ GPs need to identify patients 'at risk' of CHD

THE CORONARY HEART DISEASE NATIONAL SERVICE FRAMEWORK

This was published by the Department of Health in March 2000 and has been designed to 'transform the prevention, diagnosis and treatment of coronary heart disease'.

Coronary heart disease is among the biggest killers in this country. More than 1.4 million people suffer from angina. Some 300,000 have heart attacks every year. Heart disease is much more common in deprived areas, yet treatment and care are often better in more prosperous areas. This 'postcode' lottery of care is unacceptable and the NSF attempts to end it.

What do National Service Frameworks (NSFs) do?

National Service Frameworks have been created to set national standards and define service models for a specific service or care group, put in place programmes to support their implementation and establish performance measures against which progress within an agreed time-scale will be measured. This was the second NSF to be produced.

What does the CHD National Service Framework state?

This framework sets out a programme designed to achieve the Government target of cutting coronary heart disease and stroke by an ambitious 40% by 2010. It sets 12 standards for the prevention, diagnosis and treatment of coronary heart disease; describes service models; and explains how the standards can be delivered and how progress will be monitored, with milestones and goals.

What does this mean for GPs?

By April 2001, all practices should have created a register of CHD patients and then provide structured care within nationally accepted guidelines. GP teams also had to identify patients who are at risk of coronary heart disease and then offer them appropriate advice and treatment to reduce their risks. Regular audits on this information have to be performed. Although this has obviously involved a considerable amount of work in many practices, it is important as these measures are a start towards improving the quality of care for patients with ischaemic heart disease.

A major survey has revealed a large gulf between milestones set out in the NSF and the standards actually being reached in general practice

(BMJ 2001;321:1463). In this study, research nurses analysed the records of 548 GPs across the UK and found 24,431 patients with a diagnosis of CHD. The study showed that 35% of men and 52% of women had no record of cholesterol levels; and at least 40% of patients actually tested had total cholesterol levels greater than 5 mmol/l. About one-half were taking aspirin, one-fifth of patients with a history of MI were taking beta-blockers and less than one-fifth of the disease population were taking statins. These findings obviously suggest that many GPs still have alarming amounts of work to do if they are to meet the NSF milestones.

The NHS statin prescribing bill has been estimated to increase by at least £2b a year if GPs stick to the NSF targets. Prescribing for statins has already risen by 78% since the NSF's launch in 2000.

Should all age groups be targeted?
A study has shown that no hypertensive patients under 45 years have a 10-year cardiovascular risk >30% *(BJGP 2001;51:571–4)*. Virtually no health benefits result from assessing and treating blood pressure in patients less than 45 years of age. If the assessment and treatment of blood pressure was confined to patients over 65 years, this would prevent 85% of preventable cardiovascular disease.

What are the negative parts of this NSF?
This is a very lengthy document consisting of 124 pages with another 283 pages containing eight appendices! It is written with a lot of repetition and contains a large amount of 'management jargon' which is not always easy to follow. The main document is not referenced, although it does claim to provide evidence-based advice.

Many of the current deficiencies in providing adequate secondary prevention care to coronary heart disease patients is often due to poor funding; for example, low prescription rates for statins, long waiting times for exercise ECGs and angiograms. It is unclear how undertaking regular audits will actually improve this! The NSF has been described as a blueprint for audit rather than a guideline for patient management, and the main audit burden is going to fall on general practices.

An interesting editorial in the BMJ *(BMJ 2001;323:246–7)* comments on how unrealistic the NSF targets are. In addition, it states that if patient-centred medicine is accepted as a desirable core of general practice, patients should then have the right to make their own health choices.

WEBSITE FOR NSF

www.doh.gov.uk/nsf/coronary.htm

AIMS OF THE NATIONAL SERVICE FRAMEWORK:

❖ Create disease registers
❖ Produce locally agreed protocols
❖ Provide structured care
❖ Perform regular audits

SUMMARY POINTS FOR THE NSF FOR CHD

❖ 12 standards covered in NSF
❖ Aim to reduce heart disease
❖ Involve primary and secondary care
❖ Clear and challenging targets

HEART FAILURE

Heart failure, like hypertension, is a very common but poorly managed condition. 50% of patients with heart failure are undetected, 50% of those detected are not treated and 50% of those treated are not adequately controlled!

Despite improvements in treatment the prognosis for patients with heart failure remains poor, the risk of death annually is 5–10% in patients with mild symptoms and 30–40% in those with advanced disease.

An echocardiogram is still the investigation of choice for heart failure, as clinical examination is neither sensitive nor specific. However, the majority of GPs still have very poor access to out-patient echocardiograms.

What are the best treatments for heart failure?
There are now so many different drugs known to benefit patients with heart failure that treatment can often become confusing and complex for both the patient and the doctor.

Diuretics
For many years, diuretics have been an important part of symptomatic treatment for patients with heart failure and evidence of fluid retention. However, their long-term effects on mortality rates and other endpoints are not known (it would be unethical to trial now).

Angiotensin-converting enzyme inhibitors
ACE inhibitors (ACEI) have been evaluated extensively in randomised controlled trials (e.g. CONSENSUS, RESOLVD studies) comprising a large number of patients with heart failure, and were found to reduce mortality and morbidity. Benefits also extend to different patient groups: such as elderly patients, women, patients with or without coronary artery disease, with different degrees of functional impairment and with a history of diuretic and digoxin use. In the absence of clear contraindications these drugs should therefore be used as first-line agents in all patients with left ventricular dysfunction who do or do not have symptoms.

Many GPs still do not regularly monitor renal function, even in the most vulnerable patients (*BMJ 1999;318:234-7*). It has been recommended that patients should be screened for risk factors predisposing them to uraemia (for example, old age, peripheral vascular disease, or concomitant treatment with non-steroidal drugs). Renal function should be checked before and 7–10 days after ACE inhibitors are started in all patients and thereafter annually only in those with risk factors.

Despite the evidence for their effectiveness, angiotensin converting enzyme inhibitors are underused in primary care. Doctors' perceptions of the risks of these drugs in patients with heart failure are often exaggerated; however the introduction of these drugs has been shown to very rarely cause problems (*BMJ 2000;321:1113-6*).

Angiotensin-II receptor antagonists
The ValHeFT trial showed a 13% relative-risk reduction in the combined endpoint of all-cause mortality and morbidity in patients with chronic heart failure on valsartan compared with placebo. However, valsartan had no significant effect on the endpoint of mortality alone.

The ELITE II study (*J Card Fail 1999;5:146–54*) showed that losartan is no more effective than captopril in reducing mortality in elderly patients with heart failure. These drugs are often used in patients who are intolerant of ACE inhibitors, usually because of a cough.

Beta-blockers
Beta-blockers have been evaluated in nearly 10,000 patients with chronic heart failure in over 20 randomised clinical trials (e.g. MERIT-HF and CIBIS-II trials) and have been shown to decrease the risk of death and the need for hospital admission. These benefits were attained in patients already taking ACEI and diuretics, with ischaemic and non-ischaemic disease and with different degrees of functional impairment, although clinical trials have generally carefully selected stable patients.

Even in carefully selected and treated patients there is often an initial deterioration in symptoms, often followed by subsequent improvement. Owing to the complexities of initiating, titrating and monitoring treatment with beta-blockers in patients with heart failure, this treatment should generally be given only by experienced doctors or in specialised clinics. The choice of beta-blocker (selective versus non-selective versus carvedilol) remains controversial and is currently under investigation in randomised trials.

Digoxin
One study has shown that digoxin can provide some symptomatic benefit in patients in sinus rhythm with heart failure. However, it does not appear to improve mortality (*NEMJ 1997;336:525-33*).

Spironolactone
The RALES study (*Lancet 1999;341:709-17*) showed that patients who received spironolactone in addition to their usual treatment had a decreased mortality of 30%. The patients in this study had severe heart failure persisting despite standard therapy. More trials are still needed before spironolactone can be recommended as a routine treatment for heart failure.

Summary
General practitioners have a vital role in the early detection and treatment of the main risk factors for heart failure – namely, hypertension and ischaemic heart disease – and other cardiovascular risk factors, such as smoking and hyperlipidaemia. The Framingham study has shown a decline in hypertension as a risk factor for heart failure over the years, which probably reflects improvements in treatment. Early detection of left ventricular dysfunction in 'high risk' asymptomatic patients (e.g. those who have hypertension or atrial fibrillation) and treatment with angiotensin-converting enzyme inhibitors can minimise the progression to symptomatic heart failure.

ACRONYMS OF IMPORTANT CARDIOVASCULAR TRIALS

CONSENSUS - Co-operative North Scandinavian Enalapril Survival Study
RESOLVD - Randomised Evaluation of Strategies for Left Ventricular Dysfunction
ValHeFT – Valsartan Heart Failure Trial
ELITE - Evaluation of Losartan in the Elderly [study]
MERIF-HF - Metoprolol CR/XL Randomised Intervention Trial in Congestive Heart Failure
CIBIS - The Cardiac Insufficiency Bisoprolol Study
RALES - Randomized Aldactone Evaluation Study

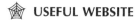 **USEFUL WEBSITE**

www.bsh.org.uk/bshx – British Society for Heart Failure

📋 **SUMMARY POINTS FOR HEART FAILURE**

❖ Heart failure is underdetected and undertreated
❖ Affects 10% of people over 75 years old
❖ ACE inhibitors are standard treatment
❖ ACE inhibitors are still under-prescribed
❖ Target risk factors in all patients

ATRIAL FIBRILLATION

There is an increased incidence of atrial fibrillation (AF) with increasing age, one study suggests a prevalence of 2.4% in patients over the age of 50 years (*BJGP 1997;47:285–9*). Atrial fibrillation is an independent risk factor for developing a stroke; its presence increases the risk of stroke fivefold. Patients with atrial fibrillation who do sustain a stroke have a higher mortality rate, greater disability, a longer duration of hospital stay and a lower rate of discharge to their own home.

The prevalence of atrial fibrillation increases with age, which obviously means the proportion of strokes attributable to atrial fibrillation also increases with age – about 24% in people aged 80–89 years. However, community-based studies show that atrial fibrillation is still underdiagnosed and undertreated.

Should patients with atrial fibrillation be prescribed warfarin?

It is recommended that patients who are at a high risk of stroke should be identified and targeted for anticoagulation in the absence of contraindications (*Lancet 1999;353:4–6*), see Box on p. 21. This risk should be reviewed at regular intervals, at least annually. High-risk patients should receive warfarin (INR (international normalised ratio) 2.0–3.0) if possible; patients at moderate risk should receive either warfarin or aspirin, depending on each individual case; and low-risk patients should receive aspirin.

Randomised trials have established that anticoagulation with warfarin is associated with a relative reduction in risk of stroke of 68% (*Lancet 1996;648:633–8*). Aspirin has been shown to be less effective in stroke reduction among high-risk patients, but is more convenient and theoretically safer then warfarin. One systematic review of long-term anticoagulation and aspirin in patients with AF showed for the first time that aspirin is probably as effective at preventing fatal and non-fatal cardiovascular events as warfarin (*BMJ 2001;322:321–4*). However, larger trials need to be undertaken before a change in the current practice can be recommended. There is no evidence that adding aspirin to warfarin confers any additional benefit.

Although anticoagulation in those aged over 75 is associated with a greater risk when the INR is maintained at 2.0–4.5, the SPAF III (Stroke Prevention in Atrial Fibrillation) trial showed that anticoagulation to a lower INR of 1.5–3.0 is both safe and effective in reducing the risk of stroke in this age group.

Guidelines for the management of atrial fibrillation have been published by the American College of Cardiology, the American Heart Association and the European Society of Cardiology. This document describes the classification, investigation and recommended treatments for atrial fibrillation (*Eur Heart J 2001;22:1852–923*).

Why are some patients with atrial fibrillation not anticoagulated?

Despite evidence in the published literature, anticoagulation is underused in clinical practice, partly because it is not known whether trial efficacy translates into clinical practice. The patients in the trials were highly selected and had very close monitoring and follow-up. Although the trials were designed to provide an estimate of treatment efficacy, they have been widely interpreted as being studies of warfarin treatment. There is a counter-argument that the benefits of warfarin were actually underestimated, since patients randomised to the warfarin arms of the studies who actually did sustain a stroke often had subtherapeutic INRs. However, a community-based study showed that stroke and haemorrhage rates were comparable to those in randomised studies (*BMJ 2000;320:1236–9*).

Other reasons for the poor prescribing of warfarin to patients with atrial fibrillation may include concern over cerebral haemorrhage, the problems associated with initiating therapy in elderly housebound patients and the inconvenience of safely monitoring anticoagulation in the community. One small study demonstrated that patients on warfarin could manage their INR at home as safely as at a hospital anticoagulation clinic (*Lancet 2000;356:97–102*). This was made possible by reliable, easy-to-use machines using capillary blood samples. Longer term studies are needed to assess the feasibility of this method, but home management would obviously have many advantages.

One study has highlighted a considerable variability between physicians and patients in their weighing up of the potential outcomes associated with anticoagulation for atrial fibrillation (*BMJ 2001;323:1218–21*). It showed that for anticoagulation treatment to be acceptable, patients required less reduction in risk of stroke and were more tolerant of an increase in the risk of bleeding than physicians.

However, a study of elderly patients in general practice showed that nearly 40% of patients with atrial fibrillation preferred not to receive anticoagulation when they were given information about stroke risk and consequences (*BMJ 2000;320:1380–4*). The findings of this study suggest that guidelines for the management of atrial fibrillation should be modified to incorporate patients' preferences in treatment decisions, particularly with regard to the consequences of anticoagulation treatment.

 USEFUL WEBSITE

www.eurheartj.com – Guidance on atrial fibrillation

RISK OF STROKE IN NON-RHEUMATIC ATRIAL FIBRILLATION

High Risk (12% annually)
- ❖ All patients with a previous history of a transient ischaemic attack (TIA) or cardiovascular accident (CVA)
- ❖ All patients aged over 75 years with diabetes, hypertension or ischaemic heart disease
- ❖ All patients with clinical evidence of valve disease or heart failure

Medium Risk (8% annually)
- ❖ All patients under 65 years with diabetes, hypertension or ischaemic heart disease
- ❖ All patients over 65 years who have not been identified in the high risk group

Low Risk (1% annually)
- ❖ All other patients under 65 years

SUMMARY POINTS FOR ATRIAL FIBRILLATION

- ❖ Risk of AF increases with age
- ❖ Associated with five-fold risk of stroke
- ❖ Patients at high risk of stroke need warfarin
- ❖ Patient education regarding risks and benefits of warfarin is important
- ❖ Many patients would choose not to take warfarin

STROKE

Stroke is the third highest cause of death in the United Kingdom and the biggest single cause of major disability. Treatment in the UK is far from satisfactory. Stroke can occur at any age, but half of all strokes occur in people over 70 years old. About 80% of all acute strokes are caused by cerebral infarction; the remainder are caused by haemorrhage. More than 50% of patients are physically dependent on others 6 months after a stroke.

It has been estimated that there will be a 30% absolute increase in the number of patients experiencing their first stroke in 2010 compared with the figures for 1983. The International Stroke Trial highlighted that the UK centres had the poorest survival from stroke in the world.

The cost to the NHS and Social Services of stroke is about £2.3b per year, nearly twice that for coronary heart disease. However, the government and charities spend around £5m per year on stroke research, compared to £43m on heart disease. Stroke prevention is actually one of the most cost-effective of all cardiovascular interventions in primary care.

The Department of Health produced the National Service Framework for elderly people in April 2001, which contains a substantial chapter on stroke. A better service for stroke is supposed to be delivered by April 2004.

What is the value of stroke units?
Stroke units are known to improve outcome by concentrating patients in a unit with appropriate expertise. Patients treated in stroke units are less likely to die and more likely to recover fully or partially from a stroke (*BMJ 1997;314:1151–9*).

The Third National Sentinel Stroke Audit for 2001–2 has recently been published by the Royal College of Physicians, which provides an overview of progress in the management of stroke to date. It highlights the failure of the NHS to provide adequate numbers of beds in stroke units – the mean number of acute stroke beds was four and the median number zero!

Even in the community, the audit has shown that only 31% of trusts have specialised community stroke teams. Evidence from RCTs shows that a focused community rehabilitation team with adequate resources, linking with a state-of-the-art stroke unit, reduces the length of stay and, in moderately and severely disabled patients, reduces disability and institutional care, when compared with management by a stroke unit alone (*Stroke 2000;31:2989–94*).

National Service Framework for Elderly People and Stroke
Stroke is covered in Standard Five of the NSF. This aims to reduce the incidence of stroke in the population and ensure that those who have had a stroke have prompt access to integrated stroke-care services. It states there are four key areas for the development of integrated stroke services, namely: prevention; immediate care; early and continuing rehabilitation; and long-term support.

Primary prevention
Hypertension is the most prevalent and modifiable risk factor for stroke in primary prevention, with its treatment substantially reducing the risk of stroke. As the risk factors for stroke are similar to those for coronary heart disease, primary care teams have a very important role in primary stroke prevention.

The NSF emphasises the need for GPs to identify patients at high cardiovascular risk and it proposes the creation of GP registers, based on those created through implementing the NSF for coronary heart disease. In addition, GPs should put in place models of care to enable the systematic recording of risk factors in high-risk patients, provide and document the delivery of appropriate advice, support and treatment, and offer a regular review to those at risk of stroke.

Secondary prevention
The main interventions with proven benefit are aspirin, cholesterol reduction in patients with existing coronary heart disease and carotid endarterectomy in people with severe carotid artery stenosis. In addition, people with atrial fibrillation have been shown to benefit from oral anticoagulation (or aspirin in the case of contraindications to anticoagulants).

Hypertension persisting after 1 month should be treated according to the British Hypertension Society guidelines. All patients should receive aspirin (if there are contraindications then dipyridamole or clopidrogel could be considered). The effect of reducing cholesterol in patients with a prior stroke but no history of coronary heart disease is, as yet, still uncertain.

Immediate care

The NSF states that all patients with acute stroke require urgent admission to hospital and should have a computed tomography (CT) brain scan within 48 hours. There is strong evidence that patients treated in stroke units are less likely to die and more likely to recover fully or partially from a stroke (*BMJ 1997;314:1151–9*). The NSF therefore states that all patients with an acute stroke should be managed on an acute stroke unit (currently, less than one-quarter of patients are being treated in specialist stroke units).

Interventions for acute ischaemic stroke

These are summarised in the Box on p. 26. Early use of aspirin reduces the chance of death and dependency and improves the chance of a complete recovery (*Lancet 1997;349:1569–81*). There has been no evidence to show that immediate anticoagulation is beneficial.

Thrombolysis trials have shown very conflicting results. Tissue plasminogen activator (tPA) can reduce the risk of dependency but it increases the risk of death (from intracerebral haemorrhage and from any cause). It is recommended that tPA is only given in specialist centres, within 3 hours of the stroke and as part of randomised controlled trials.

An interesting qualitative study in the BMJ highlighted that knowledge of stroke is still very poor amongst both stroke patients and the general public (*BMJ 2002;324:1065–8*). None of the available written patient information about stroke actually conveys the importance of early presentation to hospital.

Early and continuing rehabilitation

The NSF emphasises the need for efficient liaison between hospitals and primary care. Secondary prevention measures are a key part of any care plan, and must continue following discharge. By April 2002 every general hospital that cares for stroke patients should have plans for a specialised stroke service.

Long-term support
The NSF states that patients and carers needing long-term, ongoing support after the stroke should have access to a stroke-care coordinator who can provide advice, discuss discharge needs and facilitate access to further rehabilitation services.

By 2004, Primary Care Trusts will have to use protocols to identify, treat and refer stroke patients, and every general practice will have established clinical audit systems for stroke. It is still unclear at present how this is going to be fully implemented. Success can obviously only be achieved if there is adequate provision of staff, education, training and finance to carry out the programme.

Antihypertensives for stroke prevention
The PROGRESS (Perindopril pROtection aGainst REcurrent Stroke Study) has shown for the first time that antihypertensive therapy can prevent the recurrence of stroke even in patients without raised blood pressure. This study was presented at the European Society of Hypertension in June 2001. It enrolled 6,100 patients who had suffered a haemorrhagic or ischaemic stroke or transient ischaemic attack within the past 5 years. They were randomised to receive placebo or drug therapy (perindopril plus indapamide). After 4 years of follow-up, the primary endpoint of stroke recurrence had been reduced by 28% in the drug-treated group. There were significant reductions in stroke recurrence in both the hypertensive and non-hypertensive patients.

The LIFE (Lorsartan Intervention For Endpoint reduction in hypertension) study was recently published which showed that blocking angiotensin-II receptors reduced the risk of stroke by an impressive 25% compared to atenolol (*Lancet 2002;350:995–1003*).

USEFUL WEBSITES

www.rcplondon.ac.uk/pubs/strokeaudit01-02.pbf – Summary report on
the National Sentinel Stroke Audit, Royal College of Physicians
www.dcn.ed.ac.uk/csrg/ – Cochrane Stroke group website
www.nottingham.ac.uk/stroke-medicine/ – British Association of Stroke
Physicians
www.doh.gov.uk/nsf/olderpeople.htm – National Service Framework for
Older People
www.stroke.org.uk – The UK Stroke Association

INTERVENTIONS FOR ACUTE ISCHAEMIC STROKE

Beneficial
❖ Stroke units
❖ Aspirin

Trade-off between benefits and harms
❖ Thrombolytic treatment

Likely to be ineffective or harmful
❖ Immediate systemic anticoagulation
❖ Acute reduction of blood pressure

DIABETES MELLITUS

The prevalence of diagnosed diabetes within the UK is about 3%. The incidence is rising, especially as a result of the expanding ageing population and an increasing incidence of obesity. Up to 25% of people of Asian origin >60 years have diabetes.

Diabetes is a leading cause of blindness, kidney failure and limb amputation and greatly increases the risk of coronary heart disease and stroke. Diabetes accounts for >8% of the acute sector costs – it has been estimated that the average cost of inpatient care for a diabetic patient is more than six times that for a non-diabetic.

How is the diagnosis of diabetes confirmed?
The WHO introduced new criteria for the definition, diagnosis and classification of diabetes in June 2000. The methods for diagnosing diabetes are as follows:

With symptoms (polyuria, thirst, unexplained weight loss):
* A random venous plasma glucose concentration ≥11.1 mmol/l, or
* A fasting venous plasma glucose concentration ≥7.0 mmol/l, or
* A 2-hour venous plasma glucose concentration ≥11.1 mmol/l 2 hours after 75 g anhydrous glucose in an oral glucose tolerance test (OGTT)

With no symptoms:
* Diagnosis must not be based on a single glucose determination. At least one additional glucose result on another day with a value in the diabetic range is essential. This can be either fasting, from a random sample or from the 2-hour OGTT. If the fasting or random values are not diagnostic, the 2-hour value should be used.

There has been some concern about the implications of these changes for diabetes care; earlier diagnosis will increase the total number of people with diabetes but most of these will be diet-controlled. In the long term, complications should be reduced to the benefit of the individual and to the health service.

Why is diabetes important in primary care?
The majority of diabetic patients are routinely managed in primary care. GPs have a crucial role in both the management and follow-up of their patients with diabetes.

Secondary care diabetes services are stretched and many patients still complain of long clinic waits and insufficient time with clinical staff. It is therefore very unlikely that secondary care will be able to cope with the expanding numbers of diabetic patients.

What has happened to the NSF for diabetes?
The National Service Framework for diabetes is very much anticipated; the intention to develop this NSF was announced in 1999. The Standards for the NSF were published in December 2001; however, the Delivery Strategy is still awaited and is expected late in 2002/early 2003. Despite a Government promise at the beginning of the year that the second half of the NSF would be ready in the summer of 2002, it has recently emerged that it will not be ready until the end of 2002. The final content of the NSF and effective implementation will obviously be influenced by available resources. The Government has announced that it would not ring-fence funding for diabetes care, which has obviously angered both GPs and patients. It is likely to suggest that primary care takes on the routine care of most patients with diabetes. More resources and financial incentives will be needed for this to be delivered.

What are the Standards of the NSF?
The Standards of the NSF for diabetes provide an overview of the 'way forward' for diabetes care, but provides little information on how these Standards are to be delivered. There are 12 Standards presented:

1.	Prevention of type 2 diabetes
2.	Identification of people with diabetes
3.	Empowering people with diabetes
4.	Clinical care of adults with diabetes
5 & 6.	Clinical care of children and young people
7.	Management of diabetic emergencies
8.	Care of diabetics during their admission
9.	Diabetics and pregnancy
10, 11. & 12.	Detection and management of long-term complications

NICE has recently produced guidance on screening type 2 diabetics for renal complications and retinopathy, which have recommended eye tests and renal function tests annually.

What are the key elements of effective diabetes care?
These can be summarised as having:
- A planned programme of care for all patients with diabetes
- Clear management plans agreed with each patient, tailored to

meet the needs of the individual and their carers
* Practice-based diabetes registers to facilitate regular call and recall of patients

Healthcare professionals have a responsibility to provide appropriate education to equip people with diabetes with the knowledge, skills, attitudes and motivation to effectively manage their diabetes care and modify their lifestyle in such a way as to maximise their well-being.

Is there evidence that improved glycaemic control leads to a reduction in complications?

There is increasing evidence to confirm that meticulous glycaemic control can prevent or delay the onset of the complications of diabetes. The impact of these complications can also be greatly reduced if they are detected early and appropriately managed. Thus, regular surveillance for and early diagnosis of the complications of diabetes are also important. There are two very important studies regarding this:

1.   DCCT (Diabetes Control and Complications Trial)

This is an important study which demonstrated that patients receiving intensive insulin treatment for their diabetes had fewer microvascular complications (*Diabetes 1996;45:1289–98*). The long-term, follow-up of these patients was later published (*NEJM 2000;342:381–5*) which showed that these benefits persist. However, the improved glycaemic control was not completely advantageous to patients as it resulted in the need for more frequent basal metabolism (BM) testing and increased frequency of insulin injections. Many patients also gained weight and had an increased frequency of hypoglycaemic episodes, so it actually resulted in a huge disruption to their lifestyles.

2.   UKPDS (UK Prospective Diabetes Study)

This was a massive study involving over 5,000 type 2 diabetic patients over a 20-year period, which studied whether intensive control of blood glucose after diagnosis of diabetes was beneficial (*Lancet 1998;353:837–53*). It demonstrated that better glycaemic control reduced microvascular complications and that intense management of cardiovascular risk factors reduced macrovascular complications. Essentially, the lower the levels of blood glucose, HbA1C and BP, the lower the risk of complications.

Should there be a screening programme for type 2 diabetes?

The UKPDS study also showed that about 50% of patients had early signs of complications at the time of diagnosis of their diabetes. This therefore raises the question of whether screening for diabetes should be introduced; if diabetes is diagnosed earlier then, theoretically, there would be a reduced incidence of complications. This issue is clearly discussed in a BMJ Education and Debate article (*BMJ 2001;322:986–8*). This article concludes that, at present, there is no justification for universal diabetes screening in the UK. However, there is some support for screening and intensive treatment for those population subgroups in which undiagnosed diabetes is especially prevalent and the cardiovascular risk is high, provided the systems for organisation and management are optimised.

The NSF is expected to set GP targets for screening – in patients who are obese, have CHD, have a family history of diabetes or are of Asian descent. Primary care teams will play an important part in helping those with diabetes achieve better control and in detecting the earliest signs of complications, through regular systematic surveillance.

How important is treating hypertension in diabetic patients?
A study using the UKPDS data showed that any reduction in blood pressure for type 2 diabetic patients reduces the risk of complications (*BMJ 2000;321:412–20*). Intensive BP control is at least as (probably even more) important as intensive treatment of glucose levels in the reduction of complications in diabetic patients. The blood pressure target from the UKPDS study has been set at 140/80 mmHg.

It has been estimated that the number of diabetics taking antihypertensive medication would need to double in order to meet the targets of 140/80 mmHg!

The HOPE (Heart Outcomes Prevention Evaluation) study showed that adding ramipril to high-risk diabetic patients provides vascularprotective and renoprotective effects independent of its effect on hypertension (*Lancet 2000;355:253–9*).

Do diabetic patients have a higher risk of cardiovascular disease?
Patients with diabetes, especially type 2, have a greatly increased risk of cardiovascular disease compared with non-diabetics. This is clearly illustrated in the Joint British Societies Coronary Risk Prediction charts. Four out of five deaths in patients with type 2 diabetes are caused by cardiovascular disease. It is important to institute statin and aspirin therapy in patients with type 2 diabetes and established cardiovascular

disease. The current recommendation is to prescribe statins to patients with a 30% risk over 10 years of a CHD event.

In view of the high risk of cardiovascular disease in people with diabetes, particularly those with type 2 diabetes, the careful management of other cardiovascular risk factors – including smoking, physical inactivity, obesity and especially hypertension – in their annual diabetes review is essential.

What are the glitazones?
A new class of drugs for type 2 diabetics called 'glitazones' have fairly recently been introduced; rosiglitazone (Avandia) and pioglitazone (Actos) were launched in 2000. They work by reducing the body's resistance to the action of insulin and enable a more efficient use of insulin. They are licensed for combination use with a sulphonylurea or metformin (which are contraindicated for use with insulin).

These new agents offer a real alternative in the treatment of obese patients who do not achieve sufficient blood-glucose control with metformin and are expected to postpone the need for insulin therapy in type 2 diabetics for some years. They also hold out the possibility that through treatment of insulin resistance, the macrovascular complications of type 2 diabetes may be reduced.

What does all this mean for patients?
It is well known that in practice it is very difficult to maintain any reductions in glucose concentrations and blood pressure, even with multiple drug combinations. It is a daunting prospect for any diabetic patient to consider taking metformin, ramipril, atorvastatin, aspirin, other oral hypoglycaemics and other antihypertensives on a regular basis!

Many diabetes experts are calling for proposed clinical targets in the diabetes NSF (*BMJ 2002;324:1577–80*) to be practical and geared towards individual patients. One consultant has estimated that the targets of an HbA1c of 7% and a BP of less than 140/90 mmHg could mean up to 10% of patients needing nine different medications.

The compliance of diabetic patients is poorer than expected – one study (*Diabet Med 2002;19:279–84*) collected anonymous information on prescriptions from diabetic patients in Dundee, which showed that only one-third of patients comply with single medications and about one-tenth comply with two medications!

The future of diabetes care in the UK will be challenging to primary care. Although clear therapeutic goals have been defined, doctors may need to negotiate realistic goals with individual patients regarding their optimal treatment.

USEFUL WEBSITES

www.diabetes.org.uk – Diabetes UK (formally the British Diabetic Association)
www.audit-commission.gov.uk – Audit Commission report
www.nsc.nhs.uk – National Screening Committee website – evaluation of Type 2 diabetes mellitus screening against the National Screening Committee Handbook criteria

---

SUMMARY POINTS FOR DIABETES

- ❖ Incidence of diabetes is rising
- ❖ New criteria for diagnosis of diabetes (June 2000)
- ❖ 75% diabetic patients are routinely managed in primary care
- ❖ Meticulous glycaemic control can reduce complications
- ❖ Careful management of other cardiovascular risk factors is essential
- ❖ NSF for diabetes is still awaited

OSTEOPOROSIS

Osteoporosis is defined as a skeletal disease characterised by low bone mass and deterioration of the microarchitecture of bone tissue, which makes bone more fragile and hence increases the risk of fracture.

Osteoporosis affects approximately 40% of women over 70 years of age in the UK. It is emerging as one of the biggest health problems in postmenopausal women – resulting in more deaths in older women than cancer of the cervix, uterus and ovaries combined. The annual cost to the NHS of osteoporotic fractures has been estimated at £1.5b, a hip fracture costs about £20,000 per fracture. Approximately 20% of patients die within a year of fracturing the neck of a femur as a result of osteoporosis.

A low level of awareness of the benefits of early identification for risk factors, together with the pressure to reduce prescribing costs, often results in ineffective disease management. It is not surprising therefore that any clinical interventions to both prevent and treat osteoporosis have been very topical recently.

The National Service Framework (NSF) for older people addresses the need for action on the prevention and treatment of osteoporosis. It also acknowledges that preventing osteoporosis in high-risk patients has a significant effect on both the number and severity of fractures.

How are patients at high risk of osteoporosis identified?
Osteoporosis can be reliably identified by bone densitometry, which is still the 'gold standard' for both the measurement of disease and the response to therapy. Unfortunately, the availability of dual-energy, X-ray absorptiometry (DEXA) scanning machines is still very variable across the UK, despite only costing the NHS £20–45 per scan. DEXA scans have been shown to predict future fracture rate with a high specificity but low sensitivity. It is recommended that DEXA scanning should be used for patients at a high risk of developing osteoporosis rather than for screening the general population (see Box on p. 36).

A previous fragility fracture is a strong independent risk for further fracture and is, in itself, an indication for treatment for osteoporosis without the need for bone mineral density measurement. However, one audit found that most patients who have an osteoporotic fracture are not started on treatment for the secondary prevention of osteoporosis (*Ann Rheum Dis 1998;57:378–9*).

How important is corticosteroid-induced osteoporosis?

In most patients on long-term oral corticosteroid treatment, there is a fall in bone mass and bone mineral density. Longitudinal studies have shown that the most rapid rate of bone loss occurs in the first year of treatment, and thereafter bone loss continues at a rate of two to three times normal on long-term therapy in older subjects. As many as 40% of patients on long-term steroids may develop a fracture secondary to osteoporosis.

The exact dose of corticosteroid that induces clinically significant bone loss is not yet well established. Studies in patients have consistently demonstrated a clinically important fall in bone density in patients taking 7.5 mg prednisolone a day. One study indicated that only 14% of patients treated with oral corticosteroids are also prescribed therapy to prevent bone loss (*BMJ 1996;313:344–6*).

The National Osteoporosis Society has produced guidelines on the management of glucocorticoid-induced osteoporosis, which, where possible, are based on current clinical evidence (see their website). In the UK, the most commonly used therapies for glucocorticoid-induced osteoporosis are hormone-replacement therapy and bisphosphonates.

What drug interventions can be used to prevent and treat osteoporosis?

The Royal College of Physicians issued guidelines in 1999 for the prevention and treatment of osteoporosis. In the 18 months following the release of these guidelines, new clinical trial data became available for existing and new pharmacological interventions. Hence, an 'Update on pharmacological interventions for the prevention and treatment of osteoporosis' has been prepared by the original Guidelines Writing Group, in collaboration with the Bone and Tooth Society, and endorsed by the Royal College of Physicians. This report also includes a useful algorithm for the management of individual patients, derived from an evidence-based synthesis of different pharmacological interventions.

Prophylaxis against osteoporosis obviously needs to be continued long term. There is no evidence that bone protection lasts much beyond current use for any treatment option, so long-term costs (both to the patient and financially) have to be considered. The side-effects and method of administration must therefore be acceptable to the patient if compliance is to be optimal. Thus the increasing range of treatments and the greater acceptability of these options are very important.

Bisphosphonates

Cyclical etidronate (Didronel), alendronate (Fosamax) and risedronate (Actonel) are all licensed for the prevention and treatment of osteoporosis (and corticosteroid-induced osteoporosis). There are, at present, no randomised controlled trials comparing the relative efficacy of these agents. Generally, cyclical etidronate may be best for patients with mainly lumbar spine disease, while alendronate is beneficial in patients with more severe disease involving both lumbar spine and femoral neck (and also for patients who may prefer once-weekly therapy). The optimal duration of treatment with bisphosphonates has not yet been established.

Selective oestrogen-receptor modulator therapy (SERMs)

Raloxifene mimics the beneficial effects of oestrogen on the bone but blocks the oestrogen effect on the uterus and breast tissue. The effect of Raloxifene in reducing vertebral fractures is similar to that of bisphosphonates, and its effect on bone mineral density (BMD) is similar to that of oestrogens. It does not cause uterine bleeding or gastrointestinal side-effects, and does not raise concerns about breast disease (JAMA 1999;282:637–45). The precise place for Raloxifene in the prevention and management of osteoporosis in general practice is still a matter for debate.

Hormone-replacement therapy (HRT)

Earlier assumptions that taking HRT would reduce the risk of fracture in the future have unfortunately not been confirmed; oestrogen-induced skeletal benefits probably disappear within 6–10 years of stopping treatment. 10 years after HRT has been stopped, bone density and fracture risk are similar in women who have not taken HRT. Therefore, women would need to take oestrogens from their menopause until at least their early 70s to reduce their risk of osteoporotic fractures.

However, oestrogen can be a cost-effective treatment option for postmenopausal women. Numerous studies have shown that oestrogen reduces the risk of hip fracture by about 30% and of spine fracture by about 50%. The reduction in fracture risk by oestrogen exceeds that expected based on bone density alone. The bone protection gained from HRT treatment has also recently been confirmed in the Women's Health Initiative Study (JAMA 2002;288:321–33). It demonstrated a lower hip fracture rate (10 per 10,000 person-years vs 15 per 10,000 person-years for placebo). Combined HRT also reduced the clinical vertebral fracture rate by one-third compared to placebo. The total reductions of osteoporotic fractures in this study were 24%.

Calcium and Vitamin D

Calcium and vitamin D supplements may slow down the rate of bone loss in elderly women who already have a low BMD. However, in patients with established osteoporosis this effect is not enough. Calcium can complement the other treatments (SERMs, bisphosphonates, oestrogen) though. It is recommended that those people at risk of osteoporosis should maintain an adequate intake of calcium and vitamin D, and any deficiency should be corrected by increasing dietary intake or taking supplements. Elderly patients, especially those in residential or nursing homes, may routinely benefit from supplements.

Statins

Finally, one observation found that inhibition of hydroxymethylglutaryl coenzyme A reductase with statin therapy may reduce the risk of fracture (*JAMA 2000;283:3205–10*). This therefore raises the possibility that patients requiring statins for their cardiovascular disease may derive additional benefit in terms of osteoporosis prevention!

 USEFUL WEBSITES

www.doh.gov.uk/osteorep.htm – DoH guidelines on prevention and treatment (produced by the RCP)
www.nos.org.uk – National Osteoporosis Society
www.doh.gov.uk/nsf/olderpeople.htm – National Service Framework for Older People

RISK FACTORS FOR OSTEOPOROSIS

❖ Early menopause
❖ Hysterectomy < 45 years
❖ Long-term prednisolone ≥ 7.5mg/day
❖ Malabsorption disorder (e.g. coeliac disease)
❖ Premenopausal episodes of amenorrhoea
❖ Lean body habitus
❖ Strong family history
❖ Cigarette smoking

SUMMARY POINTS FOR OSTEOPOROSIS

❖ Annual cost of osteoporosis to NHS is £940 million
❖ Often underdiagnosed and suboptimally managed
❖ Several effective medical interventions available
❖ Poor compliance with treatment is a problem

HYPERLIPIDAEMIA – IMPORTANT TRIALS

Lowering the concentration of low-density lipoprotein (LDL) -cholesterol and raising that of high-density lipoprotein (HDL) -cholesterol reduces the progression of coronary atherosclerosis and may even induce regression. There is evidence that lowering total cholesterol by 20–25% is effective in both the primary and secondary prevention of clinical manifestations of coronary heart disease (CHD).

Statins have a role in the primary prevention of coronary events in patients at increased risk. A statin should be considered for patients with a total cholesterol of ≥5 mmol/l and a CHD risk ≥30% over 10 years.

For the primary and secondary prevention of CHD, statin treatment should be adjusted to lower the serum total cholesterol concentrations to below 5 mmol/l or by 20–30% (or LDL-cholesterol concentrations to below 3 mmol/l or by 30%), whichever results in the lower concentration.

PRIMARY PREVENTION TRIALS
There are some key, important trials supporting the evidence.

The West of Scotland Coronary Prevention Study (WOSCOPS)
(J. Shepherd, et al., NEJM 1995;333:1301–7)

Randomised controlled trial involving 6,595 men (many of whom were smokers) aged 45–64 years with high cholesterol levels (average 7.0 mmol/l) and no previous history of myocardial infarction (MI). They received either placebo or pravastatin and were followed up for 5 years.

Pravastatin was found to reduce the risk of:
- First heart attack or coronary death by 31%
- Non-fatal heart attack by 31%
- Cardiovascular death by 32%
- Death from any cause by 22%
- Revascularisation procedures by 37%

The Air Force/Texas Coronary Atherosclerosis Prevention Study
(J. R. Downs, et al., JAMA 1998;279:1615–22)

Randomised, double-blinded trial involving 5,608 men and 997 women with average cholesterol levels of 5.71 mmol/l and no previous history of cardiovascular disease. They received either placebo or lovastatin and average follow-up was for 5.2 years.

Lovastatin was found to reduce the risk of:
- First acute major coronary event by 37%
- Incidence of CHD by 40%
- Revascularisation procedures by 33%

Both these studies illustrate that lipid levels alone (except for those with extreme elevations) are relatively weak individual predictors of cardiovascular risk. It therefore follows that any prevention strategy based primarily on lipid levels will require a very large number of patients to be treated in order for a significant number to benefit.

SECONDARY PREVENTION TRIALS

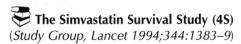 The Simvastatin Survival Study (4S)
(*Study Group, Lancet 1994;344:1383–9*)

This was the first landmark trial of LDL-cholesterol lowering with statins for the secondary prevention of CHD. It was a randomised, controlled, double-blinded trial involving 4,444 men and women aged 35–69 years and from 94 centres in Denmark, Finland, Norway and Sweden. Patients were randomised to take placebo or simvastatin. All patients had a history of myocardial infarction and/or angina and mild to moderately high total cholesterol levels of 5.8–8.0 mmol/l. The patients were followed up for a mean of 5.4 years.

Simvastatin was found to reduce the risk of:
- Death by 30%
- Coronary death by 42%
- Major coronary events by 34%
- Revascularisation procedures by 37%

Cholesterol and Recurrent Events (CARE)
(*F. M. Sacks, et al., NEJM 1996;335:1001–9*)

Another randomised controlled trial of 4,159 men and women aged 21–75 years, all of whom had all suffered a heart attack in the previous 2 years and had an average total cholesterol of 5.4 mmol/l. Patients were randomised to receive either pravastatin or placebo and were followed up for 5 years.

Pravastatin was found to reduce the risk of:
- CHD death/non-fatal MI by 24%
- CHD death by 19%
- Fatal MI by 37%
- Stroke by 28%
- Revascularisation procedures by 26%

The Long-term Intervention with Pravastatin in Ischaemic Disease (LIPID)
(Study Group, NEJM 1998;339:1349–57)

This was a trial similar to CARE but with higher patient numbers. This double-blinded, randomised, controlled trial compared the effects of pravastatin with those of placebo over a mean follow-up period of 6.1 years in 9,014 patients who were 31–75 years of age. The patients had a history of MI or unstable angina and cholesterol levels of between 4 and 7 mmol/l.

Pravastatin was found to reduce the risk of:
- CHD death/non-fatal MI by 24%
- CHD death by 21%
- Overall mortality by 22%
- Revascularisation procedures by 20%

Subgroup results
Some of the subgroup analyses of these three key studies are important:
1. **Diabetic patients** – All three studies confirmed that statins are of benefit to diabetic patients. As the primary effect of statin therapy is to lower LDL particle number, the findings actually point to LDL being of major importance in the pathogenesis of atherosclerosis in diabetes.

2. **Women** – Although women develop coronary heart disease at a later age than men, women have still been found to benefit at least as much as men in these trials. The numbers of women compared to men are lower in the trials.

3. **Older patients** – There is still scanty evidence regarding the benefits of treating raised cholesterol in patients over 75 years. However, people aged 65–75 years do obtain benefit from statin therapy. As most coronary events occur in older people, even moderate reductions in relative risk will lead to marked gains in

terms of absolute numbers of events avoided.

4. **Cerebrovascular accidents** – These were significantly reduced both in the CARE and LIPID studies. Further studies are essential to determine whether statins can prevent vascular events in patients with cerebrovascular disease (and no CHD).

Should every patient with any cardiovascular risk factor receive a statin?
This is potentially a very expensive question to answer! It is clear that priority for treatment must be given to those whose arterial disease is already evident, but the relative benefit from treatment is remarkably constant across all groups of patients.

The recently published Heart Protection Study confirmed that treating patients at high risk of cardiovascular events with statins reduces the risk of MI, stroke and revascularisation by about one-third, **even** in patients with normal or low cholesterol levels (*Lancet 2002;360:7–22*). It is clear that it is the cardiovascular risk which is important rather than the actual level of cholesterol. If a patient is at a high enough cardiovascular risk that is worth reducing by one-third, then it is worth considering statin treatment regardless of their actual cholesterol level. Results from this study have estimated that 5 years of simvastatin treatment would prevent about 70–100 people per 1000 from experiencing at least one major vascular event and longer treatment would produce further benefit.

This trial is also important as it targeted patients who are underrepresented in other trials, including over-70s, women and diabetic patients. The relative-risk reduction in events was remarkably consistent among all of these patients.

The authors of the Heart Protection Study have said that statins could benefit three times the number of patients currently receiving them – thus tripling the statins drug bill. However, on the other side, the wider prescribing of statins could potentially save 10,000 lives from cardiovascular disease. The Department of Health is apparently considering reviewing the current guidance in light of this study, which may lead to a new publication by NICE.

It is obviously possible to argue that virtually anyone who needs to take aspirin really ought to be taking a statin as well!

Important additional measures to drug treatment

Appropriate lifestyle modifications should be identified and continued indefinitely in all patients worthy of risk assessment (even if their risk is below 30% over 10 years). In primary prevention, stopping smoking alone may often reduce the CHD risk sufficiently to eliminate the need for statin treatment (*BJGP 1999;49:217–18*). Other appropriate measures include weight reduction, reducing the intake of saturated fat and increasing that of polyunsaturated fat, regular physical exercise and, when appropriate, additional measures to reduce BP and control blood glucose.

Diet can decrease levels of both cholesterol and triglycerides. However, patients at high CHD risk should not be denied statin treatment – diet should be regarded as an adjunct therapy. Patients should reduce their saturated fat intake and replace them with carbohydrates, poly-unsaturated fats or monounsaturated fats. Products 'low in cholesterol' are unimportant, as they should be low in unsaturated fat; dietary cholesterol does not contribute greatly to blood cholesterol levels.

Which statin should be used?

Pravastatin and simvastatin have an advantage in terms of weight of clinical evidence for long-term safety and effectiveness. The dose required to lower LDL-cholesterol concentrations varies substantially between the different statins. At current maximum doses, atorvastatin appears the most effective followed by simvastatin then pravastatin and fluvastatin (*Am J Cardiol 1998;81:582–7*). In addition, atorvastatin and simvastatin appear to have the greatest effect of lowering plasma triglycerides' concentrations.

Patients should be prescribed the lowest licensed dose initially, and which should be taken in the evening for maximum effect. Measurement of total or LDL-cholesterol concentrations should be performed 6 weeks after dosage adjustments are made and then annually when the desired lipid concentrations are achieved.

USEFUL WEBSITES

www.bcs.com – British Cardiac Society
www.pccs.org.uk – Primary Care Cardiovascular Society
www.hyp.ac.uk/bhs – British Hypertension Society (includes copies of CHD risk charts)
www.bhf.org.uk – British Heart Foundation

SUMMARY POINTS FOR HYPERCHOLESTEROLAEMIA

❖ Lowering cholesterol by 20–25% is beneficial
❖ Only treat for primary prevention if CHD risk >30%
❖ Cost of statin prescribing is increasing fast
❖ Less than one-third of patients with CHD currently receive statins
❖ Women also benefit from statins
❖ Treatment is of proven benefit for patients under 75 years of age

---

CHAPTER 2: RESPIRATORY DISEASES

ASTHMA

Asthma is still underdiagnosed and poorly treated despite an increased awareness of the condition. Asthma has been estimated to cost the NHS £850m a year, with half of these costs arising as a result of acute asthma attacks. Over 18 million working days are lost to asthma each year. Most patients with asthma are managed in primary care. The British Thoracic Society guidelines are an example of very successful guidelines and are due to be updated soon.

How safe are inhaled steroids?
The amount of inhaled steroid absorbed in the body is very low, but systemic side-effects can occur – e.g. osteoporosis, growth retardation and cataracts. Side-effects are unlikely with low-dose inhaled steroids (<400 mg beclometasone/day in children and <1000 mg/day in adults). All children receiving inhaled steroids should have their height measured regularly, and any children needing high maintenance doses are best supervised by a paediatrician. Children with a viral associated wheeze should not be prescribed inhaled steroids. The most important safeguard for patients is to have their asthma controlled regularly, and the dose of inhaled steroid stepped down once control of symptoms is achieved (*Drug Ther Bull Jan 2000*).

The Cochrane Airways Group has reviewed six randomised, controlled trials (RCTs) looking at patients with asthma or chronic obstructive airways disease (COAD) who are on steroids. No significant rise in bone turnover was found in any of the studies up to 3 years after steroids were first prescribed, provided they had been given at recommended blood transfusion service British Thoracic Society (BTS) levels.

What are the National Institute for Clinical Excellence (NICE) guidelines for childhood asthma?
In August 2000, NICE produced guidelines for the use of inhaler devices in children under 5 years with chronic asthma. The main recommendations are:
- Pressurised metered-dose inhalers with a spacer system (with a facemask if necessary)
- A dry powder could be considered for children aged 3–5 years
- Choice of inhaler should be governed by specific individual need and likelihood of good compliance

Which new drugs are available to treat asthma?

Leukotriene receptor antagonists – montelukast (Singulair) and zafirlukast (Accolate) – are a new class of oral asthma therapies that have anti-inflammatory and bronchodilator properties. They have been introduced since the National Asthma guidelines were written in 1995. Currently they seem to be best used as add-ons to low- or high-dose inhaled steroids where control of persistent asthma symptoms has not been achieved (Steps 3 and 4 of the guidelines).

However, a systematic review recently examined the evidence for the efficacy and glucocorticoid sparing effect of oral antileukotrienes in asthmatic patients (*BMJ 2002;324:1545–8*). This found that there is a shortage of relevant trials testing antileukotrienes as add-on treatment, and showed that these drugs may modestly improve the control of asthma. There is still little evidence to support their use as a substitute to increasing the dose of inhaled glucocorticoids. This review concluded that until further evidence is available, the 'gold standard' of asthma treatment should remain the use of inhaled glucocorticoids at the lowest effective dose.

Do self-management plans have a role in asthma management?

Asthma lends itself to the use of guided self-management plans based on the BTS guidelines. There is plenty of evidence which shows that the use of self-management plans for asthma can lead to a reduction in hospitalisation rates, time off work and improvement in symptom control. Nurses with advanced qualifications in asthma provide self-management plans significantly more frequently than other nurses.

However, a study in the BMJ showed that the concept of patient self-management plans received a lukewarm response from GPs, practice nurses and patients (*BMJ 2000;321:1507–10*). Many patients are not actually interested in self-management plans; many believe they are already managing their asthma adequately! Asthma patients generally do not regard their condition as a chronic disease that needs regular monitoring and therapeutic adjustments, they prefer to manage it as an intermittent acute disorder. Many patients do not even wish to attend for regular asthma reviews – 45% of patients questioned said they neither had nor wanted regular asthma reviews (*Asthma 2000;5:141–4*).

How well is asthma controlled in primary care?

The ultimate goal is to help patients lead a normal life, free from symptoms and with no limitations on activities. According to the

'National Asthma Campaign's Needs of People with Asthma' survey, there are as many as 1.4 million people in the UK whose asthma control is less than satisfactory (*Asthma 2000;5:133–7*).

This study showed that 42% of the asthma population have their daily life affected by symptoms related to their asthma. Perhaps of more concern, patients still seem to have very low expectations about their asthma. One study showed that 87% of patients were either very satisfied or fairly satisfied with their asthma care (*Asthma 2000;5:141–4*). However, 44.5% reported activity limitation and 87.5% experienced asthma symptoms during the night; obviously suggesting that patients' perspectives on their disease and its treatment differs substantially from that of medical professions!

What is the best way of identifying suboptimal control of asthma?
Although objective measurements of peak expiratory flow rate are important in assessing the severity and control of asthma, a symptom-based assessment is also very useful in clinical practice (*BJGP 2000;50:7–12*). The three best questions to use are:
- Have you had difficulty sleeping because of your asthma?
- Have you had your asthma symptoms during the day?
- Has your asthma interfered with your usual activities?

A recent survey – the ACE (Asthma Control and Expectations) survey – highlighted that patients have much lower expectations of asthma control and treatment than are laid out in asthma management guidelines (*Int J Clin Pract 2002;53:89–93*). As a result, many accept a life with unnecessary symptoms and activity limitations (see Box on p. 47). Healthcare professionals therefore have a role in improving asthma management by helping to raise patient expectations of what is achievable in terms of asthma control.

 USEFUL WEBSITES

www.gpiag-asthma.org – GPs in asthma group
www.brit-thoracic.org.uk – British Thoracic Society

🗋 SUMMARY POINTS FOR ASTHMA

❖ Essential to learn BTS guidelines
❖ CFC-free inhalers are replacing CFC inhalers
❖ NICE guidelines for childhood asthma are realistic
❖ Patients are not keen on self-management plans
❖ Patient expectations of asthma control are very low

Key Findings of the ACE Survey

- Of patients who said they usually felt well:
    - around 1/3 experienced daily symptoms
    - 51% accepted limitations on their lifestyle

- 32% of patients modify their behaviour when they feel their asthma is getting worse to avoid symptoms

- 89% of patients do not discuss their lifestyle limitations with their healthcare professional

SMOKING CESSATION

Smoking is the single greatest cause of preventable illness and premature death in the UK, and leads to direct medical costs of £1.7b each year. Cigarette smoking will cause about 450 million deaths worldwide in the next 50 years. It is therefore a top healthcare priority, especially as there has been a recent increase in the number of smokers. The NHS Plan states that a comprehensive smoking cessation service has been in place since 2001.

Around one in four adults smoke, with much higher levels in deprived sections of society. However, giving up permanently is difficult; although two-thirds of smokers want to quit, and about one-third try each year, only 2% actually succeed.

On average, 70% of smokers consult their GP each year, so primary care teams need to be involved with smoking cessation programmes. The authors of the Sheffield table have even estimated that the statin bill could be reduced by 85% if everyone stopped smoking!

What are the updated smoking cessation guidelines?
In December 2000, Thorax published updated guidelines for tackling cigarette dependence (*Thorax 2000;55:987–99*). They recognise that GPs have a pivotal role if the NHS is to deliver a noticeable drop in smoking rates. These guidelines are based on strong evidence from randomised trials supplemented by studies examining what can be achieved in routine clinical practice.

The guidelines recommend that all GPs give brief advice at least once a year to all their patients who smoke, and if they respond positively they should then be referred to a smoking cessation clinic and considered for either nicotine replacement therapy (NRT) or Zyban. GPs will therefore need to keep up-to-date records of patients' smoking status, advice they received and the response to that advice.

What are the advantages of stopping smoking?
There are obviously huge benefits from stopping smoking. Widespread cessation of smoking in the UK has already approximately halved the lung cancer mortality that would have been expected if former smokers had continued to smoke.

Underscoring the health benefits of smoking cessation is the report by

Doll et al. based on a comparison of two case-control studies conducted 40 years apart in the United Kingdom (BMJ 2000;321:323–9). Even smokers who stop at age 50 or 60 years avoid much of their excess risk of developing lung cancer. The benefits of cessation become progressively greater with a younger age of quitting; stopping smoking before middle age avoids more than 90% of the risk attributable to tobacco.

How effective are smoking cessation treatments?

Helping smokers to stop is actually one of the most cost-effective interventions in the NHS today (BMJ 2001;323:1140–1). The cost-effectiveness of smoking cessation treatments has been calculated at just over £600 per life-year gained for treated smokers aged 35–44 and £750 for those aged 45–54 years. By comparison, statin therapy to lower blood cholesterol concentrations ranges from about £4,000 to £13,000 per life-year gained.

The NHS Centre for Reviews and Dissemination (University of York) has produced a systematic review of smoking cessation treatments. The results also show that both NRT and bupropion are cost-effective treatments in terms of cost per life-year saved.

Smoking cessation treatments have been established throughout the NHS and are an integral part of the Government's plans to reduce deaths from coronary heart disease and cancer. In England between April 2000 and March 2001 about 127 000 smokers set a quit date and 48% of these stopped at 1 month. This has been achieved by just over 500 new staff and at a total cost of £21.4m.

A wide array of effective smoking cessation treatments are available. A BMJ article provides an up-to-date and comprehensive review of the effectiveness of smoking cessation treatments (BMJ 2000;321:355–8).

Nicotine replacement therapy (NRT)

This treatment aims to replace the nicotine obtained from cigarettes, thus reducing withdrawal symptoms when stopping smoking. Nicotine replacement is available as chewing gum, transdermal patch, nasal spray, inhaler, sublingual tablet, and lozenge. A Cochrane review of over 90 trials found that nicotine replacement helps people to stop smoking. Overall, it increased the chances of quitting about 1.5–2 times, whatever the level of additional support and encouragement. Since all the trials of nicotine replacement have included at least brief advice, this is the minimum that should be offered. More intensive support seems to be more effective; for example, NRT prescribed after GPs brief advice can result in up to 10% of smokers stopping, but NRT together with support from specialist counsellors can result in up to 20% of smokers stopping.

There is little direct evidence that one nicotine product is more effective than another. Thus the decision about which product to use should be guided by individual preferences. The Government announced in April 2001 it would allow NRT to be available on NHS prescriptions. This decision fulfilled the commitment the Government made in the NHS Plan.

What is bupropion (Zyban)?
This was initially developed as an antidepressant. One hypothesis of its mode of action is that it works by increasing levels of dopamine and noradrenaline in the brain, thereby counteracting the reductions in these chemicals that result from nicotine withdrawal. The efficacy of bupropion as an aid to smoking cessation has been investigated in two randomised, double-blinded, placebo-controlled trials (*NEJM 1997;337:1195–202 and NEJM 1999;340:685–91*). These patients received regular counselling sessions in addition to bupropion. Results have indicated that up to 30% of smokers succeed with bupropion and that these results are sustained over a year.

Zyban is relatively well tolerated; contraindications to it include epilepsy, pregnancy and concomitant antidepressants. The risk of fits has been estimated at about 1 in 1,000 people, which is actually the same risk as for amitriptyline and imipramine. Zyban may also increase the risk of fits through interactions with other drugs that lower the seizure threshold; including antipsychotics, antidepressants, systemic steroids, antimalarial drugs and theophylline.

At least 500,000 patients have received Zyban since it was launched in the UK in June 2000. During this time there have been about 160 reports of seizures; approximately half of which occurred in patients who already had a history of seizures or were at risk of them. More concerning is the small number of deaths reported among people taking Zyban. These cases are currently being investigated by the Committee on the Safety of Medicines (CSM); it is felt that the individual's underlying condition may actually have been the cause of death in the majority of cases. The recommended dosage of Zyban was reduced in June 2001; the CSM has stated that the dose should be increased from day seven of treatment (rather than day four).

It has been suggested that to prescribe Zyban, patients should answer yes to following questions:

- Do you want to stop smoking?
- Is it very important for you to stop?
- Would you be prepared to stop smoking in the next 2 weeks?

Most patients are being prescribed Zyban in designated smoking cessation clinics where regular counselling and follow-up can be provided, but this varies enormously across regions.

There is little evidence to support the superiority of bupropion over NRT for smoking cessation; one double-blind study indicated that the NRT patch is less effective than bupropion, while another unblended study found no difference between NRT gum and bupropion; further RCTs are clearly needed.

There is currently not enough evidence to recommend the use of NRT and bupropion together.

What are the NICE recommendations for smoking cessation treatments?

In April 2002, NICE recommended the use of bupropion and NRT for smokers who wish to quit. The guidance states that NRT or bupropion should normally only be prescribed when smokers have made a commitment to stop smoking on or before a certain date ('target stop date'), in conjunction with advice and encouragement to help them quit.

First prescriptions of NRT or bupropion should only be enough to last until 2 weeks after the target stop date. Normally, this will be 2 weeks for NRT. For bupropion it will be 3–4 weeks, this is because bupropion should be taken for about 1 week before the target stop date. Smokers should only be given a second prescription for NRT or bupropion if they can show they are still trying to stop smoking.

Other treatments

The effectiveness of other treatments – namely: aversion therapy, acupuncture, hypnotherapy, and exercise – is as yet uncertain.

What is the cycle of change and how can it be used for smoking cessation?

There are undoubtedly certain times when a patient will be more receptive to advice on stopping smoking. Smoking cessation should not be regarded as a dichotomous process (cessation or not), but rather as a continuum that entails several stages. DiClemente and Prochaska's cycle of readiness to change (see Figure on p. 54) has been used to describe the psychological processes involved in many patterns of human behaviour and lends itself very well to smoking cessation (*J Consult Clin Psychol 1991;59:295–304*). It is important to know the 'cycle of change' as it can be applied to various aspects of clinical practice, and can be very useful to discuss in the viva examination!

Precontemplation
This is the stage at which the patient is happy at being a smoker and does not contemplate stopping. Although brief intervention at this stage may not persuade them to give up, it may help them question their habit and move them nearer to the next stage.

Contemplation
This is the stage at which the patient is dissatisfied with being a smoker and is thinking about giving up (70% of adult smokers are at this stage!). During this stage, it can be effective to make the idea of quitting relevant to the patient, for example a patient recently diagnosed with heart disease.

Preparation
This is the stage at which the smoker is making serious plans to stop. It is therefore important to be supportive; discussion about smoking cessation treatments is most beneficial at this stage.

Action
This is the stage when maximum support should be given, as it is at this stage when the attempt to stop smoking is made.

Maintenance
This is the stage at which the patient tries to prevent relapse. This is often the most difficult time as enthusiasm often wears off quicker than withdrawal symptoms.

Relapse
This is obviously when the patient's attempt to stop smoking has been unsuccessful. This can either mean permanently giving up the idea of quitting smoking or thinking about it again in the future, whereby the patient would then re-enter the cycle at the precontemplation stage once more.

NB.

If the doctor or healthcare professional is unaware of where their patient is in this cycle of change, then any time and effort given regarding smoking cessation may be wasted.

What is the role of doctors in smoking cessation?

Tobacco dependence is also a chronic relapsing condition; like other addictions and chronic diseases, it warrants repeated clinical intervention. An important challenge is to integrate the available, evidence-based, and cost-effective treatment of smoking cessation therapies into medical practice. The number of people successfully quitting smoking after using the smoking cessation services has actually been found to have more than doubled from April to September 2000 when compared with 1999.

In addition, by taking a few moments to identify where the patient is in the cycle of change, and tailoring the advice accordingly, the GP may be able to make each intervention more effective still.

 USEFUL WEBSITES

www.update-software.com/ccweb/cochrane/revabstr/g160index.htm – Cochrane reviews
www.nhs.uk/nhsplan – The NHS Plan
www.open.gov.uk/mca/mcahome.htm – Medicines Control Agency (for further information on the CSM)
www.nice.org.uk – NICE guidance

DiClemente and Prochaska's cycle of change

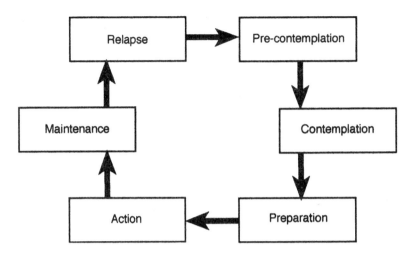

┌───┐
│ ▢ **SUMMARY POINTS FOR SMOKING CESSATION**

❖ Over 75% of smokers consult their GPs annually
❖ Only 2% smokers manage to give up by themselves
❖ Smoking cessation clinics have promising results
❖ Zyban can help up to a third of smokers to stop smoking
❖ Assessing smokers' motivation to quit is important
❖ Consider the 'cycle of change'
└───┘

INFLUENZA

During the winter months there is usually an outbreak of influenza, which results in a huge increased workload for both primary care teams and hospitals. Even when the incidence is low, it has been estimated that 3–4,000 deaths in the UK each year are from influenza related causes.

What are the benefits of the influenza vaccine?
There is plenty of evidence to support the effectiveness of the vaccine; it reduces mortality and morbidity in high-risk groups. In May 2000 the policy on influenza vaccination was altered and the vaccine is now recommended for:
* All people over 65 years
* All people in long stay residential accommodation
* All people with:
  * Chronic respiratory disease, including asthma
  * Chronic heart disease
  * Chronic renal disease
  * Diabetes mellitus
  * Immunosuppression due to disease or treatment.

What are the benefits of the influenza vaccine?
There is plenty of evidence to support the effectiveness of the vaccine; it reduces mortality and morbidity in high-risk groups. In May 2000 the policy on influenza vaccination was altered and the vaccine is now recommended for:
* All people over 65 years
* All people in long-stay residential accommodation
* All people with:
  * Chronic respiratory disease, including asthma
  * Chronic heart disease
  * Chronic renal disease
  * Diabetes mellitus
  * Immunosuppression due to disease or treatment.

Various studies have demonstrated that the influenza vaccine can reduce mortality by around 40% compared with matched controls. Health authorities were set a target of achieving a minimum of 65% uptake of immunisation in over 65-year-old patients for winter 2001/2, and 70% for winter 2002/3.

A study showed a marked reduction in hospital admission for various diseases in people who had received the influenza vaccination (*Lancet 2001;357:1008–11*). In particular, there was a 46% reduction in admissions for influenza and a lower mortality from all causes (53–56% reduction).

When should Relenza be prescribed?
In November 2000, NICE recommended that zanamivir (Relenza) should be used to treat 'at risk' adults when influenza is circulating in the community and if they present within 36 hours of developing symptoms.

'At risk' adults are defined as those with:
*   Chronic respiratory disease
*   Significant cardiovascular disease
*   Diabetes mellitus
*   Age over 65 years

This recommendation reverses the Institute's ruling last year that there was insufficient evidence of the drug's efficacy in high-risk individuals to make it worth prescribing on the NHS (*BMJ 1999;319:1024*).

What is the evidence for Relenza?
Relenza is a neuraminidase antiviral compound which works by diminishing the replication of the influenza virus within host epithelial cells. It can be used for both influenza types A and B. The recommendations have been written following an overall pooled analysis of eight trials involving 800 adults at high risk and new research by GlaxoSmithKline.
The pooled analysis showed a:
*   Reduction in the duration of symptoms by 1.2 days (6 to 5 days)
*   Reduction in duration of pyrexia by 0.5 days (2.5 to 2 days)
*   6% reduction in complications for which antibiotics were needed

When should Relenza be prescribed?
*   If flu has been shown to be circulating in the community
*   Only to patients at high risk
*   Within 36 hours of developing symptoms

Flu is considered to be circulating in the community when consultations for flu rise above 50 a week per 100,000 population, as monitored by the Royal College of General Practitioners' weekly returns' monitoring service. The Public Health Laboratory Service must also have identified the circulation of a flu virus.

Who will be responsible for prescribing Relenza?
These recommendations by NICE could potentially lead to a dramatic increase in GPs' workload during the winter months. It has been suggested that pharmacists and nurses will be allowed to prescribe zanamivir under the generalised directions of a doctor, provided they are satisfied that the patient needs it and satisfies the criteria. Telephone triaging by practice nurses may also be set up; the nurses will work to a protocol and ask standard diagnostic questions. However, the question then arises regarding the person directly responsible for the patient if there is a complication with taking the drug; often this will be the patient's GP.

It has been estimated that only 30% of self-diagnosed flu is actually due to influenza, and as there is no cheap, effective diagnostic test available many people may be unnecessarily be prescribed or unnecessarily request Relenza.

Why is there opposition to prescribing Relenza?
The evidence to support Relenza is still from small studies and many of the trials did not specifically recruit high-risk patients. Relenza's own product characteristics' statement said it had been unable to determine that the drug was effective in elderly patients and those with chronic conditions such as asthma and diabetes. In addition, there has been no published trial comparing Relenza's effect on influenza symptoms with symptomatic therapy (e.g. ibuprofen and paracetamol).

There have been reports of fatal adverse reactions in patients with COAD and asthma in the USA. It has therefore been recommended that if Relenza is to be prescribed for patients with airways disease, it should only be done under careful supervision with short-acting bronchodilators available. Any persuasive evidence of Relenza's cost-effectiveness is still lacking – NICE's own guidance states 'no reliable data are available as to the impact on the use of Relenza on hospitalisation or mortality'.

NICE originally refused to allow the drug to be prescribed on the NHS in 2000 and the BMJ has criticised NICE for responding to 'political clout'. The Drugs and Therapeutics Bulletin will still continue not to recommend Relenza as part of treatment of influenza as it is 'unconvinced of the benefits'.

Finally, one study has found that most elderly people cannot actually use the inhaler device correctly (*BMJ 2001;322:577–9*). One of the authors of the study has advised that GPs need to spend at least 15 minutes teaching their elderly patients how to use the device; this is not really realistic.

 USEFUL WEBSITES

www.phls.co.uk/facts/influenza/flu.htm – Up-to-date information from the Public Health Laboratory Service
www.rcgp-bru.demon.co.uk – Influenza surveillance website
www.nice.org.uk – NICE guidelines available online

☐ **SUMMARY POINTS FOR INFLUENZA**

❖ Influenza leads to about 3,000 deaths annually
❖ Influenza vaccine is safe and effective
❖ NICE recommends use of Relenza
❖ Weak evidence to support Relenza

CHAPTER 3: OBESITY

Obesity is rapidly becoming a major threat to health. The prevalence of obesity (defined as a body mass index (BMI) >30 kg/m^2) in the UK is increasing; approximately 1 in 5 of the UK population is now obese and this is predicted to rise to 50% of the population by 2030. More people now die prematurely from obesity related conditions than road traffic accidents in the UK!

What are the problems with obesity?
Obesity results in a huge financial burden to healthcare. Each year 30,000 premature deaths can be linked to obesity; the problem costs the NHS £500m annually in patient care and a staggering £2b in sickness absence.

Obesity is a significant aetiological factor in many common diseases. These include diabetes, hypertension, hyperlipidaemia, ischaemic heart disease and stroke. Obesity is associated with increased mortality, particularly from cardiovascular disease (*NEJM 1999;341:1097–105*). The medical costs of obesity have been estimated to account for 5–8% of all healthcare expenditure.

The National Audit Office published a report in February 2001 entitled 'Tackling Obesity in England', which stated that national guidelines should be produced on the management of overweight and obese patients in primary care.

It has been recognised for several years that a large waist circumference is also a predictor for type 2 diabetes. Carrying excess fat, particularly deposition of visceral fat, is known to promote insulin resistance and other features of the metabolic syndrome (notably type 2 diabetes).

Is obesity increasing in children?
Reports suggest that the prevalence of obesity among children is also increasing – presently one in five 9-year-olds and one in three 11-year-old girls are overweight. This trend towards obesity in British children has produced the country's first recognised cases of type 2 diabetes in White adolescents.

The American Heart Association Committee has recently recommended that doctors should increase children's physical activity, prevent or treat obesity, counsel children and their parents as well as checking for high blood pressure and high cholesterol concentrations (*Circulation*

2002;106:143–60). This is likely to be appropriate for British children in the not-to-distant future; which is both alarming and has huge resource implications for GPs.

What are the benefits of a modest weight reduction?
For many obese people, achieving their ideal body weight is unrealistic and impossible. However, significant benefits can be gained from even a 10% of body-weight loss, which is more achievable and sustainable. These benefits include a reduction in blood pressure, reduction in total cholesterol (including rise in HDL-cholesterol) and reduced risk of developing diabetes.

What is the role of the primary healthcare team in obesity treatment?
Unfortunately, only one in five obese patients ever receives treatment for their obesity, and those who do have a 90% chance of failure.

Primary healthcare teams often feel very frustrated when dealing with patients with weight problems, mainly because treatment is long-term and relapse is very common. The National Obesity Forum recently produced guidelines on the management of obesity in primary care because governments had failed to take action on this issue. Many GPs responded to the Forum by stating they are not responsible for patients' weight and it is not really part of their job to help people tackle their weight problems.

It is easy to argue either way; however, it may be useful to compare losing weight with stopping smoking and there are proven benefits from this. In the longer term, it may well prove to be cost-effective to consider helping our obese patients to lose weight.

What drugs are available to treat obesity?
Many of the drugs used in the past were centrally acting appetite suppressants, which are either addictive or associated with pulmonary hypertension and valvular heart disease, so are no longer used.

Orlistat
Orlistat is an intestinal lipase inhibitor that blocks the absorption of about 30% of dietary fat. In clinical trials of up to 2 years' duration it resulted in an average weight loss of about 10%, compared with 6% in the placebo group (*Lancet 1998;352:167–72*). There is good evidence to support its effect on weight reduction both in short term and 1–2 years post-treatment. Other benefits of orlistat include a reduction in LDL and

total cholesterol, a reduction in blood pressure and improvements in insulin resistance and blood glucose control in diabetic patients. A study of orlistat in patients with non-insulin diabetes mellitus demonstrated that 43% patients reduced their sulphonylurea dose and 12% patients actually stopped their oral diabetic medication.

The licensing criteria for the drug require patients to lose at least 2.5 kg in 4 weeks prior to starting treatment, and they should only continue with the drug if they achieve a weight loss of at least a further 5% of their body weight after the first 12 weeks of treatment and a cumulative weight loss of at least 10% after the first 6 months.

NICE have produced guidance on the use of orlistat. They have agreed it can be prescribed, as long as doctors abide by the strict conditions of its product licence and that it is only used for patients who are either clinically obese or overweight (BMI $\geq$28 kg/m^2) with other health-related health problems (such as type 2 diabetes or hypertension).

Roche, who produce orlistat, have a provided a free phone number (0800 731 7138) so patients are registered and given dietary and lifestyle advice. They are also contacted regularly to provide additional support and encouragement, which seems to be very beneficial.

Sibutramine
Another new anti-obesity drug, sibutramine (Reductil), became available in June 2001. A UK general practice-based study assessed its long-term weight reduction efficacy, tolerability and safety with encouraging results (*J Fam Pract 2001;50:505–12*). While 20% of placebo patients lost at least 5% of their body weight, this figure was 39% of patients taking 10 mg sibutramine and 57% taking 15 mg sibutramine.

The STORM (sibutramine trial of obesity reduction and maintenance) trial differs from other weight-loss trials as its objective was to test whether treatment with sibutramine could prevent weight regain among patients who had already achieved a weight loss of more than 5% of their body weight (*Lancet 2000;356:2119–25*). The study showed that 43% of the patients treated with sibutramine maintained at least 80% of their body weight loss compared with only 16% in the placebo group. In addition, significant changes in cardiovascular disease risk factors were noted, including reduced triglyceride concentrations, increased HDL-cholesterol concentrations and reduced cholesterol:HDL-cholesterol ratio.

Sibutramine works by inhibiting the reuptake of the neurotransmitters noradrenaline and serotonin, thereby leading to increased feelings of satiety after eating. The UK licence for sibutramine specifies a maximum treatment period of 12 months and has similar constraints to its use as for orlistat. It is contraindicated in patients with coronary heart disease, peripheral vascular disease and inadequately controlled hypertension or hyperthyroidism.

NICE have also produced recommendations on the use of sibutramine. However, the Drugs and Therapeutic Bulletin have, however, questioned this NICE guidance. It reviewed the clinical trial data and announced that the drug's 'limited' benefits, coupled with its many side-effects, contraindications and stringent requirements for monitoring, make it 'difficult and impractical' for GPs to prescribe (*Drug Ther Bull 2001;39:89–91*).

 USEFUL WEBSITES

www.nice.org.uk – NICE guidelines
www.nao.gov.uk – 'Tackling Obesity in England' report
www.nationalobesityforum.org.uk – National Obesity Forum

☐ SUMMARY POINTS FOR OBESITY

❖ Prevalence of obesity dramatically increasing
❖ Obesity is huge financial burden to healthcare
❖ Primary care teams need to be more involved
❖ Numerous benefits gained from losing small amounts of weight
❖ Orlistat and sibutramine have been approved by NICE

CHAPTER 4: PSYCHIATRY

MENTAL HEALTH NATIONAL SERVICE FRAMEWORK

- Sets national standards for mental health services
- Based on clinical evidence and sets out best practice for promoting mental health and treating mental illness
- Accompanied by £700m for mental health services (1999–2002)
- Aims to iron out unacceptable variations around the country
- Proposes further integration of health and social services

7 Standards of care

1. To promote mental health for all, working with individuals and communities. Combat discrimination against individuals and groups with mental health problems, and promote their social inclusion.

2. Any service user who contacts their primary healthcare team with a common mental health problem should:
   - Have their mental health needs identified and assessed
   - Be offered effective treatments, including referral to specialist services for further assessment, treatment and care if they require it.

3. Any individual with a common mental health problem should:
   - Be able to make contact round the clock with the local services necessary to meet their needs and to receive adequate care
   - Be able to use NHS Direct, as it develops, for first-level advice and referral on to specialist helplines or to local services.

4. All mental health service users of a Care Programme Approach (CPA) should:
   - Receive care which optimises engagement, anticipates or prevents a crisis and reduces risk
   - Have a copy of a written care plan which:
     - includes the action to be taken in a crisis by the service user, their carer and their care coordinator
     - advises their GP how they should respond if the service user needs additional help
     - is regularly reviewed by their care coordinator
     - allows the user to be able to access services 24 hours a day, 365 days a year.

5.   Each service user who is assessed as requiring a period of care away from their home should have:
     • Timely access to an appropriate hospital bed or alternative bed or place, which is:
          • in the least-restrictive environment consistent with the need to protect them and the public
          • as close to home as possible.

6.   All individuals who provide regular and substantial care for a person on CPA should:
     • Have an assessment of their caring, physical and mental health needs, repeated on at least an annual basis
     • Have their own written care plan, which is given to them and implemented in discussion with them.

7.   Prevent suicide. Ensure that health and social services play their full part in the achievement of the target in saving lives. Reduce the suicide rate by at least one-fifth by 2010.

Criticisms
For many, the NSF arrived far too late. After years of chronic under-funding the expectation of achieving far-fetched idealistic targets within a short period seems unattainable.

Much of the document could easily be a party political broadcast on mental health. Should politics play such a large role?

Can 24-hour access be sufficiently foolproof with the use of NHS Direct?

Discrimination is not an easily audited subject, how can you show you have improved it, in a reliable and reproducible way?

 Reforming The Mental Health Act, December 2000

This White Paper sets out the Government's plans for new mental health legislation. It will:
• Form part of new arrangements for improving the quality and consistency of health and social care services for the many people who suffer from mental health problems; and
• Provide a new structure for the application of compulsory powers of detention for the assessment and treatment (previously termed 'sections') for the small minority of those who pose a serious threat

to the safety of others as a result of their mental disorder

New mental health legislation will provide a single framework for the application of compulsory powers for care and treatment. This will include:
- Common criteria
- Common pathway for assessment
- Approval of a plan of care and treatment by the Mental Health Tribunal
- An improved and more consistent set of safeguards for all patients

The White Paper comprises two parts. This is to distinguish arrangements for high-risk group patients.

Reforms are a response to:
- Media publicity regarding dangerous and severely personality-disordered (DSPD) patients and the tragic toll of homicides and suicides
- Public confidence in care in the community has been undermined by failures in services and failures in the law
- The current 1983 Mental Health Act is largely based on a review of mental health legislation which took place in the 1950s, outmoded laws have failed properly to protect the public, patients or staff
- Under existing mental health laws, the powers for compulsory treatment are for patients in hospital only, whilst the majority of patients today are treated in the community
- Severely ill patients have been allowed to drift out of contact with mental health services and have been able to refuse treatment
- Existing legislation has also failed to provide adequate public protection from those whose risk to others arises from a severe personality disorder

Of course, the vast majority of people with mental illness represent no threat to anyone. Many mentally ill patients are among the most vulnerable members of society. But governments have a duty to protect individual patients and the public, if a person poses a serious risk to themselves or to others.

PART 1 – SUMMARY
- Improving the quality and consistency of health and social care services

- Extra investment in services and national standards of care by April 2001, almost 500 extra secure beds, over 320 24-hour staffed beds, 170 assertive outreach teams and access to services 24 hours a day, 7 days a week, for all those with complex mental health needs. (It is unclear whether these standards were met.)
- The NHS Plan announced a further £300m investment to provide better and faster care for people with mental health problems who need treatment and support, including new services for children and adolescents.
- New national standards for the care and treatment of mental illness in the Mental Health NSF
- More effective and accessible community-based support
- Principles of common law do not always provide the sort of robust framework needed to protect people from the effects of serious mental disorder and to enable action necessary to prevent serious harm
- Governments have a duty to set out a clear framework in mental health legislation for determining when and how care and treatment for mental disorder may be provided without consent, in the best interests of a patient or to prevent serious harm to other people

PART 1 – AREAS DISCUSSED

Safeguarding human rights
- Includes powers to place significant restrictions on the personal liberty of patients; in particular, the freedom to refuse care and treatment
- New mental health legislation must be fully compatible with the Human Rights Act 1998
- Revised broad definition of mental disorder covering any disability or disorder of mind or brain, whether permanent or temporary, which results in an impairment or disturbance of mental functioning
- Matched by criteria that set clear limits to the circumstances in which compulsory powers may be used
- Diagnosis of mental disorder alone would never be sufficient to justify the use of compulsory powers
- Use of compulsory powers will generally only be appropriate if a person is resisting care and treatment is needed, either in their best interests or because without care and treatment they will pose a

significant risk of serious harm to other people
- Sets out what should be covered in the care and treatment plan

New safeguards
- New independent tribunal to determine all longer term use of compulsory powers
- New right to independent advocacy
- New safeguards for people with long-term mental incapacity
- New Commission for Mental Health
- Statutory requirement to develop care plans

New procedures for use of compulsory powers
New three-stage process that applies in all cases, except for offenders (whom assessment will be ordered by the Court, and for prisoners by the Home Secretary):

Stage 1 – Preliminary examination
- When a patient needs further assessment or urgent treatment by specialist mental health services and, without this, might be at risk of serious harm or pose a risk of serious harm to other people
- Decisions to begin assessment and initial treatment of a patient under compulsory powers will be based on a preliminary examination by two doctors and a social worker or another suitably trained mental health professional

Stage 2 – Formal assessment and initial treatment under compulsory powers
- Patients will be given a full assessment of his or her health and social care needs, and receive treatment set out in a formal care plan
- Initial period of assessment and treatment under compulsory powers will be limited to a maximum of 28 days
- After that, continuing use of compulsory powers must be authorised by a new independent decision-making body, the Mental Health Tribunal, which will obtain advice from independent experts as well as taking evidence from the clinical team, the patient and his or her representatives and other agencies, where appropriate.

Stage 3 – Care and treatment order
The Tribunal (or Court in the case of mentally disordered offenders) will be able to make a care and treatment order, which will authorise the

care and treatment specified in a care plan recommended by the clinical team. This must be designed to give therapeutic benefit to the patient, or to manage behaviour associated with mental disorder that might lead to serious harm to other people. The first two orders will be for up to 6 months each; subsequent orders may be for periods of up to 12 months.

Care and treatment in the community
- Introduce new provisions so that care and treatment orders may apply to patients outside hospital
- Will mean that patients need not be in hospital unnecessarily and need not suffer the possible distress of repeated unplanned admissions to acute wards
- Will be no powers for patients to be given medication forcibly except in a clinical setting
- Steps will be specified in community orders to prevent patients, if they do not comply with their order, becoming a risk to themselves, their carers or the public
- New legislation will also introduce a new duty covering the disclosure of information about patients suffering from mental disorder between health and social services agencies and other agencies, e.g. housing agencies or criminal justice agencies

Better information and advice
- Every patient will be informed about the particular powers that apply in his or her case
- Patients who want to challenge the use of compulsory powers will continue to have the right to free legal representation
- Will also give them a new right of access to advice and support from independent specialist advocacy services – 'The New Patient Advocacy Liaison Service'

New safeguards for children and young people
- Mental Health Tribunal will be required to obtain specialist expert advice on both health and social care aspects of the proposed care plan, and to consider whether the location of care is appropriate
- Decisions taken in respect of children will be subject to a clear principle that the interests of the child must be paramount
- Changes in the provisions regarding the right of a young person between the ages of 16 and 18 years to refuse consent to care and treatment for mental disorder

New safeguards for people with long-term mental incapacity
- Potentially vulnerable to abuse or neglect, must ensure their best interests are properly considered and protected
- Can only be achieved through an independent consideration of the care they receive for their mental disorder
- Place a duty on the clinical supervisor responsible for the care and treatment of a patient with long-term mental incapacity to carry out an assessment and obtain an independent second opinion

A new Commission for Mental Health
- To look after the interests of all people who are subject to care and treatment under powers laid down in the Act
- Will carry specific responsibilities for monitoring the use of formal powers, providing guidance on the operation of those powers and assuring the quality of statutory training provided for practitioners with key responsibilities under the new legislation and for specialist advocacy services

PART 2 – HIGH-RISK PATIENTS
- Patients who pose a significant risk of serious harm to others
- Vast majority of people treated under mental health legislation are treated in their own best interests, in many cases to protect them from self-harm
- By contrast, there are a smaller number of people with a mental disorder who are characterised by the risk that they present to others
- This group includes a very small number of people detained under civil powers, and others who are remanded or convicted offenders
- Within this wider group are a number of individuals whose risk is as a result of a severe personality disorder

A narrow interpretation of the definition of the 'treatability' provision in the 1983 Act, together with a lack of dedicated provision within existing services, means that current arrangements for this group are inadequate both to protect the public and to provide the individuals themselves with the high-quality services they need.

The criteria
- New criteria for compulsory treatment under the Act will form a key part of these changes
- Deal separately with those who need treatment primarily in their own best interests, and with those who need treatment because of the risk they pose to others

- In high-risk cases, the use of compulsory powers will be linked to the availability of a treatment plan needed either to treat the underlying mental disorder or to manage behaviours arising from the disorder.

Powers in the Criminal Justice and Court Services Act 2000, implemented in April 2001, will mean that the police and probation services will be under a new statutory duty to assess and manage relevant sexual or violent offenders.

Under new mental health legislation, the relevant statutory agencies will be able to refer the individual for an initial assessment and, if the initial criteria are satisfied, apply for a 28-day period of compulsory care and treatment to allow for more detailed assessment.

Beyond 28 days, compulsory care must be authorised by the new 'Mental Health Tribunal'

In addition to existing facilities, assessment facilities for those who are 'dangerous and severely personality disordered' (DSPD) are being established for the in-depth assessment needed for this group.

Treatment
Under new legislation, the Tribunal (or Court for offenders) will be able to make a care and treatment order, which will authorise the care and treatment specified in a care plan recommended by the clinical team.

The first two orders will be for up to 6 months each; subsequent orders may be for periods of up to 12 months.

Where treatment is authorised under the legislation, individuals will be transferred to appropriate NHS facilities, taking account of any security risks they pose. Wherever possible, treatment will be specifically aimed at addressing the underlying mental disorder. But in all high-risk cases, treatment will be designed both to manage the consequences of a mental disorder as well as to enable the individuals themselves to work towards successful reintegration into the community.

Safeguards
All those detained under compulsory powers will also have the right to:
- Free legal representation
- Access to independent specialist advocacy services

- Provisions to cover the use of certain specified treatments for mental disorder and all long-term treatment without consent.

Developing services for the DSPD

A recent spending review across the Department of Health (DoH), Home Office and Prison Service includes an additional £126m from 2000 to 2003 for the development of new specialist services for those who are high risk as a result of a severe personality disorder.

- Committed to a series of pilot projects to test out new approaches
- Assessment process is already being piloted in both NHS and Prison Service high-security settings and the first treatment pilot will began in 2001
- During the years 2000 to 2003 this will provide: an extra 320 specialist places across Her Majesty's Prisons (HMP)/NHS; and 75 hostel places
- Introduction of new arrangements for the provision of information to the victims of mentally disordered offenders who have committed serious violent or sexual offences and who have been given a care and treatment order by the Courts rather than a prison sentence

 USEFUL WEBSITE

www.doh.gov.uk/mentalhealth – gives full document

 Draft Mental Health Bill, July 2002

Following the initial White Paper on reforming the Mental Health Act, the Draft Mental Health Bill was published in July 2002. Proposed legislation is the first major overhaul of the system since the 1950s and has been published in draft form to allow 12 weeks of consultation.

After the 16 September 2002 deadline, it will be up to the Government to decide whether to include the bill in its legislative programme for the next parliamentary year.

Department of Health. Draft mental health bill. London: Stationery Office, 2002.

The bill can be accessed at the website below and was discussed in an editorial (*BMJ 2002;325:2–3*) entitled 'Detaining dangerous people with mental disorders'.

USEFUL WEBSITE

www.doh.gov.uk/mentalhealth

Summary

- The White Paper on reforming the Mental Health Act that preceded the draft bill attracted a great deal of attention because of its overriding emphasis on public safety
- The fact that it was not well received is hardly surprising, and proposals for managing dangerous people with severe personality disorder were described as glaringly wrong and unethical
- The ministerial foreword accompanying the draft bill seeks to reassure us that the new law will promote patients' rights and protect them
- The term 'dangerous people with severe personality disorder' often used in the White Paper does not receive a single mention in the draft bill
- The procedure for compulsion is similar to that described in the White Paper
- This involves a single pathway with three distinct stages: a preliminary examination; a period of formal assessment lasting up to 28 days; and then treatment under a Mental Health Act order
- Four conditions must be satisfied before any compulsory powers can be used:
  1. There must be a mental disorder
  2. This must be of a nature or degree warranting medical treatment
  3. Treatment must be necessary for the health or safety of the patient or the protection of others
  4. Appropriate treatment must be available for the disorder
- 'Mental disorder' is defined as 'any disability or disorder of mind or brain which results in impairment or disturbance of mental functioning'
- The broad definition of mental disorder means that dangerous people with severe personality disorder are included; it also raises the possibility of compulsory treatment for sexual deviancy and alcohol/drug dependence
- The 'treatability test', which many will recall is used to exclude some patients with psychopathic disorder and mental impairment from treatment under the current Act, is also absent
- The draft bill may not go as far as the White Paper in advocating compulsory powers to manage behaviours arising from the disorder, but the broad 'medical treatment' definition probably

allows for this
- Principles require that patients are involved in decisions made about them, decisions are made fairly and openly and that any treatment given imposes the minimum level of intrusion. In certain circumstances, however, including matters of public protection, these principles may be 'disapplied'
- Another important difference is that a patient who is at substantial risk of causing serious harm to others can be given medical treatment if this is necessary for the protection of those persons
- In all other instances the condition that treatment cannot be provided without using the Act must also be satisfied
- The development of services for dangerous people with severe personality disorder at Whitemoor and Frankland prisons shows that this must be on the Government's agenda
- The draft bill has safeguards including rights of appeal, as one would expect
- Access to advocacy services and safeguards for certain patients treated informally who are not capable of consenting are welcome additions, but it is doubtful whether the proposed safeguards are robust enough

Criticisms
- The Mental Health Alliance, a group of over 50 voluntary organisations that has worked with the Government to try to update the Mental Health Act 1983, says that it is disappointed with the Government for ignoring its concerns and that it fears the new proposals will make the current services even worse
- Mental health experts have rejected the Government's proposals to lock up hundreds of people with untreatable personality disorders who may not have committed a crime
- They say the proposals are fundamentally flawed and a waste of public money that would be better spent on improving services for patients
- The Royal College of Psychiatrists together with the Law Society has called the proposals 'fundamentally flawed' as well as 'costly and complex' and almost impossible to implement
- It has been said that 600 extra full-time psychiatrists would be required to run the new 'Mental Health Review Tribunals' alone, clearly an almost impossible task

DEPRESSION

This has always been an exam favourite, we frequently encounter it in general practice and therefore it is no surprise that it features in nearly every paper.
*   See BJGP in Feb and Nov of 1999
*   Common: 5–10% of people
*   Much of the published research in primary care revolves around the poor pick-up of depression and lack of treatment instigation
*   Detection is obviously paramount to successful treatment and possibly resolution
*   Many studies look at various short questionnaires that can be used in clinical practice. These allow for the screening and therefore detection of people with depression. Using validated tools allows GPs to be more accurate in their diagnosis

Detection criteria (simplified): (Oxford Textbook of Medicine: third edition)
Over the last 2 weeks, both of the following features should be present for a diagnosis of major depression
*   Depressed mood
*   Anhedonia – loss of interest or pleasure

And at least 4 of the following:
*   Weight or appetite change
*   Early waking and diurnal mood variation
*   Psychomotor agitation or retardation
*   Fatigue
*   Feelings of worthlessness/guilt
*   Reduced ability to concentrate
*   Recurrent thoughts of death/suicidal ideas

PAPERS

1. Effects of a clinical-practice guideline and practice-based education on detection and outcome of depression in primary care: Hampshire Depression Project (HDP) randomised controlled trial.
(C. Thompson, et al., Lancet 2000;355:185–91)

*   This large, well-constructed RCT tested the hypothesis that 'the most effective strategy to reduce this burden has been believed to be education of primary-care practitioners'

- They tested this assumption by assessing the effectiveness of an educational programme based on a clinical-practice guideline in improving the recognition and outcome of primary-care depression.
- Education was delivered to practice teams and quality tested by feedback from participants and expert raters. This involved 4 hours of education to GPs in the intervention group.
- The primary endpoints were recognition of depression, defined by the hospital anxiety and depression (HAD) scale, and clinical improvement. Analysis was by intention to treat.
- 21,409 patients were screened, of whom 4,192 were classified as depressed by the HAD scale.
- The education was well received by participants, 80% of whom thought it would change their management of patients with depression
- The sensitivity of physicians to depressive symptoms was 39% in the intervention group and 36% in the control group after education
- The outcome of depressed patients as a whole at 6 weeks or 6 months after the assessment did not significantly improve
- Results disappointingly negative, failing to show any increase in recognition or patient recovery rates
- In an editorial (*Lancet*) GPs were accused of not following guidelines

Shortly afterwards, an editorial entitled 'Why can't GPs follow guidelines on depression?' appeared in the BMJ discussing the issues raised by the study (*BMJ 2000 320;200*).

Issues discussed and points raised:
- Findings of the HDP herald the need for a major change in thinking about improving the management of depression in primary care
- Results conflict with the positive findings of other studies (note the HDP had more participants)
- Such intensive training as used in the HDP cannot be delivered through our existing education systems
- A review of 45 guidelines for depression showed they all have three common recommendations:
  - Practitioners seek cases of 'major depressive disorder'
  - Treatment is advised if patients have enough symptoms for long enough (even if social causes are identified)

- Most recommend tricyclics antidepressants (TCAs) as first-line treatment (in dose equivalents of 125 mg/day of amitriptyline and continuing for 4 months after recovery)

Problems exist with these recommendations:
- Diagnosis is not easy to make in primary care, symptoms change quickly and the cut-off levels for duration are somewhat arbitrary
- Practitioners vary significantly in the threshold at which they treat. Many practitioners doubt the effectiveness of antidepressants in the face of social problems. Guidelines are based on an RCT of amitriptyline versus placebo: patients with 'major' depression responded, whilst those with minor depression did not, irrespective of whether the depression was endogenous or non-endogenous (i.e. attributed to social problems). Other research shows social factors in the short-term are associated with persistence of depression
- Patients are often reluctant to accept drugs. Much of the public believe that depression is due to adverse life events and that counselling should be offered. Most think that antidepressants are addictive. Explains why patients take subtherapeutic doses of tricyclics and discontinue early. Advent of selective serotonin-reuptake inhibitors (SSRIs) has increased the proportion taking therapeutic doses, but they still do not continue treatment for the recommended duration.

May explain why the recognition of depression and subsequent drug treatment in primary care is not associated with better outcomes. The author states the '...negative findings of the HDP must be viewed in this context'. The effectiveness of SSRIs for minor depression has not been established in primary care. Neither has the effectiveness of counselling been wholly validated.

2. Antidepressant drugs and generic counselling for treatment of major depression in primary care
(C. Chilvers, et al., BMJ 2001;322:772–5)

- Objective was to compare the efficacy of antidepressant drugs and generic counselling for treating mild to moderate depression in general practice
- RCT with patient-preference arms (i.e. allowed to choose rather than be randomised), followed up at 8 weeks and 12 months

- 31 general practices in the Trent region with 103 patients randomised and 220 patients in preference arms
- Study looked at the Beck Depression Inventory Score (validated), time to remission and global outcome assessed by a psychiatrist

Concluded
- Statistical tests showed no significant differences in effectiveness, so authors state that generic counselling seems to be as effective as antidepressants for mild to moderate depressive illness
- Patients receiving antidepressants may recover more quickly
- GPs should allow patients to have their preferred treatment
- 12 months after starting treatment, generic counselling is as effective as antidepressants
- Patients who choose counselling may benefit more than those with no strong preference

Criticisms
- Data interpretation should be regarded with caution due to small sample sizes and difficulties in follow-up
- Study placed few constraints on either the drug treatment or the type of counselling, other than that the counselling should be provided by an experienced mental health professional in six sessions
- Therefore compared non-standardised antidepressant use with non-standardised counselling by experienced professionals

3. The effectiveness of exercise as an intervention in the management of depression
(D. A. Lawlor and S. W. Hopker, BMJ 2001;322;763–7)

- Systematic review of RCTs to determine the effectiveness of exercise as an intervention in the management of depression
- Analyses was difficult as all studies were methodologically flawed
- How do you 'blind' treatment in which you have to partake?
- Difficult to separate the fact that people may socially interact when they exercise and that this may act as a benefit
- No apparent difference existed between aerobic and non-aerobic exercise
- Concluded that the effectiveness of exercise in reducing symptoms of depression cannot be determined because of a lack of good quality research with adequate follow-up and that, as usual, a well-designed RCT is needed

- Does this mean that 'exercise on prescription' for depression is futile or do you carry on funding beneficial social interaction and hope for some health promotion?

4. Effectiveness of teaching general practitioners skills in brief cognitive behaviour therapy (CBT) to treat patients with depression: randomised controlled trial
(M. King, et al., BMJ 2002;324:947–50)

- In brief, this study looked at whether a short period of education on CBT would have an impact on patients suffering from depression
- CBT is as effective as pharmacotherapy for treating depression, with the benefit of reduced rates of long-term relapse
- It is also effective in depressed patients presenting to GPs
- CBT is effective when delivered by GPs who have received extensive instruction
- It was an RCT involving 84 GPs and 272 patients in North London
- The patients enrolled had scored above the threshold for psychological distress on the hospital anxiety and depression scale
- A training package of 4.5 days on brief cognitive behaviour therapy
- The GPs and patients then completed the Depression Attitude Questionnaire (general practitioners) and the Beck Depression Inventory (patients)
- The results not surprisingly showed doctors' knowledge of depression and attitudes towards its treatment showed no major difference between intervention and control groups after 6 months. The training had no discernible impact on patients' outcomes
- They concluded that GPs may require more training and support than a basic educational package on brief CBT to acquire the skills to help patients with depression
- We, however, already know from other studies that most doctors do not have the time or inclination to carry out such comprehensive training
- Problems with the study related to a small sample size due to loss of follow-up, although power calculations suggested the data was still reliable
- Also, they found that trained doctors probably referred more to secondary care, suggesting training may have had a paradoxical effect in making GPs feel unable to deal with more complex cases

5. General practice based intervention to prevent repeat episodes of deliberate self-harm: cluster randomised controlled trial
(O. Bennewith, et al., BMJ 2002;324:1254–7)

- This large English study looked at whether a GP-based intervention on self-harm can reduce its incidence. We know that:
  - About two-thirds of patients consult their GPs in the 3 months after an episode of deliberate self-harm
  - Deliberate self-harm is a serious clinical problem in England and Wales, accounting for an estimated 140,000 hospital presentations each year
  - 15–23% of patients will be seen for treatment of a subsequent episode of deliberate self-harm within 1 year
  - 3–5% of those who harm themselves die by suicide within 5–10 years
- RCT involving 98 practices were assigned in equal numbers to an intervention or a control group
- The intervention comprised a letter from the GP inviting the patient to consult, and guidelines on the assessment and management of deliberate self-harm for the GP to use in consultations. Control patients received the usual GP care
- 1,932 patients participated. The patients were registered with the study practices and had attended accident and emergency departments at one of the four hospitals after an episode of deliberate self-harm (patients lived within the catchment area of four general hospitals in Bristol and Bath)
- Primary outcome was an occurrence of a repeat episode of deliberate self-harm in the 12 months after the index episode. The study also looked at the number of repeat episodes and time to first repeat
- The results showed the incidence of repeat episodes of deliberate self-harm was not significantly different for patients in the intervention group compared with the control group
- Similar findings were obtained for the number of repeat episodes and time to first repeat
- The treatment seemed to be beneficial for people with a history of deliberate self-harm, but it was associated with an adverse effect in people for whom the index episode was their first episode
- They concluded the hypothesis that patients who had previously harmed themselves benefited from the intervention was inconsistent with previous evidence and should be treated with caution

- As usual, more research is needed on how to manage patients who deliberately harm themselves, to reduce the incidence of repeat episodes
- As to what is the most effective management in general practice of patients with self-harm, nobody knows
- The role of the GP is very important in the aftercare of patients who deliberately harm themselves, as more than half of them will receive no psychiatric follow-up

6. Suicide rate in young men in Scotland is twice that in England and Wales
(Framework for the Prevention of Suicide and Self Harm can be found at www.show.scot.nhs.uk)

- Action is to be taken in Scotland in an attempt to halt an alarming rise in suicides among men, which have increased by more than 70% in the past 30 years
- Deaths from suicide of men under the age of 34 in Scotland now accounts for more deaths of young men than road traffic accidents
- More than 50% of 600 suicides/year in Scotland occur in men under 44 years of age
- Rates are twice as high as those in England and Wales
- Poverty and unemployment in Scotland are considered to be important factors
- Suicide rates among women in Scotland have fallen slightly since the 1970s and are now three times lower than rates among men
- But the rate of women succeeding is twice that in England and Wales
- The Scottish Health Department has published a consultative report that sets out a series of proposals on how the problem can be tackled
- Practical suggestions include making popular sites for suicide less accessible
- Plans to establish a telephone helpline and referral service

7. Spiritual beliefs may affect outcome of bereavement: prospective study
(K. Walsh, et al., BMJ 2002;324:1551)

- This study looked at the whether spirituality can help with bereavement
- Religious belief affects the outcome of bereavement in families

coping with the death of a child and in older people who are bereaved of a spouse
- Research is often retrospective, and causal connections are difficult to establish
- It was a prospective cohort study of people about to be bereaved with follow-up continuing for 14 months after the death
- 135 relatives and close friends of patients admitted to the centre with a terminal illness from a Marie Curie centre for specialist palliative care in London participated
- Outcome was based upon core bereavement items, a standardised measure for the intensity of grief, measured 1, 9 and 14 months after the patients' death
- They found people reporting no spiritual belief had not resolved their grief by 14 months after the death
- Participants with strong spiritual beliefs resolved their grief progressively over the same period
- People with low levels of belief showed little change in the first 9 months but thereafter resolved their grief
- Strength of spiritual belief remained an important predictor after the confounding variables were controlled for (age, sex, etc.)
- Although the degree of closeness to the person who died and the level of emotional distress before the death increased feelings of grief, neither affected the rate at which the grief was resolved
- They concluded that people who profess stronger spiritual beliefs seem to resolve their grief more rapidly and completely after the death of a close person than do people with no spiritual beliefs

Limitations
- Fell short of statistical significance, but strength of spiritual belief remained an important predictor
- Sample size was small and so restricts the number of potential confounders that can be explored
- The difficulty of recruiting a large sample of people for what is obviously a difficult and emotive time

POST-NATAL DEPRESSION

(Drug Ther Bull, May 2000)

- Common, affects 70,000 women/year in the UK, approximately 13% of deliveries
- Little evidence for aetiology; antenatal, personal and social factors more relevant
- Many recover spontaneously
- 50% still depressed at 6 months
- One-third go on to develop a chronic, recurrent mood disorder
- Associated with disturbances in the mother–infant relationship, which in turn has an adverse impact on child cognitive and emotional development
- Must distinguish between common maternity 'blues' (= emotional lability, peak between third to fifth day postpartum and over by day 10)
- Depression more likely if previous psychiatric/family history, social problems, bereavement
- Remember to routinely use 'The Edinburgh Post-natal Depression Score' (validated detection tool)
- Conclusion of *Drug Ther Bull* article states that the following are effective:
  - Non-directive counselling by the health visitor
  - CBT
  - Antidepressants all effective
  - TCAs appear to be safe with breast-feeding
  - SSRIs are only secreted in small quantities in breast milk; the article states they are probably OK at the usual doses, but baby should be closely monitored and mother advised to stop breast-feeding if she is on a high dose
  - Refer if psychotic/suicidal to mother and baby unit

SCHIZOPHRENIA

 How to manage the first episode of schizophrenia
(Editorial, BMJ 2000;321:522–3)

- The article quoted a '1% lifetime prevalence'
- Among the leading causes of disability worldwide
- 2–4 per 1,000 patients (*Clin Evid 2001*)
- £2.6b estimated to be the cost in the UK per year
- First onset typically in twenties
- Can remain undetected for 2–3 years in many
- Insidious onset hinders diagnosis, particularly when there is a 'background of premorbid disorders'
- Growing evidence that early stages of schizophrenia are critical in forming and predicting the course and outcome of the disorder
- Aim of primary treatment is rapid remission, and strategies that cause a minimum of side-effects should be used
- 80% will recover, but 70% will have a second psychotic episode within 5–7 years
- Early withdrawal of drug is not recommended and should be slowly tailed off
- Clozapine is used if typical antipsychotics do not help
- Most patients have difficulty reintegrating into the community
- CBT is useful in reducing persistent delusions and hallucinations
- Focusing on early detection and intervention in schizophrenia offers the opportunity to make a real difference to the lives of our patients and their families
- We cannot afford to miss it

THE NEW ANTI-PSYCHOTIC DRUGS

Reviewed in *BJGP* September 1999
(T. Kendrick, BJGP 1999;49:745–9)

Benefits of the atypical antipsychotics

- They do not cause extrapyramidal side-effects, which represents a major advance in the treatment of schizophrenia
- Clozapine is effective in 30–70% of patients resistant to traditional treatments; it remains to be seen whether the other atypical drugs also confer this benefit
- Clozapine also seems to be beneficial for the negative symptoms of schizophrenia, including apathy and social withdrawal. Time will tell whether this is a true effect and whether it extends to other atypicals
- Risperidone may be more effective among younger patients who have a depressive component to their psychotic illness
- The atypicals are expensive, but may be more cost-effective if they reduce specialist treatments and hospital admissions

Prescribing issues for the atypical antipsychotics

- Clozapine is restricted to treatment-resistant patients; however, the other atypicals, especially risperidone and olanzapine, are increasingly being used as first-line agents, especially among treatment-naive patients
- All other psychotropic drugs must be withdrawn before clozapine may be commenced
- Co-prescribing of traditional antipsychotics negates the benefits of the atypical drugs
- Clozapine patients must have regular blood counts, initially weekly
- ECGs before and during treatment are mandatory when prescribing sertindole (available on a named-patient basis for those patients already stabilised on the drug in whom other anitpsychotics are inapproprite.)
- Extreme caution is advised if prescribing atypicals for patients with heart disease
- Avoid concurrent prescribing of antihistamines, diuretics, tricyclics and antiarrhythmics, especially in the elderly
- Hypokalaemia must be corrected before prescribing an atypical
- Patients should be warned to avoid concurrent use of over-the-counter antihistamines

NB.

Also see *Clinical Evidence* 2001 for further evidence from systematic reviews.

Atypical antipsychotics, patients value the lower incidence of extrapyramidal side-effects
(S. Kapur and G. Remington, BMJ 2000;321:1360)

This editorial appeared in the BMJ alongside a systematic review of atypicals, points raised were:
- No clinically significant evidence of superiority in efficacy, or for that matter tolerability, for atypical antipsychotics as a group
- Atypical antipsychotics account for nearly three out of four new prescriptions for antipsychotics in North America
- Atypicals have a lower incidence of extrapyramidal side-effects
- Extrapyramidal side-effects are not just incidental 'side' effects but the central factor in many patients' agendas
- Extrapyramidal effects by themselves have been related to a poor outcome, a compromised compliance, secondary negative symptoms, cognitive parkinsonism, and depression as well as the long-term risk of tardive dyskinesia
- May turn out that the real superiority of atypicals is not in their antipsychotic abilities but in their ability to control ancillary symptoms related to mood, cognition, hostility and a higher level of compliance
- Atypical agents have their own new side-effects such as weight gain and diabetes

NICE guidance June 2002

- NICE has recommended the more widespread use of atypical antipsychotic drugs for patients with schizophrenia, on the grounds of fewer side-effects and equal efficiency
- The recommendations were made after a review of over 200 trials
- NICE has said that older antipsychotic drugs were associated with a higher incidence of extrapyramidal side-effects compared with newer antipsychotics (such as amisulpride, olanzapine and risperidone)
- If, however, patients are achieving good control without unacceptable side-effects with typical antipsychotics, they should not change their medication
- The National Schizophrenia Fellowship said more than 80% of the

210,000 people with schizophrenia are currently denied access to antipsychotics, on grounds of cost
* Direct treatment costs of schizophrenia in England and Wales are estimated to be in excess of £1b (about 3% of the total NHS expenditure)
* The yearly cost of maintenance on older style antipsychotics is £70, whereas for atypical drugs it is £1220
* NICE estimates that the cost for the NHS of making these drugs freely available will be £70m a year
* The cost will be offset by an expected shift away from inpatient care to cheaper community-based care

EATING DISORDERS

- Rates: 1/2,000 anorexia, 20/2,000 bulimia, 40/2,000 'partial' syndromes (*BJGP 2000;50:38083*)
- Psychological interventions such as cognitive behavioural therapy (CBT) and anti-depressants such as SSRIs have been shown to be effective treatment options
- Early intervention produces better outcome
- Binge eating – eating in a period of time an amount of food that is larger than most people would eat in a similar period/situation. May have a sense of lack of control

Diagnostic criteria for anorexia nervosa
- Overconcern with shape and weight, with intense fear of becoming fat
- Active maintenance of low weight (body mass index <17.5) by strict dieting, excessive exercising and possibly self-induced vomiting
- Amenorrhoea for a minimum of 3 months (if not taking the combined oral contraceptive pill, COCP)

Diagnostic criteria for bulimia nervosa
- Characteristic overconcern with shape and weight
- Frequent binges (bulimic episodes)
- Extreme behaviour to prevent weight gain (self-induced vomiting, purgative and diuretic abuse, fasting)

Atypical eating disorders
- Disorders that do not fulfil the above criteria (i.e. binge eating without extreme weight controlling behaviour)

The SCOFF questionnaire: assessment of a new screening tool for eating disorders
(*J. F. Morgan, et al., BMJ 1999;319:1467*)

The SCOFF QUESTIONS (one point for every yes; a score of ≥ indicates a likely case of anorexia nervosa or bullimia.)
1. Do you ever make yourself **S**ick because you feel uncomfortably full?
2. Do you ever worry you have lost **C**ontrol over how much you eat?
3. Have you ever lost more than **O**ne stone over a one month period?
4. Do you believe yourself to be **F**at when others say you are thin?
5. Would you say **F**ood dominates your life?

- The researchers found that 'setting the threshold at two or more positive answers to all five questions provided **100% sensitivity** for anorexia and bulimia, separately and combined (all cases, 95% confidence interval 96.9% to 100%; bulimic cases, 92.6% to 100%; anorectic cases, 94.7% to 100%), with **specificity of 87.5%** (79.2% to 93.4%) for controls'

Psychiatry

ALCOHOL

- We know from population studies that non-drinkers and heavy drinkers have higher all-cause mortality rates than light drinkers, this is known as the U-shaped curve
- The RCP/RCGP/RCPsych advise men and women to drink less than 21 and 14 units a week, respectively
- The UK government, however, recommends no more than 4 and 3 units a day, respectively
- 1 unit is 8–10 g of alcohol
- It is estimated that 20/1,000 people are physically dependent
- In systematic reviews of all-cause mortality, the risk was lowest for men drinking 7–14 units a week and for women drinking under 7 units a week (*J Clin Epidemiol 1999;52:967–75*)
- In a recent review by a group of statisticians (*BMJ 2002;325:191*):
  - The level of alcohol consumption that carries the lowest mortality ranges from 0 in men and women aged under 35 to 3 units a week in women aged over 65 and 8 units a week in men aged over 65
  - The level of alcohol consumption that carries a 5% increase in mortality rises with age from 8 to 20 units a week in women and from 5 to 34 units a week in men
- Alcohol problems are estimated to cost Scotland £1b a year through reduced productivity and the costs of crime, accidents, damage to property and health service costs from injury and illness
- Latest figures show that 1 in 3 men in Scotland and 1 in 7 women in Scotland are exceeding recommended drinking levels
- Most worrying is the increase in alcohol use amongst young people
- More 12–15-year-olds are reporting drinking and at greater amounts than 10 years ago
- The heaviest drinking occurs among people aged 16–24 years
- The Health Education Board for Scotland stated, 'A 15 year old in France is likely to drink as frequently as a 15 year old in Scotland but is half as likely to get drunk as often'.

Key sources:
1. Royal Colleges of Physicians, Psychiatrists, and General Practitioners. Alcohol and the heart in perspective: sensible limits reaffirmed. London: Royal Colleges, 1995.
2. Inter-Departmental Working Group. Sensible drinking. London: Department of Health, 1995.

The CAGE questionnaire
- Have you ever felt you should Cut down on your drinking?
- Have people ever Annoyed you by criticising your drinking?
- Have you ever felt Guilty about your drinking?
- Have you ever had to have a drink first thing in the morning to steady your nerves or to get rid of a hangover (Eye opener)?

If answer 'Yes' to two or more then there is an 80–90 % chance that a drinking problem exists.

1. Alcohol consumption and mortality from all causes, coronary heart disease, and stroke: results from a prospective cohort study of Scottish men with 21 years of follow up
(C. L. Hart, et al., BMJ 1999;318;1725–9)

- 5,766 men aged 35–64 screened in 1970–3 who answered questions on their usual weekly alcohol consumption
- Aim was to define mortality from all causes, coronary heart disease, stroke and alcohol-related causes over 21 years of follow-up related to units of alcohol consumed per week
- Risk for all-cause mortality was similar for non-drinkers and men drinking up to 14 units/week
- Mortality risk then showed a graded association with alcohol consumption
- No strong relation between alcohol consumption and mortality from coronary heart disease
- Strong positive relationship between alcohol and risk of mortality from stroke
- Men drinking 35 or more units have double the risk of stroke compared with non-drinkers
- No clear evidence of any protective effect for men drinking less than 22 units/week
- Different relations between alcohol consumption and mortality than previous studies
- Some, but not all, of this could be accounted for by alcohol-related increases in blood pressure
- Overall, risk of all-cause mortality was higher in men drinking 22 or more units/week

2. Editorial: Dying for a drink
(BMJ 2001;323:817–18)

Focused on developing strategies to reduce suicide amongst those with alcohol-use disorders.

Points raised:

- There is a consistently reported high prevalence of alcohol-use disorders among people who committed suicide (e.g. 56% in New York, 43% in Northern Ireland)
- Lifetime risk of suicide is 7% for alcohol dependence
- In the Northern Ireland suicide study (case-control psychological autopsy), the estimated risk of suicide in the presence of current alcohol misuse or dependence was eight times greater than in the absence of current alcohol misuse or dependence
- 89% of suicides with alcohol dependence in the Irish study had at least one other comorbid mental disorder
- The 5-year report of the National Confidential Inquiry into Suicide and Homicide by People with Mental Illness recently revealed that 40% of people who committed suicide in England and Wales who had been in contact with mental health services within 1 year of death had a history of alcohol misuse (53% in Scotland) and 19% had misused both alcohol and drugs (26% in Scotland)
- 'The combination of mental illness and substance misuse is probably the greatest clinical problem facing general adult mental health services' suggests that 'a coordinated approach to training, service planning, and research is needed to improve the ability of the general service to address this problem'
- Therefore, after attempted suicide (deliberate self-harm) and presentation to mental health services, the detection and effective treatment of alcohol-use disorders are important aspects of suicide prevention
- The Irish study also revealed that a lower risk of suicide was associated with a higher religious commitment
- However, after adjustment for psychiatric disorders, the 'protective' effect did not remain, suggesting that the protective effect of religious commitment may be partially mediated by the reduced likelihood of a committed individual developing a psychiatric disorder (including alcohol-use disorder)
- The author states that healthcare professionals should be aware of the potential influence of religious commitment on behaviour affecting health

DRUG MISUSE

Drug Misuse and Dependence – Guidelines on Clinical Management.
Department of Health, 1999

This guideline, first published in 1991, was updated in 1999 in the light
of recent advances. As many of you are probably aware, a great
discrepancy of services exists throughout the UK. Many of the points in
the plan caused a lot of controversy and still remain topical in the GP
press. In summary from the guidelines:

- Total number of drug misusers presenting to treatment in the 6
  months ending March 1998 was around 30,000
- 54% of those users presenting were in their twenties
- 1 in 7 (15%) were aged under 20 years
- Ratio of males to females was 3:1
- 55% reported heroin as their main drug of misuse
- Methadone was the next most frequently reported main drug of
  misuse with 13%, followed by cannabis and amphetamines, both
  with 9%
- Self-reported drug use amongst those aged 16–59 years in England
  and Wales in 1996, showed that approximately 1 in 10 had used
  illegal drugs in the last year, and that 1 in 20 (6%) had done so in
  the last month
- People who are involved in drugs may have multiple social and
  medical problems
- Doctors everywhere must expect to see drug misusers presenting
  for care and will need to be vigilant in looking for signs of drug
  misuse in their patients
- It is the responsibility of all doctors to provide care for both
  general health needs and drug-related problems, whether or not
  the patient is ready to withdraw from drugs
- This should include the provision of evidence-based interventions
  such as hepatitis B vaccination
- Medical practitioners should not prescribe in isolation, but should
  seek to liaise with other professionals who will be able to help
  with factors contributing to an individual's drug misuse
- A multidisciplinary approach to treatment is therefore essential
- Where there are no local specialist services with which a shared
  care agreement can be developed, it is the responsibility of the
  health authority to ensure that appropriate services are in place
- Doctors are not to be pressurised into accepting responsibility

Useful contact numbers for GPs and patients
ADFAM National (National Charity for the Families and Friends of Drug Misusers) – tel. 020 7928 8900
Alcohol Concern – tel. 020 7928 7377
Cocaine Anon – tel. 020 7284 1123
Council for Involuntary Addiction, helpline for general public – tel. 0151 949 0102; helpline for professionals – tel. 0151 286 9884
Drug Prevention Advisory Service, Head Office – tel. 020 7217 8631
Narcotics Anonymous (NA) UK Service Office, Helpline – tel. 020 730 0009
National Drugs Helpline (provides 24-hour free and confidential advice, including information on local services) – tel. 0800 776600. (Also provides an email question and answer service through website, www.nbh.org.uk. This service is available 24 hours a day, every day throughout the year, including Bank Holidays.)
Parents Against Drug Abuse Helpline – 08457 023 867
Release (this is a legal advice helpline to support drug users, their family and friends and professionals) – tel. 0207 729 9904
Resolve – tel. 0808 800 2345
TACADE (Advisory Council on Alcohol and Drug Education) – tel. 0161 836 6850

Cannabis trial launched in patients with multiple sclerosis (MS)
- The world's biggest clinical trial of the cannabis plant started in January 2001 at Derriford Hospital, Plymouth
- Looking at the control of pain and tremors in multiple sclerosis
- The Cannabis in Multiple Sclerosis (CAMS) study is sponsored by the Medical Research Council
- Approved by the Government, which has arranged for the drug to be imported from Switzerland
- A parallel study will examine the effect of the drug on lower urinary tract symptoms
- Cannabis has been a Schedule 1 drug since 1971, when the WHO pronounced it medically useless
- Two years ago a House of Lords select committee argued that more research was necessary in view of reports of the drug's efficacy in controlling pain and tremor in multiple sclerosis

BMA calls for Government action on drugs and driving
(BMJ 2002;324:632)

- The BMA has called on the UK Government to develop a

campaign to highlight that taking drugs whether prescribed, over the counter, or illegal can impair driving capacity in a similar way to alcohol
- The BMA has recommended that the Government should coordinate scientific research to establish effective drug-testing devices and should educate the public on the association between taking some drugs and impaired driving ability
- To help publicise the problem, the BMA has developed a website that reviews trends in road traffic fatalities and injuries, as well as research on drugs and driving performance.
- The website highlights research from the Transport Research Laboratory warning that the number of people involved in fatal collisions who tested positive for illegal drugs increased sixfold between the 1985–7 and 1996–9
- The number of people testing positive for cannabis increased from 3% to 12%. Over the same period, the incidence of use of medicinal drugs and alcohol remained similar.
- Driving while unfit under the influence of drugs is an offence in the United Kingdom, and a driver faces the same penalties as for driving under the influence of alcohol
- However, the law does not currently state any legal limits for drugs, as it does for alcohol, making it difficult to enforce legislation
- The BMA is calling for this dilemma to be resolved by the development of appropriate testing devices
- The BMA's initiative arose from a resolution passed at its annual meeting of representatives in 2001 to consider ways of supporting the police in their fight against drugs and driving

USEFUL WEBSITE

www.bma.org.uk – This allows access to the BMA's drugs and driving website

BMA calls for action on 'drug driving'
(BMJ 2001;323:70)

- The BMA wants to raise awareness about the number of road traffic crashes caused by drivers using illicit drugs
- A Government commissioned study showed that the number of crash victims testing positive for illicit drugs had risen sixfold in the past decade

- Illegal drugs were found in 1 in 5 of those killed on the road
- 9% of drivers had driven after taking drugs ranging from cannabis to cocaine
- Of a representative sample of 1,000 adults aged 17–39, 87% said that they had accepted a lift in a car driven by someone they knew had used illicit drugs
- The number of people driving while under the influence of drugs was increasing, whereas the number of people arrested for drink driving had fallen as it became socially unacceptable to drink and drive
- Doctors had a responsibility to report to the authorities any patients who they knew were taking drugs that would impair their driving, in the same way as they would report patients with epilepsy.

COUNSELLING

Q. What is counselling?
A. It is helping patients to identify, understand, come to terms and cope with their problems.

Skills needed:

Listening	Summarising
Empathising	Interpreting
Reflecting	Confronting
Clarifying	Motivating

Various counselling styles	
• Directive	Counsellor acts prescriptively
• Informative	Counsellor provides information to help decision-making
• Confrontational	Counsellor challenges unhelpful thinking/behaviour
• Cathartic	Counsellor encourages expression of hidden thoughts/fears/guilt
• Catalytic	Counsellor encourages patient to establish own goals/take control
• Supportive	Counsellor provides acceptance, empathy, concern for patient's anxieties and needs
• Rogerian	Counsellor provides non-directive listening rather than advice, encouraging patient to make decisions based on own judgement

It has been known in the MRCGP exam to be asked for working examples of the above techniques, for example: 'Give an example of the use of catalytic intervention'

Who does it?

GP — uses counselling skills generally in the course of normal surgery

Attached counsellor — longer interviews with protected time
- need to ensure competence
- need to ensure integration in the primary healthcare team (PHCT)

Does it work?

Evidence suggests counselling in general practice is an effective therapy for psychosocial problems and minor affective disorders.

Some trials (not all) show that doctors:
- Identify more problems
- Prescribe fewer drugs
- Investigate less
- Refer less

Patients:
- Get relief from symptoms
- Cope better with feelings
- Cope better with life
- Consult less often

More information is needed on the value of types of counselling and the skills of counsellors.

What is the case against?
- It has been said that doctors may avoid contact with difficult patients by referring
- Patients may therefore feel rejected in some cases and fail to attend
- Some patients may feel worse after counselling
- Financial costs are sometimes prohibitive, nationally the service offered on the NHS is patchy

NICE guidelines on Ritalin
- Used as part of a comprehensive treatment programme for children with a diagnosis of severe attention deficit–hyperactive disorder (ADHD)
- Institute said that an estimated 1% of school-aged children (69,000 children aged 6–16 in England and 4,200 in Wales) meet the diagnostic criteria for severe, 'combined-type' ADHD

- 48,000 of those are not currently receiving methylphenidate (Ritalin and Equasym), and if all the children were to be prescribed it for a trial period, the cost of the drug would be an estimated £7m
- Should be diagnosed by a child psychiatrist or a paediatrician with expertise in the disorder, with involvement of children, parents, carers and the child's school
- Should receive regular monitoring, and when improvement has occurred and the child's condition is stable, treatment can be discontinued, under careful specialist supervision
- The only drugs licensed for treating ADHD in the UK are methylphenidate and dexamfetamine, although tricyclic and other antidepressants are sometimes prescribed

CHAPTER 5: THE ELDERLY

NATIONAL SERVICE FRAMEWORK (NSF) FOR OLDER PEOPLE

The original document is over 100 pages long, therefore the salient points have been summarised here with respect to General Practice. This NSF is a 10-year strategy to ensure fair, high quality, integrated health and social care services for older people. It is designed to support independence and promote good health. Aims to promote and engender that older people and their carers are always treated with respect, dignity and fairness. The National Director for Older People, Professor Ian Philp, will lead NSF implementation.

The four themes in this NSF are:
1. Respecting the individual
2. Intermediate care
3. Providing evidence-based specialist care
4. Promoting an active, healthy life

Prior to this NSF, some action has already taken place through other initiatives:

Improving standards of care
- In rest/nursing homes, through the new National Care Standards Commission and through the *Better Care, Higher Standards* Charters

Extending access to services
- Free NHS sight tests for those aged 60 and over
- Improved access to cataract services
- Extension of breast screening to women aged up to 70
- Carers' access to services in their own right has been ensured through the *Carers and Disabled Children Act 2000*
- *Care Direct* (Government pilot), a one-stop shop gateway to information about social care, health, housing and social security benefits, which will complement *NHS Direct*
- DoH issued *Fair Access to Care Services* guidance to councils in Spring 2001 setting out how they should develop fair and consistent eligibility criteria for adult social care services

Developing services which support independence
- *Promoting Independence Grant* supports councils to help more people to retain their independence for longer.
- *Supporting People* is a new initiative to help vulnerable people live independently in the community by providing a wide range of housing support services

Helping older people to stay healthy
- Free influenza immunisation for everyone aged 65 and over
- Improve oral health in older people and increase access to dentistry through *Modernising NHS Dentistry*
- Routine breast cancer screening is being extended to women up to the age of 70
- *Keep Warm, Keep Well* campaigns to prevent deaths in winter and increased Winter Fuel Payments of £200. This is paid to every household with someone over 60 years of age, regardless of whether they are retired or not.

Ensuring fairer funding
- End the anomaly that people in nursing homes may have to pay for their nursing care; it will be provided on the same basis as other NHS services, free at the point of use
- 3 months property disregard and by raising the capital limits when councils may step in with financial support
- Deferred payment scheme, to be introduced from October 2001, will give people more choice in how they pay for residential accommodation
- Aim to give people a valuable breathing space between entering a care home and selling their home, if that is their wish

Developing more effective links between health and social services
- The Health Act 1999 allowed partnership between Health Authorities and councils to improve services at the interface of health and social care
- Local Strategic Partnerships (LSPs) have been established across the country since April 2001
  - Committed to improving the quality of life
  - Refocusing of mainstream services and resources
  - LSPs will bring together the public, private, voluntary and community sectors and service users to provide a single over-arching local framework that will allow NSFs to be implemented

The NSF itself had eight standards, each accompanied with details of arrangements that would allow it to be implemented. (As you go through, note the standards which have any additional funding in order to aid implementation.)

STANDARD 1: ROOTING OUT AGE DISCRIMINATION

NHS services will be provided, regardless of age, on the basis of clinical need alone. Social care services will not use age in their eligibility criteria or policies, to restrict access to available services.

- Negative staff attitudes also impact on the quality of care
- Palliative care services have not been available to older people in some areas
- This may be related to the fact that palliative care services have been concentrated on those with cancer rather than terminal stages of a chronic disorder
- Elderly people from black and minority ethnic groups can be disadvantaged and are likely to suffer more discrimination in accessing services
- Concerns have been raised about resuscitation policies with older people more likely to be denied cardiopulmonary resuscitation (CPR) on the grounds of age alone; Guidelines from the BMA, RCN and Resuscitation Council suggest regular audits of local CPR policies in order to prevent age related discrimination
- Denying access to services on the basis of age alone is not acceptable
- Decisions should be made on the basis of health needs and ability to benefit, rather than age
- National guidance has been developed since May 2001 to assist with the audits of age-related policies
- Age discrimination may not always be explicit

STANDARD 2: PERSON-CENTRED CARE

NHS and social care services treat older people as individuals and enable them to make choices about their own care. This can be achieved through the single assessment process, integrated commissioning arrangements and integrated provision of services, including community equipment and continence services.

The plan focused on key areas of improvement, where need was identified, they are summarized below.

Personal and professional behaviour
- Staff should be polite and courteous at all times, e.g. using the older person's preferred form of address and relating to them as a competent adult
- Procedures are in place to identify and if possible meet, any particular needs and preferences relating to gender, personal appearance, communication, diet, race or culture and religious/spiritual beliefs
- Personal hygiene needs are met with sensitivity, intimate interventions carried out in privacy
- Patients allowed to wear their own clothes in hospital and able to have personal effects at their bedside (space/safety permitting)

Dignity in end-of-life care
- Control of painful and distressing symptoms
- Rehabilitation and support as health declines
- Social care to maintain access to safe and accessible living environments, practical help, income maintenance, social networks and information
- Spiritual care – availability of pastoral or spiritual carers reflecting the faiths of the local population
- Provide evidence-based complementary therapies
- Psychological care to anticipate, recognise and treat any psychological distress of the patient or carer
- Bereavement support and counselling

The single assessment process
- Proposed by The NHS Plan
- Introduced in April 2002, for health and social care for older people
- Covers health and social care for older people
- Standardised assessment process is in place across all areas and agencies
- Raised standards of assessment
- Designed to identify all of their needs
- Less duplication and worry for the patient
- Can be carried out by one front-line professional
- If other professionals need to be involved this will be arranged to provide a seamless service
- Assessment scales and tools are validated

Integrated community equipment services
- Audit Commission estimated that nearly 1 million people need equipment to help them live independently
- Demand for disability equipment is increasing due to ageing population and user expectation
- The NHS Plan set out an intention to achieve single, integrated community equipment services by 2004 and to increase by 50% the number of people able to benefit; comes with increased funding

Integrated continence services
- Primary and community staff involved in the identification and initial assessment and care
- Specialist services to provide expert advice when condition does not respond to initial treatment
- Availability and provision of continence aids/equipment and access to bathing/laundry services

STANDARD 3: INTERMEDIATE CARE

Older people will have access to a new range of intermediate care services at home or in designated care settings, to promote their independence by providing enhanced services from the NHS and councils to prevent unnecessary hospital admission and effective rehabilitation services to enable early discharge from hospital and to prevent premature or unnecessary admission to long-term residential care.

- A new layer of care, between primary care and specialist services
- To prevent unnecessary hospital admission, support early discharge and reduce or delay long-term residential care
- To improve physical functioning, build confidence, re-equip with the skills they need to live safely and independently at home
- Rehabilitation reduces re-admittance to hospitals and long terms in residential care
- Rehabilitation improves survival rates and physical and cognitive functioning
- 63% of older people permanently enter nursing home care, 43% of those entering residential care homes come direct from hospital
- Older people will be the main but not exclusive beneficiaries of these services
- Should involve rapid assessment, diagnosis and immediate treatment followed by appropriate referral

- Will include counselling, intensive support at home for a short period, community nursing and therapy services ('hospital at home')
- Well-managed intermediate care can improve recovery rates, increase patient satisfaction and reduce impact on the primary care team
- Strongest evidence is for stroke rehabilitation and geriatric/orthopaedic rehabilitation (more patients being discharged home compared with conventional care)

STANDARD 4: GENERAL HOSPITAL CARE

Older people's care in hospital is delivered through appropriate specialist care and by hospital staff who have the right set of skills to meet their needs.

Emergency response
- Older people should be transferred from A&E as soon as possible
- The NHS Plan commitment is that no patient should stay longer than 4 hours in A&E (by 2004)

Early assessment
- Should identify the further care the older person requires
- Will include investigation, observation and multidisciplinary assessment
- Input from geriatricians, specialists in stroke, falls and mental health or other disciplines including specialist nurses, therapists, pharmacists and social workers, may be required
- Clinical Leaders (Modern Matrons) for Older People to oversee care

Appropriate surroundings
- Separate room always available for private discussions and to make personal telephone calls
- Building design or re-design should take the need for privacy into account
- More four-bedded bays
- Single rooms for the most vulnerable
- Space provided for therapy equipment, or a small gym, comfortable day rooms and specially adapted kitchens
- 95% of NHS accommodation will be single sex by 2002

STANDARD 5: STROKE

The NHS will take action to prevent strokes, working in partnership with other agencies where appropriate. People who are thought to have had a stroke have access to diagnostic services, are treated appropriately by a specialist stroke service, and subsequently, with their carers, participate in a multidisciplinary programme of secondary prevention and rehabilitation.

- Each year 110,000 people in England and Wales have their first stroke (30,000 have further strokes); biggest cause of severe disability and the third most common cause of death in the UK
- 30% of patients die in the first month after a stroke
- After a year, 65% of surviving stroke patients can live independently, 35% are significantly disabled
- Around 5% are admitted to long-term residential care
- Risk increases with age but young people affected too
- 10,000 people under 55 years and 1,000 people under 30 years have a stroke each year
- African-Caribbean and South Asian men are about 40% and 70% more likely to have a stroke
- Socio-economic group V have a 60% higher chance of having a stroke than group I
- Mortality rates from stroke are 50% higher in socio-economic group V than in group I
- Strong evidence that people who have a stroke are more likely both to survive and to recover more function if admitted promptly to a hospital based stroke unit
- Apparently the NSF states this can be achieved at no overall additional cost to health and social care!
- Every DGH which cares for people with stroke has plans to introduce a specialised stroke service. This has been in place since April 2002.
- By April 2003 RCP guidelines for stroke care will be in place and audited
- By April 2004 PCG/Ts will have ensured that:
    - Every GP is using protocols agreed with local specialist services
    - Patients identified as being at risk are identified and treated
    - Rapid referral and management of those with a transient ischaemic attack (TIA) – guidelines in place

Population approaches to preventing stroke
* Similar to those for coronary heart disease – increasing levels of physical activity, encouraging healthy eating, supporting smoking cessation and identifying and managing high blood pressure

Preventing strokes in individuals at greater risk

Main risk factors	
Cardiovascular disease	hypertension, atrial fibrillation, CHD previous stroke or TIA, peripheral vascular disease, carotid stenosis
Metabolic	diabetes, hyperlipidaemia and obesity
Lifestyle	alcohol misuse, poor diet, low level of physical activity and smoking

* Risk of stroke for people with hypertension can be reduced by 37% through treatment
* Atrial fibrillation increases the risk of having a stroke by 3–7 times
* 13% of people who have had a stroke are in atrial fibrillation
* In the younger population risk factors include sickle cell disease, congenital heart disease, abnormalities of blood clotting and arterio-venous malformations of the brain.

Long-term support
Can continue over a long time and until maximum recovery has been achieved.

Some will need ongoing support and have access to a stroke care co-ordinator who can provide advice, arrange reassessment, co-ordinate long-term support or arrange for specialist care.

Any patient reporting a significant disability at six months should be re-assessed and offered further targeted rehabilitation, if this can help recover further function.

STANDARD 6: FALLS

The NHS, working in partnership with councils, takes action to prevent falls and reduce resultant fractures or other injuries in their populations of older people. Older people who have fallen receive effective treatment and rehabilitation and, with their carers, receive advice on prevention, through a specialised falls service.

- Falls are the leading cause of mortality due to injury in older people aged over 75 in the UK
- 14,000 people a year die in the UK as a result of an osteoporotic hip fracture
- Osteoporotic fractures occur most commonly in the hip, spine and wrist
- One-third of women and one-twelfth of men over 50 are affected by osteoporosis
- 50% of women have an osteoporotic fracture by the time they reach the age of 70
- Consequences for an individual of falling or of not being able to get up after a fall can include:
  - Psychological problems, for example a fear of falling and loss of confidence
  - Loss of mobility leading to social isolation and depression
  - Increase in dependency and disability
  - Hypothermia
  - Pressure-related injury
  - Infection
- After an osteoporotic fracture, 50% can no longer live independently
- Falls are a common symptom of previously unidentified health problems

Prevention
- Older people who have fallen are at risk of falling again
- A specialist falls services should be established for older people

Population approach to falls prevention
- Reduce incidence and impact of falls through encouraging appropriate weight-bearing and strength enhancing physical activity, promoting healthy eating and reducing smoking
- Community strategy to prevent falls should also include:
  - Ensuring that pavements are kept clear and in good repair
  - Adequate street lighting
  - Providing information, such as *'Avoiding Slips, Trips and Broken Hips'* by the Department of Trade and Industry (DTI)
  - Making property safer

 USEFUL WEBSITE

www.preventinghomefalls.gov.uk

Preventing falls in individuals
- Depends on identifying those most at risk
- Many who fall do not seek medical help but may be identified through risk factors
- Interventions should target both multiple risk factors for individuals (intrinsic risk factors) and environmental hazards to be successful

Intrinsic risk factors include
- Balance, gait or mobility problems including those due to degenerative joint disease and motor disorders such as stroke and Parkinson's disease
- Taking four or more medications, in particular centrally sedating or blood pressure lowering drugs
- Visual impairment
- Impaired cognition or depression
- Postural hypotension

Risk factors in the home environment include
- Poor lighting, particularly on stairs
- Steep stairs
- Loose carpets or rugs
- Slippery floors
- Badly fitting footwear or clothing
- Lack of safety equipment such as grab rails
- Inaccessible lights or windows

Assessment of risk of osteoporosis
Risk factors for osteoporosis include
- Previous fragility fracture (e.g. wrists)
- Prolonged corticosteroid therapy
- Hysterectomy, premature menopause or history of amenorrhoea (not treated to reduce risk of osteoporosis)
- Risk factors such as liver or thyroid disease, malabsorption, alcoholism, rheumatoid arthritis and male hypogonadism
- Family history of osteoporosis (including maternal hip fracture)
- Low body mass <19 kg/m^2
- Smoking

Treating osteoporosis
- When patients are identified as being at high-risk bone mineral density measurement should be carried out in line with the RCP Clinical Guidelines

- All patients get lifestyle advice on nutrition (calcium and vitamin D), regular weight bearing exercise, stopping smoking and avoiding alcohol
- Drug interventions: HRT, selective oestrogen receptor modulators (SERMS) and bisphosphonates will be most cost-effective when prescribed in high risk older people
- Frail or housebound people with previous fragility fractures may benefit from supplements of calcium and vitamin D to help prevent hip fracture

STANDARD 7: MENTAL HEALTH IN OLDER PEOPLE

Older people who have mental health problems have access to integrated mental health services, provided by the NHS and councils to ensure effective diagnosis, treatment and support, for them and for their carers.

- Cost of care for Alzheimer's Disease (AD) in 1993 was estimated at over £1 billion
- Considerable variation across the country exists in mental health services for older people
- Under-detection of mental illness in older people is widespread
- Depression in people aged 65 and over is especially under-diagnosed
- Mental and physical problems interact in older people making diagnosis and management difficult
- Older people from black and minority ethnic communities need accessible and appropriate mental health services
- Assessments may be culturally biased
- Information about services may not be effective if this relies on translated leaflets or posters rather than more appropriate mechanisms
- There may be distrust of agencies by some black and minority ethnic communities
- Older people with learning disabilities may have difficulty obtaining appropriate mental health care
- Family or paid carers of disabled elderly may not be alert to their mental health needs

Promoting mental health
- Standard 8 sets out the interventions at population level to promote good mental health
- Additional interventions which will promote mental health include

tackling social isolation, providing bereavement support and suicide prevention
- Key elements of suicide prevention will include health maintenance and promotion, treatment of depression in primary care and screening for suicidal ideation coupled with prevention
- Older people in residential care and nursing homes should be able to participate in a range of stimulating group or one to one activities

Depression
- 10–15% of the population aged 65 and over will have depression
- More severe states of depression are less common, affecting about 3–5% of older people
- Depression severely affects the quality of life and may adversely affect physical health
- Depression may be triggered by a variety of factors such as bereavement and loss, life changes such as unemployment, retirement and social isolation
- Older people can also become depressed because of increasing illness or frailty, or following a stroke or a fall
- Early recognition can reduce distressing symptoms and prevent physical illness, adverse effects upon social relationships, self-neglect and self-harm or suicide

Dementia
Dementia is a clinical syndrome characterised by a widespread loss of mental function, with the following features:
- Memory loss
- Language impairment (having difficulty finding words especially names and nouns)
- Disorientation (not knowing the time or place)
- Change in personality (becoming more irritable, anxious or withdrawn; loss of skills and impaired judgement)
- Self neglect
- Behaviour that is out of character (for example, sexual disinhibition or aggression)

Dementia has a number of causes, the most common of which are:
- AD – responsible for 60% of dementia cases, characterised by memory loss and difficulties with language becoming more severe over several years
- Vascular dementia – this is the consequence of strokes and/or

insufficient blood flow to the brain and causes up to 20% of cases of dementia; signs depend on area of brain involved
- AD and vascular dementia can co-exist
- Dementia with Lewy bodies – this causes up to 15% of dementia cases and is characterised by symptoms similar to Parkinson's disease as well as hallucinations
- Approximately 600,000 people in the UK have dementia (5% of the total population aged 65 and over, rising to 20% over the age of 80)
- 17,000 people with dementia are in younger age groups
- 154,000 live alone with dementia
- By 2026 there will be 840,000 people with dementia in the UK, rising to 1.2 million by 2050
- People diagnosed should be assessed under the single assessment process

STANDARD 8: THE PROMOTION OF HEALTH AND ACTIVE LIFE IN OLDER AGE

The health and well-being of older people is promoted through a co-ordinated programme of action led by the NHS with support from councils.

- NHS and local partners should re-focus on helping older people to continue to live healthy and fulfilling lives
- Growing body of evidence to suggest modification of risk factors late in life can have health benefits; longer life, increased/maintained levels of functional ability, disease prevention and an improved sense of well-being
- Integrated strategies for older people aimed at promoting good health and quality of life and to prevent or delay frailty and disability can have significant benefits for the individual and society

Action can be taken by the NHS and councils to:
- Prevent or delay the onset of ill health and disability
- Reduce the impact of illness and disability on health and well-being
- Identify barriers to healthy living (for example cultural appropriateness of services)
- Working with council services such as leisure and lifelong learning
- Health promotion activity should take account of differences in

lifestyle and the impact of cultural/religious beliefs, for example it would not be appropriate to advise a strict Muslim woman to take up a certain form of exercise which would mean that she would have to wear scant clothes for exercise or be in the same room as men.

PAPERS:

The first four articles appeared in the BMJ in March and April 2001. They focused on the care of elderly, the basis being extensive literature reviews undertaken to inform the development of the National Service Framework (NSF) for NHS care of older people in England. Some of the issues mentioned are covered in the NSF, therefore just the salient points are listed below along with any general issues that may arise.

1. Care of older people – Maintaining the dignity and autonomy of older people in the healthcare setting
(K. Lothian and I. Phile, BMJ 2001;322:668–70)

- It appeared that it is not just the lack of autonomy of elderly people within the healthcare service, but a somewhat unsettling lack of respect for their dignity
- Autonomy and dignity, although related, are differing concepts
- Dignity refers to an individual maintaining his or her self-respect and being valued by others
- Autonomy refers to individual control of decision-making and other activities
- Both the dignity and the autonomy of older people are often undermined in healthcare settings
- Negative interactions between staff and patients, a lack of regard for patients' privacy and a general insensitivity to the needs and desires of an older population all affect their 'dignity'
- 'Autonomy is threatened when patients (and their carers) are not given adequate information or the opportunity to understand fully their diagnosis and to make informed choices about their care'
- Qualitative data cited in the article suggests that attitudes of staff greatly affect both the quality of treatment of older people and the regard given to maintaining their dignity and autonomy
- Older people are becoming disempowered in healthcare settings
- Not just a problem of the UK but international
- Pessimistic viewpoints of healthcare professionals translates into a loss of dignity, identity and decision-making power for seniors

- Ageism, it appears, is as much of a problem within the NHS as it is within the population as a whole
- 'Tackling negative attitudes through exposure and education can help to preserve older patients' dignity and autonomy'
- 'Giving older people and their carers adequate information for them to make informed choices about care further increases autonomy'

The ironic realization is that the issues facing our profession in caring for the elderly are the same as those the Western world so readily counts as one of its merits, namely Autonomy, Dignity and Equality.

From articles such as those listed above and guidelines such as the NSF it is envisaged we can go some way in closing the apparent gap that exists between the young and old.

2. Promoting health and function in an ageing population
(G. R. Andrews, BMJ 2001;322:728–9)

The second article was written by an Australian academic in 'Ageing Studies'. Through a review of literature he looked at the evidence of the effectiveness of strategies for promoting health and function, particularly the benefits of exercise in old age.

- The prevalence of disability in older people is declining
- In order to maintain health and function in the elderly, the social, mental, economic and environmental determinants of health in old age must be taken into account
- The health benefits of exercise may often relate to psychosocial as well as direct health gains
- Most health benefits can be gained from regular physical activity of moderate intensity
- Health and well-being at older ages is modifiable
- Promoting health and fitness throughout life could make substantial gains
- The WHO has argued for a proactive and positive approach to dealing with the risk of chronic disease in old age
- WHO proposed a 'life course' approach for dealing with the health issues associated with ageing, and recommended implementing programmes oriented towards positive interventions in earlier life

The third article looked at the quality of mental health services for the elderly.

3. Care of older people – mental health problems
(A. Burns, et al., BMJ 2001;322:789–91)

The paper outlined the current evidence of benefit in four areas: services currently available; interventions that have been shown to be effective; rating scales that should be recommended to clinicians for detecting common mental health problems; and the needs of carers.

- Guidelines and standardised screening instruments improve recognition
- Carer interventions in people with dementia have been shown to be effective in RCTs
- Depression is the commonest mental health disorder and psychological therapies are underused
- Memory clinics significantly improve the quality of life in carers of people with dementia because of the treatment and advice they offer
- An RCT of a psychiatric liaison intervention for medical inpatients aged over 75, showed that those in the intervention group had improved physical function, fewer re-admissions to hospital or nursing home and a shorter length of stay
- A similar intervention was shown to be effective in frail, older people living at home

4. Falls in late life and their consequences
(C. G. Swift, BMJ 2001;322:855–7)

The last in this series of articles looked at falls in the elderly. The salient points were covered in the NSF, but it would be a relatively easy read if you wanted more detail.

The next few short topics were duplicated in the NSF; I have covered what has not appeared in NSF for completeness.

5. Randomised factorial trial of falls prevention among older people living in their own homes
(L. Day, et al., BMJ 2002;325:128)

- This urban Australian, RCT study looked at the effect of three interventions to prevent falls among older people

- Multiple interventions are known to prevent falls among older people, but the relative importance of the different strategies is unknown
- The prevention of falls among older people living in their own homes is an established priority in many countries; in the UK has a strong presence in the NSF for the elderly
- 1,090 people aged 70+ years and living at home were recruited
- Most were Australian-born and rated their health as good to excellent; just over half lived alone
- Three interventions (group-based exercise, home-hazard management and vision improvement) delivered to eight groups
- Seven groups received at least one intervention (1 hour/week for 15 weeks); the eighth received no intervention until after the study had ended
- Main outcome measure was time to first fall ascertained by an 18-month falls calendar
- Changes to targeted risk factors were assessed using measures of quadriceps strength, balance, vision and the number of hazards in the home
- Significant effect ($p < 0.05$) was observed for the combinations of interventions that involved exercise
- Balance measures improved significantly among the exercise group
- Neither home-hazard management nor treatment of poor vision showed a significant effect
- The strongest effect was observed for all three interventions combined, producing an estimated 14.0% reduction in the annual fall rate
- Number-needed-to treat (NNT) to prevent one fall a year ranged from 32 for home-hazard management to 7 for all three interventions combined
- Group-based exercise was the most potent single intervention tested, and the reduction in falls among this group seems to have been associated with improved balance
- The addition of home-hazard management or reduced vision management, or both of these further reduced falls

Problems
- Cost-effectiveness was not examined
- These findings are most applicable to Australian-born adults aged 70–84 years living at home who rate their health as good

- Whether or not this data can apply to the UK population is unknown (mainly middle class in Melbourne)
- The authors state that their programmes were of least intensity and, despite poor compliance, people still showed improvement (the exercises were supposed to be undertaken daily but most did them twice-weekly)
- Falls reduction may also have been mediated through social interaction, behavioural change, or both, as a result of heightened awareness during the classes
- The population studied may already have had many visual problems addressed in the free public healthcare system, since 48% of the intervention group did not require referral
- Participants in the intervention groups may also have underreported falls, and those receiving a more intense intervention, such as the group-based exercise programme, may have been even more inclined to underreport

6. Should elderly patients be told they have cancer? Questionnaire survey of older people
(A. Ajaj, et al., BMJ 2001;323:1160)

- This English questionnaire-based study examined the views of the elderly as to the level of information they would like imparted if they had a diagnosis of cancer
- Based on the premise that doctors fail to tell patients of their diagnosis, particularly if elderly
- Questionnaire elicited views on how much they would want to know, if they were diagnosed with cancer, about the type of cancer, extent of spread, treatment and prognosis, and also their wishes about informing their families. They also enquired about mobility and living circumstances to determine any association
- Patients with dementia or a history of cancer were excluded
- Of a total of 315 individuals approached, 270 (86%) completed the questionnaire
- Respondents ranged in age from 65 to 94 years
- Altogether 238 (88%) respondents wanted to be informed of the diagnosis, whereas 11% did not and 1% were indifferent
- 6.4% under 75 and 13.7% over 75 did not want to be informed, which represents a significant difference
- Of those who expressed a desire to be informed, 62% (n = 147) wanted to know as much as possible about their cancer, whereas

the remainder were more selective

- Over 70% (n = 194) of respondents wanted their relatives to be informed when the diagnosis of cancer was made
- No significant differences in attitude towards being told about cancer were found between those with different living circumstances and those who lived with a partner or not
- Individuals with limited mobility were significantly less interested in knowing they had cancer than those who walked independently either unaided or with a stick
- The authors state this may represent that mobility could be taken to reflect independence
- There was no relation, however, to walking distance, as a substantial proportion (44%) could walk only 23 metres or less

TREATMENT OF ALZHEIMER'S DISEASE (AD)

NICE Guidelines – on the use of donepezil, rivastigmine and galantamine for the treatment of AD (Jan 2001)

- Available on the NHS as part of the management for mild and moderate AD
- For patients with Mini-Mental State Examination (MMSE) score of >12/30
- Only specialists should initiate treatment
- Agreed shared-care protocol with GPs
- Reviewed at 2–4 months
- Continue only if MMSE >12

Evidence

NICE performed a systematic review of five RCTs for donepezil, five for rivastigmine and three for galantamine. Also used unpublished studies from drug companies. All three drugs show statistically significant improvement in cognitive function compared with placebo.

Typical average improvements of 1 to 2 points in MMSE (out of 30 points) over 6 months are usual compared with placebo; compared with an average decline of some 4 or 5 points per year in placebo-treated patients within trials.

RCT evidence of improvement in quality-of-life measures is less positive. There is no measure of quality of life for use in patients with dementia that has proved universally satisfactory. Evidence that quality of life has been improved by any of these drugs has therefore been mixed.

Carers report functional benefits and improvement in behavioural symptoms, such as agitation and aggression, as well as in motivation, concentration, control and independence.

Placebo effects are quite large, with as many as 30% improving on baseline outcome scores at the next assessment.

Clinical Evidence 2000

- Beneficial: donepezil
- Likely to be beneficial: rivastigmine, selegeline (one systematic review) and gingko

The Elderly

📖 Editorial: Drugs for Alzheimer's disease. Cholinesterase inhibitors have passed NICE's hurdle
(BMJ 2001;323:123–4)

- Alzheimer's disease, the commonest cause of dementia in older people, affects 4% of the over-65s and 20% of the over-80s, with around 400,000 sufferers in the United Kingdom
- The prevalence of the condition will double over the next 50 years
- NICE has reviewed the available drugs for Alzheimer's disease and declared them clinically effective in reducing the burden of disease in some patients
- Within the past 3 years, three cholinesterase inhibitors (donepezil, rivastigmine and galantamine) have been licensed in the UK for use in mild to moderate Alzheimer's disease
- These drugs are a rational therapy based on the core deficit in the disorder, that of cholinergic deficit
- These compounds represent symptomatic treatments and have been shown in several large, multicentre, randomised, double-blind, placebo-controlled trials to improve cognitive function, global outcome and activities of daily living (ADL)
- There is also accumulating evidence that they may improve non-cognitive symptoms such as psychosis and apathy
- The mean effect of drug over placebo represents an improvement in cognition roughly equivalent to stemming 6–12 months of natural decline in untreated patients
- When the drug is withdrawn the clinical gain is reversed, and there are no convincing clinical data that these drugs modify the disease
- 40–50% of patients show a definite clinical improvement (≥4 points on the Alzheimer's disease assessment scale-cognitive subscale – ADAS-cog)
- 20% show a strong response (≥7 points on the ADAS-cog, equivalent to stemming a year or more of natural cognitive decline)
- Responders are maintained above baseline for 12–18 months on both cognitive and non-cognitive measures
- NNT for significant clinical improvement are 3–7
- No reliable predictors of response have emerged, and in each patient careful assessment of benefit needs to be undertaken after 2–4 months of treatment
- Both efficacy and side-effects (mainly gastrointestinal problems)

are similar between compounds
- Initial scepticism over these compounds was fuelled by the late publication of key trial data, initial lack of clear effects on ADL scores and difficulties in determining cost-effectiveness
- Most economic analyses clearly show either cost-neutrality or cost-effectiveness in favour of these agents
- Evidence to date suggests that the modest cost of these agents (£800–£1,200 a year) would be more than offset by savings elsewhere, though not necessarily within the healthcare system

 USEFUL WEBSITE

www.nice.org.uk – Guidance No 19, January 2001

CHAPTER 6: OBSTETRICS AND GYNAECOLOGY

COMBINED ORAL CONTRACEPTIVE PILL

The combined oral contraceptive pill (COCP) has been one of the most extensively researched medicines and is still providing many areas of controversy and discussion. About 80% of British women use the COCP at some time between the ages of 16 and 24 years. The pill continues to be one of the most worried and talked about drugs, regularly making newspaper headlines. Consequently, women's fears persist out of all proportion to actual risk, and in most cases women are unaware of the pill's substantial non-contraceptive health benefits.

In addition, the medical professionals knowledge of the pill's advantages and disadvantages is still very varied. Two large cohort studies followed a total of over 70,000 women and had very reassuring results with the same mortality rates for users and non-users.

What is the risk of deep vein thrombosis to women taking the combined oral contraceptive?
The largest area of controversy is the increased risk of deep vein thrombosis (DVT) with third-generation pills.

In October 1995 the Committee on Safety of Medicines (CSM) warned that COCPs containing desogestrel or gestodene carried a small increased risk of DVT compared with other preparations so should not be used as first-line treatment. Subsequent studies have actually shown no difference in risk of thromboembolism between different pill preparations.

However, two different studies in the BMJ have used the same data and reported opposite conclusions regarding the risk of DVT in third generation oral contraceptives *(BMJ 2000;321:477–9 and 1190–5)*! However, the superior design and analysis of the more recent study *(BMJ 2000;321:1190–5)* mean that it could be the most important paper yet published on this vexed subject. It also provides vital evidence on several controversial matters, including the increased risk in first time users of oral contraceptives and the role of risk factors such as obesity and smoking. It showed that women with a BMI of at least 35 have a four-fold increased risk of DVT by taking all types of combined oral contraceptives.

A meta-analysis in the BMJ concluded that the risk with third-generation pills is 1.7 times that with second-generation pills (*BMJ 2001; 323:131–4*); however this is not the result of RCTs. An editorial in the same edition of the BMJ points out that, while debating whether the risks are one or ten in a million, it is important to remember that in most of the world the risk of death associated with pregnancy is at least 100 times greater than this.

The quoted risks of DVT are as follows:

Non-users	5 :100 000
Second-generation pill	15 :100 000
Third-generation pill	30 :100 000
Pregnancy	60 :100 000

The Department of Health actually announced in 1999 an end to the 1995 restrictions on prescribing third-generation oral contraceptive pills. The absolute risk of venous thromboembolism in women taking either second- or third-generation combined oral contraceptives remains very small and still well below the risk associated with pregnancy. Provided that the women are informed of and accept the relative risks of thromboembolism, the choice of oral contraceptive is for the woman and the prescriber to decide jointly in the light of her individual medical history and any contraindications.

The European Agency for Evaluation of Medicinal Products published a report in October 2001 based on an ongoing review of the risk of venous thromboembolism (VTE) with the COCP. The Committee found an excess risk of VTE during the first year a woman takes any combined oral contraceptive pill. The report summarised that if a woman uses any type of combined oral contraceptive pill for a year without suffering a clot then her future risk of VTE is extremely low.

Should the COCP be prescribed to patients with a family history of clots?

The value of a family history of venous thromboembolism has recently been questioned, as it actually has a poor sensitivity and unsatisfactory predictive value for identifying women with thrombophilic defects (*BMJ 2001;322:1024–5*). Universal screening is not cost-effective as 8,000 women need to be screened to prevent one VTE, and only screening women with a family history of VTE may miss a substantial number of women at increased risk of VTE while taking the COCP.

Is there an increased risk of myocardial infarction?

A recent large community based case-control study found no association between the use of the combined oral contraceptive and myocardial infarction, and no difference of risk between second- and third-generation pills *(BMJ 1999;318:1579-84)*. The risk of myocardial infarction in women taking the combined oral contraceptive seems to increase only in association with additional risk factors (e.g. smoking, diabetes, obesity, hypertension). The combined oral contraceptive pill is contraindicated in women with severe or multiple risk factors for ischaemic heart disease.

Is there an increased risk of ischaemic stroke?

In women who do not smoke and do not have hypertension, the risk of ischaemic stroke is 1.5 times higher than in non-users. However, the risk rises to threefold in women with hypertension taking the combined oral contraceptive.

Is there an increased risk of haemorrhagic stroke?

There is no increased risk in women under the age of 35 years who are non-smokers and normotensive. One study has shown that women over 35 years have a double risk of haemorrhagic stroke compared with non-users. Women who smoke and take the pill are three times more likely to have a haemorrhagic stroke, and hypertensive women have a 10–15 times increased risk.

Does taking the combined oral contraceptive pill lead to hypertension?

There is a lack of data on the effects of the low dose combined oral contraceptive on blood pressure. If a woman develops pill-induced hypertension she should consider an alternative method of contraception. The pill should not be used and also be stopped in patients with a sustained blood pressure above 160/95 mmHg.

Is the combined oral contraceptive pill contraindicated in women with migraine?

The incidence of ischaemic (not haemorrhagic) stroke is increased in women with migraine, particularly if they are also taking the combined oral contraceptive pill *(BMJ 1999;318:13–18)*. The combined oral contraceptive pill is contraindicated in patients who have migraines with focal aura (migraine with focal symptoms) or classical migraine and those patients who have severe migraines lasting over 72 hours despite treatment.

Are there benefits from taking the combined oral contraceptive pill?
It is important to remember that the pill has numerous advantages. These include:
- Excellent efficacy and acceptability
- Beneficial effects on menstrual disorders
- Suppression of benign breast disease
- Protection against endometrial and ovarian cancer
- Protection against pelvic inflammatory disease.

Any adverse effects from taking the oral contraceptive pill are reversed after 10 years cessation of the pill.

SUMMARY POINTS FOR COMBINED ORAL CONTRACEPTION

- ❖ Very safe and effective contraception
- ❖ Conflicting evidence still exists regarding thrombotic risk
- ❖ Absolute risk of DVT very small with 3rd generation pill
- ❖ Always consider patient's risk factors for CHD
- ❖ COCP still has numerous advantages and is a safe contraceptive

---

EMERGENCY CONTRACEPTION

Emergency contraception (also called postcoital contraception) is a safe and highly effective way of preventing an accidental pregnancy; it is not suitable if used as a regular method of birth control. It is very popular, one-third of women aged 18–19 years and one-quarter of women aged 20–24 years have used it at least once over the preceding 2 years.

Levonelle-2 is now the only available emergency contraception pill. It prevents pregnancy by suppressing ovulation, impairing fallopian transport of the egg and sperm (so preventing fertilisation) and also prevents implantation of any fertilised egg. Levonelle-2 appears to be very safe and there are no contraindications for its use.

Why has Levonelle-2 become available without a prescription?
A medicine must have prescription-only status if: there would be a danger to health if the substance were used without medical supervision; the product might be used incorrectly, so endangering health; and the active ingredient, or side-effects it may cause, require further investigation. The CSM advised that Levonelle-2 does not meet these criteria and so could be safely supplied by a pharmacist without medical supervision. The UK Government took this advice and from 1 January 2001 Levonelle-2 has been available, now at a cost of £25, to women over 16 years of age from pharmacies without a doctor's prescription.

What are the advantages of Levonelle-2 being available without prescription?
- Very safe medication (unlike paracetamol and ibruprofen!)
- Very effective medication
- Increases ease of access
- Patients may prefer anonymity
- Leads to reduction in unwanted pregnancies
- Supported by RCOG and BMA
- May save money by reduction in termination rates

What are the disadvantages of Levonelle-2 being available over the counter?
- Does not address issues of ongoing contraception and sexually transmitted diseases
- Lost opportunity for counselling/education
- Patients will have to pay for it
- Opposition by church/anti-abortion groups

- Need highly motivated pharmacists
- Not all pharmacies will have an area available for discussing private issues
- Has been banned in Ireland

Should Levonelle-2 be available free of charge over the counter?
It has been estimated that £1 spent on contraception actually saves £11 in subsequent NHS costs from an unplanned pregnancy, so it could be argued that offering free over-the-counter emergency contraception releases money to spend on other services.

Lambert, Lewisham and Southwark Health Authority (which has one of the highest rates of teenage pregnancies and unwanted pregnancies in the UK) has recently allowed specially trained pharmacists to dispense Levonelle-2 free rather than charging £20.

Women still need to know how, when and where they can obtain emergency contraception free of charge through established NHS routes of supply. Emergency contraception still remains available free on prescription from general practitioners, family planning clinics, youth clinics, walk-in centres, some genitourinary medicine units and accident and emergency departments.

The intrauterine contraceptive device (IUCD) is still available as an alternative to Levonelle-2, is effective for up to 5 days after unprotected intercourse and is more effective than the hormonal methods.

SUMMARY POINTS FOR EMERGENCY CONTRACEPTION

- ❖ Levonelle now obtainable without prescription
- ❖ Low incidence of side-effects
- ❖ Levonelle should be given early to improve efficacy
- ❖ IUCD still more effective

TEENAGERS AND SEXUAL HEALTH

The UK has the second highest teenage pregnancy rate in the developed world. (The USA has the highest.) Many teenagers are willing to run the risk of an unplanned pregnancy or catching a sexually transmitted disease because they fear that their parents will find out if they seek advice from their GP. Reduction in teenage pregnancy was one of the targets set for improvement during the 1990s in the Health of the Nation document; however it was not met!

What are the problems?
Teenagers are often confused about where they can obtain contraceptive advice or treatment, whether it is legal and how to actually use the different contraceptive methods. In the UK, approximately 50% of teenagers use contraception; this rate is much higher in Denmark, which suggests a poorer access and knowledge rather than lower demand in the UK. In addition, 75% of teenage mothers admit to having unplanned pregnancies.

In 1995–7 the rate of increase of gonorrhoea among 15–19-year-olds was 45% and chlamydia was 53%. The results of a questionnaire survey sent to 1,045 children aged 13–15 years showed that 54% believed they had to be over 16 years of age to access sexual health services (*BJGP 2000;50:550–4*).

A recent landmark study has shown that risky sexual behaviour has led to a dramatic increase in sexually transmitted infections (*Lancet 2001;358:1835–54*). This study showed that among 16–24-year-olds, almost 20% of men and 15% of women have already had 10 or more sexual partners.

How should GPs be able to improve teenage sexual health?
The Fraser (previously Gillick) ruling clarifies the legal position of treating children under 16 years of age without parental consent (see Box on p. 129).

It has been estimated in various surveys that at least one-quarter of teenagers do not believe their consultation will be confidential. Posters or leaflets in the surgery explaining the services available and the confidentiality issue may be useful. Patients must have easy access to emergency contraception. It can be useful to advertise local family planning and youth clinics, as many patients prefer these clinics rather than seeing their own GP.

Doctors can and should advise on the effective use of contraception for their patients. There is evidence to show that practices with young female partners have significantly lower teenage pregnancy rates (*BMJ 2000;320:842–5*).

A piece of research studying teenage pregnancies found that almost all had visited a GP in the previous year, and many of them had sought contraceptive advice during the consultation (*BMJ 2000;321:486–9*). More worryingly, teenagers who had terminations of their pregnancy were more likely to have received emergency contraception in the past.

It is clear therefore that GPs should follow up teenage patients to ensure they are using their contraception correctly. In addition, patients who receive emergency contraception should be started on regular contraception at the same time and then have clear follow-up arrangements.

Unfortunately, primary prevention strategies have not actually shown to delay the initiation of sexual intercourse or improve the use of contraception among teenagers (*BMJ 2002;324:1426–9*).

What is the recently launched multimedia campaign about teenage pregnancy?
This national campaign aims to give young people information about sex and contraception, including facts about the rising rates of sexually transmitted infections among teenagers and dispelling some 'urban myths' about sex. This is going to be achieved by using adverts in teen magazines, on local radio stations and through other media.

Specifically, the campaign messages are:
• You can get free, confidential advice about contraception whatever your age
• If you are sexually active, use contraception, because of the risk of pregnancy and infections
• You choose when to have sex, no one else

Local sexual health services are expected to see a gradual increase in demand from teenagers as a result of this campaign. To ensure the services are accessible and trusted by teenagers, best-practice guidance has been developed by the Teenage Pregnancy Unit for the commissioning and provision of effective services for young people.

It is very important that more clinics are provided for younger people, particularly as the Government wants a reconfirmation of services so they would be provided at a primary care level as well as at an acute and community level.

Contraception and young people under 16 years – the Fraser guidelines

A young person under 16 years may be given advice and may be prescribed contraception without parental consent if the following conditions are met:
- She understands the advice and is competent to consent to treatment
- You encourage her to inform her parent or guardian
- You believe she is likely to commence or continue sexual activity with or without contraception
- Her physical or mental health will suffer if she does not receive contraception advice or supplies
- Providing contraception is in her best interest

🕸 USEFUL WEBSITE

www.teenagepregnancyunit.gov.uk – Teenage Pregnancy Unit's website

---

📝 SUMMARY POINTS FOR TEENAGERS AND SEXUAL HEALTH

- ❖ UK has high teenage pregnancy rate
- ❖ Most teenagers unaware of confidentiality
- ❖ Lower teenage pregnancy rates in practices with young female partners
- ❖ Many teenagers ignorant of contraception methods and their availability

---

SEXUAL HEALTH AND CHLAMYDIA

The number of visits to genitourinary medicine (GUM) clinics has doubled over the past decade and the number of sexually transmitted infections diagnosed continues to rise.

Chlamydia is the commonest curable sexually transmitted disease in the industrialised world and is currently a huge problem in young, sexually active adults. Long-term consequences of chlamydia include increased pelvic pain, increased rate of ectopic pregnancies and increased infertility rates. This latter consequence often only becomes apparent during investigations at infertility clinics, as many patients are unaware of earlier infection with *Chlamydia* spp.

Up to 70% of women and 50% men with infections are asymptomatic. The incidence has increased by 27% in 2001/2 and by 106% over the past 5 years according to recent Public Health Service Laboratory figures (www.phls.co.uk); it has been estimated as affecting 1 in 12 women aged 16–24 years.

Why has the incidence of sexually transmitted infections, including chlamydia, increased by so much?

Some of the rise in incidence may be a reflection of improved detection and awareness. However, one of the major factors behind the recent rises in Western Europe is probably changing sexual behaviour. In addition, levels of awareness and fear of the human immunodeficiency virus (HIV) and acquired immunodeficiency syndrome (AIDS) among people have declined, and the major fear is now of unintended pregnancy rather than a sexually transmitted infection (*BMJ 2001;322:1135–6*).

How is chlamydia detected?

Chlamydia has traditionally been diagnosed by endocervical swabs, which has a poor sensitivity. The detection of chlamydial infection in women is particularly difficult because between 5 and 30% of infected women are infected only in the urethra, which is not detected by endocervical swab culture. The taking of endocervical or urethral swabs is an uncomfortable, time-consuming and relatively expensive procedure that obviously requires a pelvic examination.

New tests are emerging that are more sensitive and preferable to previous tests. The ligase chain reaction (LCR) on a sample of urine is more sensitive than endocervical swabs (90% vs. 65% sensitivity). Urine test kits are currently available only in some areas – cost is obviously the main consideration determining the general availability of these kits. However, with complications costing £50m a year, they could prove cost-effective.

Why not screen for chlamydia in UK?
There are currently successful screening programmes in the USA and Sweden, which have resulted in a lower incidence of chlamydia. Screening is currently under consideration for <25-year-olds, patients with symptoms, women seeking termination of pregnancy and women >25 years of age with a new partner.

However, there are many problems with introducing a successful screening programme in the UK. These are clearly documented in the report by the CMO's advisory group (see website). They include the psychological barriers of investigation, costs involved and methods of contact tracing. If contact tracing is not done effectively and efficiently then any screening programme would be wasted: treated patients would simply become reinfected and so negate any good done!

Before a national screening programme can be introduced there needs to be effective implementation of training and education for both staff and patients, which will have huge resource implications. Many women have never heard of chlamydia, let alone its consequences, so at present it would be very difficult to expect people to be screened for a disease they have never heard of.

Finally, screening for chlamydia is a very sensitive area as many women may feel 'targeted' by the introduction of this programme. It needs to be addressed and implemented properly for it to be successful in the UK. Ideally, for chlamydia screening to be successful there should be a multidisciplinary structured approach with comprehensive testing of an agreed 'at risk' population, with both effective and timely treatment of infected patients and effective tracing and treatment of sexual contacts.

Is screening going to be implemented soon?
The Department of Health announced in the summer of 2001 that £47.5m is to be invested over the next 5 years as part of their First National Strategy for Sexual Health and HIV. A 'target' screening programme will be phased in during 2002.

The key objectives of this strategy are to ensure that all individuals have access to the knowledge and skills necessary to achieve positive sexual health, and that services should be readily available to all who require them (*BMJ 2001;323:243–4*). The specific aims are to reduce the undiagnosed prevalence and transmission of sexually transmitted infections and HIV, to reduce unintended pregnancies and to improve social care and health for people with HIV. The proposals will increase the role of primary care and strengthen links between specialist services and other local agencies. It does still look very overambitious when considering the resources allocated to it!

Screening for chlamydia will be offered, in selected health authorities, to women attending:
- Family planning clinics
- Antenatal clinics
- For terminations of their pregnancy
- For their first smear test

Screening will also be offered to some men, such as partners of infected women. The aim will be to extend screening to GP surgeries, but careful planning is obviously needed.

How will the National Strategy for Sexual Health and HIV affect GPs?
This National Strategy will greatly increase the role GPs have in providing sexual healthcare. Every GP will need to provide:
- Sexual history and risk assessment
- Sexually transmitted infection (STI) testing for women
- Pregnancy testing and referral
- Contraceptive information and services
- Assessment and referral of men with STI symptoms
- Cervical cytology screening and referral for hepatitis B virus immunisation

Many of these services are already provided by most practices; the main change will be the introduction of screening for chlamydia.

How has the RCGP responded to the Strategy for Sexual Health and HIV?
The College has responded very favourably, as this is the first time there has been such a nationwide approach with the Department of Health acknowledging that sexual health and HIV are major public health problems. The College has also stated that the Government needs to ensure that adequate resources are made available for the proposals to become a reality.

USEFUL WEBSITE

www.doh.gov.uk/chlamyd.htm – report of the Chief Medical Officer's expert advisory group on chlamydia

---

📋 SUMMARY POINTS FOR CHLAMYDIA

❖ Chlamydia is most prevalent sexually transmitted disease (STD) in UK
❖ Highest rates in females aged 16–24 years
❖ Most infections are asymptomatic
❖ Screening programme needs to be properly implemented
❖ Continued lack of public awareness of chlamydia

HORMONE REPLACEMENT THERAPY

HRT is always a topical subject and patients are often guided by inaccurate information they have read in the lay press so it is important to be able to reassure and educate them with reference to the recent literature. Patients taking HRT are more likely to be healthier, well educated and compliant (quite different from most patients!) so it is very difficult to control bias in studies, which are still mainly observational. It has been estimated that currently one third of perimenopausal and postmenopausal women in the UK are taking HRT.

Does HRT protect patients from coronary heart disease?

This is still the most controversial area. Observational studies have reported that the risk of ischaemic heart disease may be reduced by up to 40% in women taking HRT. However, the differences are thought to be related to selection bias and therefore interpretation of these studies is extremely difficult.

The HERS (Heart and Estrogen/Progestin Replacement Study) was the first randomised prospective study of 2,763 postmenopausal women in the USA with established ischaemic heart disease. The data showed that taking combined oestrogen and progestogen had no effect on MI or coronary death after treatment for 4.1 years. This trial created a lot of debate because it reported that the overall null effect comprised what appeared to be an early adverse effect followed by a trend towards a benefit, although neither effect was actually statistically significant (*JAMA 1998;280:605–13*). Many critics of this study felt it was stopped too soon, because if the study had been extended for another year or so, looking at the graphed data, it might have extended to a 30–50% lower risk. It was also criticised for being underpowered to detect moderate differences in clinically important outcomes.

The Estrogen Replacement and Atherosclerosis (ERA) trial looking at angiographic progression of existing disease found no effect of either oestrogen alone or combined oestrogen and progestogen (*NEJM 2000;343:522–9*).

The Women's Health Initiative (WHI) study (see below) demonstrated increased relative risks for coronary heart disease (the primary outcome) and stroke, although the absolute risks were very small (*JAMA 2002;288:321–33*). For each 10,000 women taking HRT each year (compared with placebo) there would be an extra seven heart attacks, eight strokes and eight pulmonary embolisms (PEs). However, there would also be six fewer cases of bowel cancers and five fewer hip fractures.

An interesting BMJ article regarding this study highlights that, given the biological effects of oestrogen on the cardiovascular system, the lack of benefit on CHD is surprising (*BMJ 2002;325:113*). However, the findings from the WHI study only apply to this particular HRT regimen. Particularly for CHD, the dose (and possibly type) of oestrogen and the type of progesterone may well be crucial.

Various other studies have shown that patients taking HRT have lower levels of LDL-cholesterol and higher levels of HDL-cholesterol compared with patients taking a placebo. Further large randomised controlled trials, including the WISDOM (Women's International Study of long Duration Oestrogen after Menopause) trial in the UK, are underway in order to clarify the association of HRT and coronary heart disease. However, these trials will not provide definitive results for several years.

In the meantime, the British Menopause Society suggests that the recommendations of the American Heart Association, published in April 2001, should be read and considered for patients (*Circulation 2001;104:499–503*) (see Box on p. 138).

Is HRT related to breast cancer?
The risk of breast cancer is much exaggerated in the lay press, and this risk is usually the one that dissuades many women from taking HRT. Some studies have shown that women who take oestrogen after their menopause are more likely to develop breast cancer; others have established no link.

What about the recent HRT 'scare'?
There has been even more publicity than usual in the media because of the Women's Health Initiative which recruited over 16,000 women in a randomised controlled trial, looking at continuous-combined HRT versus placebo (*JAMA 2002;288:321–33*). During monitoring, the adverse events for CHD, stroke and PE rose (within the limits), but the threshold for invasive breast cancer and also the global index of overall risk versus benefit exceeded the previously set limits. This meant that the HRT arm of the study was stopped; the oestrogen-only trial is continuing.

In this study, however, the combination of conjugated equine oestrogen with medroxyprogesterone acetate was used (a preparation not available in the UK) – the data can not therefore necessarily be extrapolated to considering other forms and doses of HRT. The absolute numbers of adverse events were very low (e.g. 8 cases of breast cancer in 100,000 women studied). In addition, up to 4 years' use of HRT did not seem to increase the risk of invasive breast cancer. The study did also demonstrate that HRT prevents bone fracture and that protection increases with duration of treatment.

Studies have shown that women using hormone replacement therapy after the menopause are actually more likely to have slow-growing and highly curable types of breast cancers. An American study showed that women taking HRT had no difference in their risk of getting the fast-growing, life-threatening tumours, ductal carcinoma in situ, invasive ductal or lobular cancer, which together constitute 85–90% of all cases of breast cancer (*JAMA 1999;281:2091–9*).

Any increased risk of breast cancer only applies to women over the age of 50 years. Therefore women taking replacement HRT (e.g. post-oophorectomy) are at no higher risk of breast cancer until they reach the age of 50 years.

In summary, most women taking HRT in the UK are <60 years and do so for a relatively short time. Women at increased risk of stroke and CHD should consider reducing other risk factors (independent of HRT); HRT can be used for its other known benefits.

Does HRT increase risk of ovarian cancer?
The latest US findings showed that oestrogen-only HRT increases the risk of ovarian cancer, especially if taken for more than 10 years (*JAMA 2002;288:334–41*). However, the increased risk is small and many women have oophorectomies at the time of their hysterectomy, so this risk would only be applicable to a small number of women in the UK. This increased risk has not been demonstrated with taking combined HRT.

Does HRT offer protection against osteoporosis?
Numerous studies have shown that oestrogen reduces the risk of hip fracture by about 30% and of spine fracture by about 50%. The reduction in fracture risk by oestrogen exceeds that expected based on bone density alone. However, 10 years after HRT has been stopped,

bone density and fracture risk are similar in women who have not taken HRT.

The Women's Health Initiative study did confirm this protection (*JAMA 2002;288:321–33*). It demonstrated a lower hip fracture rate (10 per 10,000 person-years vs. 15 per 10,000 person-years for placebo). Combined HRT also reduced the clinical vertebral fracture rate by one-third compared to placebo. The total reductions of osteoporotic fractures in this study were 24%.

Do women taking HRT have a higher risk of DVT?
The excess risk of DVT in HRT users compared with non-users was estimated to be 4.1 per 1,000 women in the HERS trial (*JAMA 1998;280:605–13*). The absolute risks of DVT caused by HRT are higher in older women and those with other risk factors for venous thromboembolism.

Finally, the most commonly asked question by patients:

Does HRT cause women to put on weight?
Many women are worried about putting on weight when taking HRT. From many trials on HRT, however, it has been shown that all women put on weight after the menopause, but generally those taking HRT actually put on less weight than those in the placebo groups!

Note
At present, long-term HRT should really only be given on an individual basis, depending on the needs and risk factors of the patient. Long-term therapy can still be considered for the prevention of osteoporosis. For women starting HRT, the recommendations are to keep the starting dose of oestrogen low in women over 60 years.

AMERICAN HEART ASSOCIATION RECOMMENDATIONS ON HRT AND CARDIOVASCULAR DISEASE

Secondary prevention (i.e. in woman with established CVD)
❖ HRT should not be initiated for the secondary prevention of CVD
❖ The decision to continue or stop HRT in women with CVD who have been undergoing long-term HRT should be based on established non-coronary benefits, risks and patient preference
❖ If a woman develops an acute CVD event or is immobilised while undergoing HRT, it is prudent to consider discontinuing HRT. Reinstitution of HRT should be based on established non-coronary benefits and risks, as well as patient preference

Primary prevention (i.e. in women without CVD)
❖ There are insignificant data to suggest that HRT should be initiated for the sole purpose of preventing CVD

📋 **SUMMARY POINTS FOR HRT**

❖ Association between HRT and CHD still controversial
❖ Risk of breast cancer in HRT users often over estimated
❖ WHI study has provoked much anxiety in patients
❖ Osteoporosis protection only when taking HRT
❖ Little evidence that HRT causes weight gain

CHAPTER 7: PAEDIATRICS

CHILDHOOD VACCINATIONS

MMR vaccination

While the measles, mumps and rubella (MMR) debate persists, it appears that the vaccination rates are falling. The uptake of the MMR vaccine in babies has reduced as a result of reports suggesting possible links with autism and inflammatory bowel disease. In some areas, the vaccination rates are now even below those needed to ensure herd immunity. There is concern that the incidence of measles and mumps is increasing as a result of this reduced uptake of the vaccination. As many as one in four 4-year-olds in Surrey are currently unprotected.

Outbreaks of measles have occurred in London, where MMR uptake rates are among the worst in the country. The uncertainty around Leo Blair's immunity to measles has also heightened public fears about the vaccine.

Dr Wakefield has been at the forefront of suggesting the link between the MMR vaccine and long-term health problems, especially inflammatory bowel disease and autism. Media interest has also focused on the use of single antigen vaccines as opposed to recommending the combined vaccine. There is real concern about having the vaccines separately, since children would then be left unnecessarily at risk from these potentially serious diseases. The problems with the studies were that they were all retrospective and so subject to recall bias by the parents and carers. The original studies also involved very small numbers of children.

Four independent bodies have reviewed the evidence: CSM, Joint Committee on Vaccination and Immunisation, MRC expert group and CSM Working Party on MMR Vaccine. They all agreed that the information does not support the suggested causal associations or give any cause for concern about the safety of the MMR vaccine. In addition, a very large Finnish study followed an impressive 1.8 million individuals for 14 years from the start of the MMR vaccination programme, and it concluded that serious events are rare and are greatly outweighed by the risks of the disease. There were actually no cases of inflammatory bowel disease or autism detected in this study.

In the USA, two independent committees reviewed all the published and some unpublished research, they concluded there is no epidemiological evidence to support any link between MMR vaccine, autism and inflammatory bowel disease.

One study in London showed that, although many mothers were influenced by the adverse media publicity, many mothers thought the second dose of the MMR vaccine was unnecessary for their children. The majority of the 170 mothers said they valued their own GPs opinion the most when deciding whether to have their child vaccinated or not (*BGJP 2000;50:969–71*). This is quite worrying as another study, which was based on 500 healthcare professionals, showed that almost a half of GPs, health visitors and practice nurses felt very uneasy about giving the second dose of the MMR vaccine (*BMJ 2001;322:82–5*). In addition, one-third of the practice nurses thought that the link of the vaccine with Crohn's disease was either very likely or possible. This wide variation in knowledge regarding the vaccine may be influencing the advice given to parents.

If health professionals lack trust in advice and available evidence, how can we expect the public not to share this trust?

Is there any place for single-antigen vaccines?
Some parents and professionals still feel reticent about the MMR vaccine and would prefer the use of single vaccines. When single measles vaccine was used in the UK before 1988, there were regular epidemics of measles with 10–20 deaths each year. There is no research evidence or experience of a regimen giving measles, mumps and rubella vaccine separately to preschool children. A link between the single vaccine and autism and bowel disease has never been investigated. It is not known what the optimum time interval between doses should be, or even if it provides adequate protection against the diseases.

All single measles and mumps vaccines available in the UK are unlicensed and therefore could be unreliable. Finally, no country in the world recommends the use of single measles, mumps and rubella vaccines as an alternative to the combined MMR vaccine.

USEFUL WEBSITES

www.doh.gov.uk/mmrvac.htm – Department of Health site on MMR
vaccination
www.immunisation.org.uk – NHS Health Promotion England
immunisation website

📋 SUMMARY POINTS ON MMR VACCINE

- ❖ Reduced uptake of vaccination
- ❖ MMR vaccine is very safe
- ❖ Wide variation in knowledge and attitudes amongst health care professionals
- ❖ Numerous incorrect media reports

MENINGOCOCCAL C VACCINATION

The incidence of group C meningococcal infection has increased to account for approximately 40% of meningococcal disease. This rise is particularly prominent in teenagers, in whom mortality rates have been as high as 20%. It has been estimated that between July 1998 and June 1999 more than 1,500 cases of group-C disease occurred in the UK leading to 150 deaths.

The vaccine has an excellent safety profile in all ages and has been given to babies, young children, schoolchildren and students. The meningococcal group C conjugate vaccines were introduced into the UK primary immunisation schedule in November 1999. The impact of this immunisation campaign has been significant, with substantial reductions in meningococcal C disease in both children and young people.

The Chief Medical Officer announced in January 2002 that people aged 20–24 years should also be immunised against meningitis C. The vaccine has a good safety profile and good primary antibody responses have been shown in all age groups following immunisation (*Arch Dis Child 2001;84:383–6*).

The Department of Health is currently investigating whether it is beneficial to give the vaccine to adults. A meningitis B vaccine is currently undergoing trials, but is realistically several years away from a licence.

Although the meningococcal group B vaccine will (at best) prevent less than half of all cases of meningitis, doctors should continue to remain alert to the signs and symptoms of both meningitis and septicaemia.

CHAPTER 8: CANCER

THE NHS CANCER PLAN

The NHS Cancer Plan was introduced in September 2000. It is the first comprehensive national cancer programme and aims to improve the way in which cancer care is organised in the UK. It aims to:
- Save more lives
- Ensure cancer patients receive correct professional support and care
- Ensure patients receive the best available treatments
- Tackle the inequalities in cancer healthcare

The plan includes new targets for how quickly treatment should begin after patients see a consultant, and how soon treatment should begin after referral by a GP.

The Government believes that the targets can be met because it is proposing the creation of almost 1,00 new cancer consultant posts by 2006. The Government is also planning to increase investment in palliative care services and hospices by £50m and provide more treatment equipment and 250 new scanners.

Cancer specialists have expressed doubts about whether the NHS would be able to achieve the set targets (BMJ 2000;321:850). They have welcomed the increased funding for cancer services, but have said it is doubtful whether some of the targets could be met. For example, the target of a maximum 2-month wait from urgent GP referral to treatment for colorectal cancer may be unrealistic because presently the investigations necessary for a definite diagnosis can often take a month or more.

New targets to be introduced in stages
- Maximum 1-month wait from urgent GP referral to treatment guaranteed for children's and testicular cancers and acute leukaemia by 2001
- Maximum 1-month wait from diagnosis to treatment for breast cancer by 2001
- Maximum 1-month wait from diagnosis to treatment for all cancers by 2005
- Maximum 2-months wait from urgent GP referral to treatment for breast cancer by 2002
- Maximum 2-months wait from urgent GP referral to treatment for all cancers by 2005

How will the cancer plan affect GPs?

All primary care trusts will be expected to review their cancer screening coverage and improve the uptake, especially by ethnic minorities and deprived patient groups. A national system of cancer networks is being set up which aims to plan cancer services to meet individual needs and coordinate cancer plan initiatives at a local level. A lead clinician for cancer will be appointed for each primary care trust (PCT), this will be a GP who will have dedicated time to work for the cancer network and help to improve clinical standards. They will also help to improve communication across primary, secondary and tertiary services.

Cancer registers will also be established for each PCT and GPs will have to contribute to these. The GMC has stated that patient's consent is required before cancers can be registered, which is likely to lead to chaos (*BMJ 2000;321:849*). The UK Association of Cancer Registers have found that the most reliable and consistent data on cancers are obtained at the time of diagnosis from histopathology departments – making consent very difficult. Patients must be given clear details on how the information from their disease may be used, and they must have access to that information in order to be assured of its validity. If patients refuse to let their details go to the cancer registries then the epidemiological picture of the disease is obviously going to be distorted.

However, an amendment to the Health and Social Care Bill was passed by Parliament in May 2001 (*BMJ 2001;322:1199*), which should clear the way for health registries in the UK to continue collecting data on public health without the patient's consent. A new body is being set up under the Health and Social Care Bill, called the 'Patient Information Advisory Group'. Individual registries who want to be exempt from the council's guidance on informed consent will be able to appeal to this group, which will decide whether to recommend to the Secretary of State that they be exempt.

What role should GPs play in cancer diagnosis and treatment?

General practitioners are gradually becoming more involved in managing patients with cancer. They are concerned with the comprehensive, coordinated, and continuous care of individuals, families and, increasingly, populations. General practitioners have an important role in cancer and the British Government's desire to improve cancer outcomes relies heavily on GPs playing their part.

Diagnosing cancer in primary care is often difficult. Many cancers present with common symptoms such as persistent cough or non-specific abdominal pain, yet few patients with such symptoms turn out to have cancer. Primary care clinicians need to be able to discriminate which patients within a relatively unselected population have a higher likelihood of malignant disease. The Government has produced guidelines regarding urgent referrals of patients with suspected malignancies, and most hospital departments have created referral forms for GPs to complete as a consequence of these guidelines.

What are the problems with the GP referral guidelines?

They have been criticised as they are based on poor-quality evidence; the evidence used was from patients seen in secondary and tertiary care and then applied to primary care. As many of the guidelines are quite general the system could become overloaded very quickly, which would then be detrimental to cancer patients.

A *BMJ* editorial has highlighted that the 2-week rule for cancer referrals does not appear to be working well (*BMJ 2001;322:1555–6*). The 2-week standard is often being met at the expense of a substantial increase in waiting times for routine referrals. A retrospective study of patients with colorectal cancer found that about 30% of cases would not actually have met the referral criteria for an urgent referral (*Gut 2001;48(Suppl):A53*).

 USEFUL WEBSITE

www.doh.gov.uk/cancer

📝 **SUMMARY POINTS FOR CANCER**

❖ Over-ambitious targets in NHS Cancer Plan
❖ Lead clinician to be appointed for each PCT
❖ GPs have a crucial role in both cancer and cancer screening
❖ 2-week cancer referrals are not working well

PROSTATE CANCER

Prostate cancer is a very common disease – the incidence is rising as a result of earlier detection of the disease and an ageing population. It is the second commonest male cancer, and death rates have doubled from it over the last 20 years. Despite considerable advances in the ability to detect and treat prostate cancer, there have been no significant corresponding decreases in morbidity and mortality in the UK. Conversely, in the USA, where there is widespread prostate cancer screening with prostate-specific antigen (PSA), mortality from prostate cancer has fallen by almost 3% per annum since 1999.

Prostate cancer is increasingly detected at an earlier stage by serum measurement of PSA. However, it is still highly debatable as to whether screening for prostate cancer is worthwhile.

What are the benefits of measuring PSA levels in patients?
PSA is probably the best available blood test for detecting any cancer, although it still has somewhat limited specificity. Its value has been improved by techniques such as monitoring change in concentration with time (velocity), assessing concentration in relation to prostate volume (density), using age-adjusted upper limits and, most recently, measuring the free to total prostate-specific antigen ratio (the lower the ratio the greater the chance of prostate cancer being detected by biopsy).

What are the problems with measuring PSA levels in patients?
In terms of efficacy, about 10% of men aged 50–69 years will have raised PSA levels, but only about 25% will be confirmed to have prostate cancer, and some tumours will be missed.

Controversy continues about the treatment of apparently localised prostate cancer (*BMJ 2000;320:69–70*). However, radical treatment is generally not justified for patients with a PSA concentration over 20 µg/l, as the tumour will often extend beyond the prostatic capsule and there may be micrometastases or lymph node deposits. The grade of tumour and the life expectancy of the patient also influence the final decision. Patients with well-differentiated tumours may do well without treatment, whereas those with poorly differentiated tumours usually do badly. Most men have moderately well-differentiated tumours and are likely to benefit from radical treatment if they have a life expectancy of more than 10 years.

Certain events can result in a transient change in the serum PSA level. For example, it can fall after a long period of recumbency and can increase with prostatic biopsy, transrectal ultrasound and vigorous prostatic massage. However, a digital rectal examination alone does not appear to have any significant effect on the serum PSA level.

A recent American study examined the outcome over 14 years of men diagnosed with localised prostate cancer, and found that for men with palpable but non-metastatic prostate cancer the mean time to death was 11.7 years (*BJU Int 2000;85:1063–6*). The authors of this study actually propose an upper age limit of 62 years for a screening programme when the intent is to cure. The difficulty obviously remains that some men in their seventies and eighties will present with metastatic bone disease and will leave us wondering whether this could have been prevented by screening.

What is the optimal treatment for prostate cancer?
This is an area of great debate as there is still no clear agreement as to the optimal treatment (*BMJ 1999;318:299–300*). A Government-funded trial is commencing which will investigate the best treatment option for men who are diagnosed with prostate cancer – watchful waiting, radical surgery or radiotherapy. Also, only patients with a life expectancy of over 10 years should be considered for radical treatment. This is because prostatic cancer does not usually kill men in less than 10 years from diagnosis.

Each of the main treatments – radical prostatectomy, radical radiotherapy, brachotherapy and monitoring – has risks. Radical treatment offers the potential for cure, but can have serious side-effects, including pain, hospitalisation, varying levels of incontinence and impotence and, rarely, death. With monitoring, men will have to live with the knowledge that they have untreated cancer and with the risk of progression, which in a few cases may be fatal.

Should prostate cancer be screened for?
Media publicity and a heightened public awareness of prostate cancer have increased the profile of PSA screening. The question of whether screening should be implemented is still extremely debatable. First of all, only a minority of cancers spread beyond the gland to cause disease and shorten life expectancy. In addition, curative treatments have major side-effects (e.g. impotence and incontinence). At present, PSA testing for prostate cancer does not fulfil all of Wilson's criteria for screening (refer to section on Screening on p. 150).

A recent report found that PSA screening causes overdiagnosis rates of prostate cancer in about 29% of White men; many men whose cancers were diagnosed through PSA screening would probably have died of a disease other than prostate cancer (*J Natl Cancer Inst 2002;94:981–90*). In addition, this report stated that most of the prostate cancers (85%) detected via PSA testing in recent years would have presented clinically.

A large £13m screening trial is currently underway by researchers in Sheffield, Bristol and Newcastle upon Tyne, involving 230,000 men aged 50–69 years. They will be invited for PSA testing, along with counselling at their GP practice. Those with raised PSA levels will be offered digital rectal examination and prostate biopsy. Those with prostate cancer will be randomised to one of three treatment groups. This trial will 'help to establish whether to introduce a screening programme for prostate cancer'.

The National Screening Committee has advised against screening, as:
• Many subclinical cases would be detected
• Excess anxiety would result
• In many cases there would be no change in the overall outcome
• The PSA level can not predict whether the cancer is indolent or aggressive
• PSA has a poor specificity
• There is still a lack of consensus regarding treatment for early disease
• Physical harm of prostate biopsies
• Some cancers detected would never present clinically

There are also strong arguments towards introducing a screening programme including:
• Men's autonomy
• PSA is a cheap and readily available test
• Screening may possibly be beneficial (lack of evidence of effectiveness does not prove ineffectiveness)
• May lead to detection of early, potentially curable cancers

A recent American study has demonstrated that screening men for prostate cancer has no impact on death rates from the disease (*J Clin Epidemiol 2002;55:603*). This study examined the outcomes of more than 1,000 men with prostate cancer. Half of the patients had been screened using PSA testing alone or in combination with a rectal examination. The other half had not been screened at all. The patients were followed up for 4–9 years, and the conclusion was that PSA screening did not improve survival in men under 70 years.

What are the NHS Prostate Cancer Screening Policy recommendations?
These were implemented in July 2001 and recommend that when a patient requests a PSA test, he should be given full information on the advantages and disadvantages of testing. The National Electronic Library for Health has produced patient information leaflets – available online – these vary from a one-page summary to a detailed five-page leaflet, so can supposedly be 'tailored' to the patient's level of interest.

Under the policy, the NHS will not be inviting men for PSA testing and does not expect GPs to raise the subject of PSA testing with their asymptomatic patients. However, the Government policy states that 'any man considering a PSA test will be given detailed information to enable him to make an informed choice about whether to proceed with a test or not'. This therefore implies that asymptomatic men may have the test if they want, so there is now ambiguity about whether screening is supported and confusion about what this policy means in everyday practice.

An assumption has been made that most men will not want to be tested once they are informed of the uncertainties. However, in the feasibility study for the ProtecT (Prostate testing for cancer and Treatment) trial, around 90% of men given detailed information about the implications of PSA testing and the lack of evidence about treatment consented to a test!

The proof of the ability of PSA testing to reduce the disease-specific mortality of prostate cancer will be provided by randomised controlled trials, which are currently underway in both the USA and Europe. Unfortunately, it will be many years before these results are available and, in the interim, doctors must act on the information that is currently available in the best interests of their patients. Patients must be informed of the pros and cons of PSA testing and also the implications of a positive result before having a PSA test performed.

 USEFUL WEBSITE

www.nelc.org.uk/docs/psa/psa-frame.htm – NHS prostate cancer screening policy

---

📋 **SUMMARY POINTS FOR PROSTATE CANCER**

❖ Incidence of prostate cancer is rising
❖ Screening may occur in future
❖ Controversial treatment options exist

SCREENING

A screening procedure is one that is applied to a population to select people at risk of an unfavourable health outcome for further investigation, monitoring or advice and treatment. Informed choice with regard to screening is essential; as, although screening programmes may benefit populations, not all participants will benefit and some will even be harmed by participation (*BMJ 2002;325:78–80*).

What is informed choice?
Informed choice has two core characteristics – it should be based on relevant, good-quality information and the resulting choice should reflect the decision-maker's values. The GMC has produced guidance on the information that should be provided to people offered screening.

How do GPs contribute to cancer screening?
General practitioners occupy a critical position in ensuring the effectiveness of national cancer screening programmes, as well as providing effective and cost-effective advice on specific primary-prevention strategies. In the United Kingdom's breast and cervical cancer screening programmes, primary healthcare team members have both developed and been delegated important roles in providing information and advice to women at all stages of the screening process (*BMJ 2000;320:1090–1*).

Patients often do not understand the rationale for screening or the inevitability of some false-positive and false-negative results. General practitioners thus have an important and expanding role in ensuring their patients truly understand these issues and the need for continuing vigilance about new symptoms.

What are Wilson's criteria for screening?
These well-established criteria should ideally be met before implementing a screening programme. They are important to know and can be applied to other screening programmes as well as to different types of cancer. There are, however, very few conditions for which all the criteria can be met.

They state that:
• The condition should be common and important
• There must be a latent period or early symptomatic stage during which effective treatment is possible

- There must be acceptable and available treatment for the disease
- The untreated natural history of the disease must be known
- The screening tests must be acceptable, cost-effective, safe and reliable
- The screening test should be highly sensitive and specific
- The screening should be continuous (not just a 'one off' test)

What are the ethics of screening?
The four main principles of ethics should be applied here (they are very useful to know for the viva exam!):
- Beneficence (do good)
- Non-maleficence (do no harm)
- Autonomy
- Justice

Beneficence
The benefit of screening must outweigh any potential harm to an individual.

Non-maleficence
Personal costs include problems with false-positive results, which can lead to distress and possible unnecessary treatment. False-negatives can also occur, as no test is 100% sensitive, which can then lead to false reassurance by both patients and doctors. This may even dissuade patients from returning for future screening tests.

Misinterpretation of results can lead to a false sense of security, for example patients with normal cholesterol or normal blood pressure may continue to smoke. There are also the costs to society, the actual costs of equipment, services, treatment, etc. and also the time taken off work for people to attend for the screening test and the treatment.

Finally, there are psychological costs involved. One article showed that false-positive results in screening tests can have undesirable effects (*J Public Health Med 2001;23:292–300*). Women who had been given the 'all clear' after having had abnormal mammography results 3 years previously remained significantly more anxious than those who had normal results. This was actually sufficient to deter 15% of them from attending for mammography the next time round.

Autonomy

Some people have different health beliefs and cultures and object to being screened. This needs to be appreciated when considering individual autonomy.

Justice

Implementing screening tests may mean that funds are diverted away from other services, for example cancer treatments. The correct allocation of limited resources is very important, especially in the current climate.

 USEFUL WEBSITE

www.gmc-uk.org – GMC website

CHAPTER 9: ANTIBIOTICS

ANTIBIOTIC RESISTANCE

 Resistance to antibiotics and other antimicrobial agents. House of Lords Select Committee Seventh Report, 17 March 1998

USEFUL WEBSITE

www.parliament.uk

- Highlighted the problem of increasing resistance to antibiotics
- It stated that most antibiotic use is in two areas: in humans in the community; and in animals as growth promoters and for prophylaxis
- In the UK, most antimicrobials used in human medicine are prescribed by GPs
- Antibiotic misuse is common and studies have suggested that up to 70% of treatment courses are unnecessary or inappropriate
- Therapy is often unnecessarily prolonged, and prophylaxis is often inappropriate or given at the wrong time
- One major factor affecting the prescribing behaviour of GPs is the expectations of their patients
- Increasing resistance problems are probably related to the use of broad-spectrum agents, such as cephalosporins, and crowding of susceptible people in institutions like nursing homes
- Veterinary and agriculture practices were also analysed and are expected to change

 The Standing Medical Advisory Committee (SMAC) Report

USEFUL WEBSITE

www.doh.gov.uk/smac1.htm – full report available

Recommendations for treatment:
- No prescribing of antibiotics for simple coughs and colds
- No prescribing of antibiotics for viral sore throats
- Limit prescribing for uncomplicated cystitis to 3 days in otherwise fit women
- Limit prescribing of antibiotics agents over the telephone to exceptional cases

Further recommendations
- Support for appropriate prescribing in primary care to be provided by developing and promulgating evidence-based national guidelines for the management of certain infections, under the aegis of NICE
- Guidelines would aim to minimise unnecessary use of antimicrobial agents and that, when needed, the most appropriate antimicrobial agent and regimen are used to ensure the best possible clinical outcome and to reduce the risk of resistance developing
- National guidelines are adapted for local use during the development of Health Improvement Plans
- The best of guidelines are of no value if they are not used; so to incorporate the guidelines into everyday practice as effortlessly as possible, they recommended that these should be integrated within computerised decision-support systems as soon as possible
- A national campaign should be launched to increase public and health professionals' understanding of the problem

The national campaign mentioned above was launched shortly afterwards, and you may recall featured leaflets with a character called 'Andy Biotic'. It was a public education exercise and also provided support to doctors to encourage more appropriate prescribing. In addition, it promoted advice-seeking from community pharmacists.

Following the campaign's introduction an update report was issued in March 2001 by SMAC. It stated that the 'antibiotic resistance campaign may be in part responsible for antibiotic prescribing by GPs falling by 19% in England between 1997 and 1999'. Inevitably, the results were taken to show that the campaign was a huge success. However, it has been commented that awareness of practitioners to the problem of resistance and increased media coverage may also be responsible for the improving trend.

⌷ SUMMARY POINTS FOR ANTIBIOTIC RESISTANCE

- ❖ 50% of antibiotic use in the UK is in humans, 50% in animals
- ❖ 80% of human use is in the community
- ❖ 50% of community use is for respiratory tract infections, 15% for urinary tract infections
- ❖ Considerable local and regional variation exists in the levels of community prescribing
- ❖ In hospitals, antimicrobial agents account for 10–30% of the drugs budget

---

PAPERS

▧ 1. Antibacterial prescribing and antibacterial resistance in English general practice – cross-sectional study
(P. Priest, et al., BMJ 2001;323:1037–41)

- 405 practices in SW and NW England (38 groups)
- Design: Cross-sectional study of antibacterial prescribing and antibacterial resistance of routine isolates within individual practices and primary care groups
- Objective: To quantify the relation between community-based antibacterial prescribing and antibacterial resistance in community-acquired disease
- Main outcome measures: Correlation between antibacterial prescribing and resistance for urinary coliforms and *Streptococcus pneumoniae*
- Looked at resistance to urinary coliforms and *S. pneumoniae*
- Prescribing 20% less ampicillin/amoxicillin would lead to 1% reduction in resistant coliforms (95% confidence interval, 0.02–1.85).
- Resistance of *S. pneumoniae* to both penicillin and erythromycin remains uncommon, and no clear relation with prescribing was found
- Antibacterial resistance in urinary coliform isolates is common, but the correlation with prescribing rates was relatively low for individual practices and primary care groups
- Concluded that routine microbiological isolates should not be used for surveillance of antibacterial resistance in the community or for monitoring the outcome of any change in antibacterial prescribing by GPs, and that improved methods of assessing national antimicrobial resistance are required
- Controversially stated that trying to reduce the overall level of antibiotic prescribing in UK general practice may not be the most effective strategy for reducing resistance in the community

Commentary discussed the future of resistance
- Strategies in Europe and North America are based on the belief that the process can be reversed (or at least held in check) by using antibiotics more prudently
- Differing conclusions can be drawn from the study, e.g. the minimal variation in ampicillin and trimethoprim resistance between practices with differing rates of prescribing (and various

criteria for submitting specimens to a laboratory) does not necessarily imply that a change in prescribing would not affect resistance

- The dynamics between prescribing and resistance are exceedingly complicated.
- Mathematical modelling gives some insights:
    - Generally, resistance rates are low after a new antimicrobial drug is introduced into a community
    - Resistance then appears and increases steadily until it reaches a steady-state level
    - The rate of increase in resistance depends on the drug and how much is used, the bacteria and the nature of the community, e.g. the opportunity for cross-infection
    - If ampicillin and trimethoprim are at steady-state levels in the UK, we would expect little interpractice variation
    - Such models also predict that the decline in resistance after withdrawal of antibiotic selection pressure will be uncomfortably slow

URINARY TRACT INFECTIONS

☐ **SUMMARY POINTS FOR CYSTITIS (BY SMAC)**

❖ Each year about 1 woman in 20 will present to her GP with symptoms of cystitis

❖ About half of these women will have an infection (defined by the presence of a significant number of bacteria in the urine)

❖ Most of these infections in otherwise healthy women are caused by coliforms

❖ Uncomplicated cystitis can be treated empirically with trimethoprim

❖ If resistance is common locally, the medical microbiologist can advise on an appropriate alternative

❖ Several studies have shown that a 3-day course of treatment is as effective as a 5- or 7-day course

❖ Limiting the prescription of antibiotics for uncomplicated cystitis in otherwise healthy women to 3 days reduces selection pressure for resistance

---

ACUTE SINUSITIS

📋 **SUMMARY POINTS FOR SINUSITIS (SMAC)**

❖ Several studies, including RCTs, have shown antibiotics to be effective in proven acute sinusitis

❖ Most of these studies have used 10-day courses of antibiotics

❖ One comparative study showed that 3 days of antibiotics were as effective as 10 days

❖ Recent overviews of the treatment of acute sinusitis-like symptoms in adults in the primary care setting suggest there is no benefit from antibiotic treatment

❖ The adult with 'sinusitis-like symptoms' in primary care does not need immediate antibiotics

❖ In proven cases of acute sinusitis, 3 days of antibiotics are as effective as 10 days' treatment

---

ACUTE BRONCHITIS

📖 **Reducing antibiotic use for acute bronchitis in primary care: blinded, randomised controlled trial of patient information leaflet**
(J. Macfarlane, et al., BMJ 2002;324:91–4)

- This RCT from Nottingham looked at whether the use of written and verbal explanations as to the uncertainty of the value of antibiotics made any difference to the likelihood of patients taking them
- Acute bronchitis is a common condition that results in nearly 2 million consultations in England and Wales each year
- Defined as a 'new, acute lower respiratory tract illness in a previously well adult' (LRTI of 21 days or less, cough as the main symptom and at least one other lower respiratory tract symptom: sputum production, dyspnoea, wheeze, chest discomfort or pain)
- 75% of such GP consultations result in an antibiotic script
- 259 previously well people presenting with acute bronchitis were recruited from three practices in Nottingham
- 212 formed Group A, where the GP judged them not to need antibiotics that day, but were given a prescription to use if they got worse and standard verbal reassurance. Half of them (106) were randomised to be given an information leaflet detailing the advantages/disadvantages of antibiotics and history of an LRTI
- Group B comprised 47 patients who were judged to need antibiotics and were given a prescription and encouraged to use it
- The primary endpoint was whether the patient took the antibiotics (in the first 2 weeks) they had been prescribed, and the second was the re-consultation rate in the next month
- In Group A, fewer patients who received the information leaflet took antibiotics compared with those who did not receive the leaflet (49 vs. 63, risk ratio 0.76, 95% confidence interval 0.59–0.97, p = 0.04)
- Numbers re-consulting were similar (11 vs. 14)
- In Group B, 44/47 patients took the antibiotics
- In conclusion, most previously well adults with acute bronchitis were judged not to need antibiotics. Reassuring these patients and sharing the uncertainty about prescribing in an information leaflet supported by verbal advice is a safe strategy and reduces antibiotic use
- The use of the patient information leaflet reduced the use of antibiotics by nearly one-quarter

- This may underestimate the true efficacy of the leaflet as all patients were also reassured verbally by their GP
- Rates of re-consultation were no higher in the leaflet group and no patients required referral to hospital
- These practices were used to researching into this topic, which may make the doctors and patients unrepresentative

In his commentary, Professor Weel, from The Netherlands, argued that patients influence prescribing, and there is a strong perception among practitioners that patients in general value a prescription. He also stated that about half of the patients still used the antibiotics their GP thought they could do without, in turn leaving substantial room for improvement.

The message 'antibiotics are not required' was accompanied by the handing out of a prescription that implied a totally different message. This may trigger doubt and lack of confidence, particularly in patients who value medical as opposed to self-treatment

SORE THROAT

When should we use antibiotics?
Antibiotics have been used in the past in order to:
- Reduce severity or shorten the duration of symptoms
- Reduce the risk of complications, suppurative (quinsy, otitis media, sinusitis) and non-suppurative (rheumatic fever, nephritis)
- Satisfy non-clinical purposes, e.g. perceived patient demand terminating consultation

But:
- At least 70% of sore throats are caused by viruses
- We now have evidence to help us select those patients who probably have a bacterial infection and may benefit from penicillin

---

☐ SUMMARY POINTS FOR SORE THROAT (BY SMAC)

- ❖ Most are viral and can be left to run their course without resort to antibiotics
- ❖ Indeed, recurrence and relapse may be more common in those who have had early treatment with antibiotics
- ❖ A recent study showed that patients with sore throats were more likely to leave the consultation satisfied if they received a prescription
- ❖ However, they were no more likely to be satisfied at the end of the illness
- ❖ Those who received antibiotics were more likely to return for treatment in future attacks and were more likely to believe in the efficacy of antibiotics
- ❖ A minority of sore throats are caused by a bacterium, *Streptococcus pyogenes*
- ❖ *S. pyogenes* can lead to local abscesses and, rarely, to kidney problems and rheumatic fever
- ❖ Therefore, many doctors prescribe antibiotics for a sore throat with the intention of preventing the consequences of *S. pyogenes* infection
- ❖ Sore throats should not be treated with antibiotics, unless there is good evidence they are caused by *S. pyogenes*

PAPERS

📖 1. Penicillin for acute sore throat: randomised double blind trial of 7 days vs 3 days treatment or placebo in adults
(S. Zwart, et al., BMJ 2000;320:150–4)

- GP-based study from The Netherlands
- Randomised to 3 groups: phenoxymethylpenicillin (penicillin V; pen V) for 7 days; pen V for 3 days followed by placebo for 4 days; or placebo for 7 days
- Sore throats for less than 7 days and with three of the four 'Centor' criteria:
  - Fever
  - No cough
  - Tonsillar exudate
  - Swollen, tender, anterior cervical nodes

Showed that penicillin V for 7 days resulted in:
- Two days' shorter duration of symptoms
- Reduced incidence of complications (quinsy)
- Supports use of penicillin V in patients with three of the four Centor criteria

Arguments against using an antibiotic:
- Benefit shown is so modest that one can dispute its clinical importance
- Actual benefit is marginal/modest at best
- Harms may outweigh benefits. Bacterial resistance, allergic reactions (rashes/anaphylaxis 2–4/10,000 and death 2/100,000)
- Diarrhoea, candidiasis, unplanned pregnancy if on combined oral contraceptive pill
- Costs to NHS
- Increased patient dependence, expectation and future demands

📖 2. Open randomised trial of prescribing strategies in managing sore throat
(P. Little, et al., BMJ 1997;314:722–7)

- Designed to test three different prescribing strategies in terms of: duration of symptoms; satisfaction and compliance with treatment; and time off school and work
- Group 1: 10 days' prescription for antibiotics; Group 2: no

prescription; Group 3: prescription if symptoms did not settle in 3 days
- No significant difference in the proportion of patients better in 3 days, duration of illness, time to return to work or satisfaction
- More people in the first group thought antibiotics were effective and intended coming to the doctor in future attacks
- 69% of patients in the delayed prescription group did not use their prescriptions
- Concluded that antibiotics had a marginal clinical effect
- Prescription resulted in enhanced belief and intention to re-consult when compared to other groups

3. Reattendance and complications in a randomised trial of prescribing strategies for sore throat: the medicalising effects of prescribing antibiotics
(P. Little, et al., BMJ 1997;315:350–2)

- Aim to assess the medicalising effect of prescribing antibiotics
- Randomisation as above
- Outcome measures were number and rate of patients making a first return with sore throat, early return (within 2 weeks) and complications
- Followed up for 1 year, a higher proportion of those initially prescribed antibiotics re-presented within the year with sore throats
- Longer duration of illness also increased chance of return
- No difference between the various groups in terms of early return or complications
- Previous and current prescribing increases re-attendance

4. Antibiotics for symptoms and complications of sore throat
(Cochrane Systematic Review 2000; (4) CD000023 by Del Mar CD, Glasziou PP, Spinks AB)

- Found that prescribing antibiotics reduced the symptoms of sore throat, fever and headache by 50% in the short term, but 90% of all patients were symptom-free by 1 week
- Pooling of data (large number of patients) allowed rarer complication rates to be elicited
- Risk of rheumatic fever reduced by 30%, but unable to assess whether treatment offered protection against glomerulonephritis as numbers were still too small

- Effect of antibiotics on suppurative complications: AOM reduced by 25%, acute sinusitis by 30% and quinsy by 20%
- Concluded that antibiotics offer a modest clinical benefit
- In the Western world, it was not thought to be worth recommending the routine use of antibiotics to treat sore throats for the small reduction in rheumatic fever and glomerulonephritis

ACUTE OTITIS MEDIA

Definition: Otitis media is inflammation in the middle ear.

Subcategories include acute otitis media (AOM), otitis media with effusion (also known as 'glue ear'), recurrent acute otitis media and chronic suppurative otitis media. Acute otitis media presents with systemic and local signs and has a rapid onset.

The persistence of an effusion beyond 3 months without signs of infection defines otitis media with effusion, whereas chronic suppurative otitis media is characterised by continuing inflammation in the middle ear giving rise to otorrhoea and a perforated tympanic membrane.

- Acute otitis media is a common condition with a high morbidity and low mortality
- In the UK, about 30% of children aged under 3 years are taken to their GP with acute otitis media each year
- 97% receive antimicrobial treatment
- 1 in 10 children will have an episode of acute otitis media by 3 months of age
- Most common bacterial causes for acute otitis media are *Streptococcus pneumoniae*, *Haemophilus influenzae* and *Moraxella catarrhalis*
- Risk factors for poor outcome are young age and attendance at day-care centres such as nursery schools
- Others risks include White race, male sex and history of enlarged adenoids, tonsillitis and asthma
- Factors predisposing to poor outcome: multiple previous episodes, bottle feeding, history of ear infections in parents or siblings and use of a soother/pacifier (dummy)
- Evidence for the effect of environmental tobacco smoke is controversial
- In 80% of children the condition resolves without antibiotic treatment in about 3 days
- Complications are rare, but include hearing loss, mastoiditis, meningitis and recurrent attacks
- In the developed world, the majority of children with AOM are treated with antibiotics
- In The Netherlands only a minority are, but the outcome seems no worse
- Antibiotics give limited benefits
- Most children can be treated without antibiotics

- Pain lasts no more than 24 hours in 80% of children
- Benefits of withholding antibiotics include reduced cost, reduced side-effects and reduced antibiotic resistance

'Clinical Evidence' published by the BMJ Publishing Group included a review of the effects of treatment for otitis media and of the effects of preventive interventions. This particular section also appeared in the BMJ (25 September 1999).

KEY POINTS FOR ACUTE OTITIS MEDIA

❖ Limited evidence from one RCT that non-steroidal anti-inflammatory drugs are more effective than placebo in relieving pain in children with acute otitis media

❖ Effectiveness of antibiotics is conflicting

❖ The review found no clear evidence favouring a particular antibiotic for acute otitis media

❖ One systematic review of RCTs found greater immediate benefit but no difference in long-term outcome with short (≤5 days) rather than longer courses of antibiotics

❖ One systematic review of RCTs found that long-term antibiotic prophylaxis has a modest effect in preventing recurrences of AOM; however, which antibiotic to use, for how long and how many episodes of AOM justify treatment have not been adequately evaluated.

SUMMARY POINTS FOR AOM (BY SMAC)

❖ Reviews on AOM suggest that the benefit of routine antimicrobial use is unproved or modest

❖ A proportion of children do benefit but it is difficult to predict which ones

❖ Countries with lower rates of antibiotic prescribing for AOM show no increase in the number of complications compared with those where a prescription is usual

❖ Even if antibiotics are prescribed, there is debate about the appropriate length of treatment: 3- and 10-day courses were equally effective in one study

❖ Antibiotics are probably unnecessary in AOM

❖ Reassurance, time and adequate pain relief are required

❖ If antibiotics are prescribed, the course should be limited to 3 days

---

SUGGESTED EVIDENCE-BASED MANAGEMENT

Explain that:
- ❖ Most patients get better within 24 hours without antibiotics
- ❖ Most cases are due to viruses, which aren't killed by antibiotics
- ❖ Withhold antibiotics in mild cases
- ❖ Advise paracetamol every 4 hours in correct doses
- ❖ Offer to review child in 24–72 hours if parental/doctor concern
- ❖ Consider information leaflets
- ❖ Consider deferred prescription of antibiotic, only to be used if child is no better after 24–48 hours
- ❖ Consider antibiotic at outset if child is unduly ill, toxic or has a high fever

---

PAPERS

📚 **1. Are antibiotics indicated as initial treatment for children with acute otitis media? A meta-analysis**
(C. Del Mar, et al., BMJ 1997;314:1526–9)

Meta-analysis of controlled trials (antibiotics versus placebo):
- Early use of antibiotics conferred marginal benefit, with 17 patients requiring immediate treatment to prevent one getting pain at 2–7 days
- Antibiotics benefit only those 14% still in pain 24 hours after presentation
- Antibiotics double the risk of vomiting, diarrhoea and rashes

📚 **2. Antibiotic treatment of acute otitis media in children under two years of age: evidence based?**
(R. A. Damoiseaux, et al., BJGP 1998;48(437):1861–4)

Meta-analysis of trials of treatment for acute otitis media in children under 2 years of age:
- No significant difference in outcomes in first 7 days between antibiotic treated patients and controls
- No evidence to support the use of antibiotics in the under-2s

3. Primary care based randomised, double blind trial of amoxicillin versus placebo for acute otitis media in children aged under 2 years
(R. A. Damoiseaux, et al., BMJ 2000;320:350–4)

RCT of amoxicillin versus placebo in under-2s:
* Amoxicillin reduced the duration of pain and fever by about 1 day
* No difference in outcome at 11 days
* Seven or eight patients needed to be treated with antibiotic for one to benefit
* Very modest benefit does not justify treating every child with an antibiotic
* Watchful waiting is justified

4. Pragmatic randomised controlled trial of two prescribing strategies for childhood acute otitis media
(P. Little, et al., BMJ 2001;322:336–42)

* This clinically useful large RCT study looked at the rationale behind delayed prescriptions in general practice
* 315 children aged between 6 months and 10 years were recruited from practices in SW England
* They were randomised to receive immediate treatment or delayed treatment for 72 hours with support from standardised advice sheets (antibiotic prescription to be collected at parents' discretion after 72 hours if child still not improving)
* Outcome measures were symptom resolution, absence from school or nursery and paracetamol consumption
* On average, symptoms resolved after 3 days
* Children in the immediately prescribed antibiotic group had a shorter illness (–1.1 days), fewer disturbed nights (–0.72 days) and slightly less paracetamol consumption (–0.52 spoons/day).
* There were no differences in school absence or pain or distress scores, since the benefits of antibiotics occurred mainly after the first 24 hours when distress was less severe
* Parents of 36/150 of the children given delayed prescriptions used antibiotics, and 77% were very satisfied
* Fewer children in the delayed group had diarrhoea (14/150 (9%) vs. 25/135 (19%)).
* Fewer parents in the delayed group believed in the effectiveness of antibiotics and in the need to see the doctor with future episodes
* In conclusion, immediate antibiotic prescription provided

symptomatic benefit mainly after the first 24 hours, when symptoms were already resolving
- For children who are not very unwell systemically, a wait-and-see approach seems feasible and acceptable to parents, and should substantially reduce the use of antibiotics for acute otitis media

5. Selecting persistent glue ear for referral in general practice: a risk factor approach
(Medical Research Council Multi-centre Otitis Media Study Group, BJGP 2001 52;480:549–54)

- This study tried to establish a set of risk factors that would allow the prediction of glue ear and ensure the appropriateness of referral
- Glue ear (otitis media with effusion) is the most common reason for surgery in children
- It is also the most common cause of hearing loss in children
- Resolution occurs in about 50% of cases after 12 weeks and 75% after 24 weeks
- Most prevalent between the ages of 2 and 5 years, and in most instances it begins to regress between 6 and 7 years of age
- A set of risk factors for persistence of glue ear would be useful in helping GPs to decide which children might benefit from referral and possible subsequent specialist intervention
- This nested case-control study involved 16 ENT departments in the UK
- With the aid of audiometry and tympanometry, diagnostic information was collected on 548 children after referral by their GP
- Using cases and controls, children were classified as either having or not having persistent glue ear
- Parental reports on an extensive list of risk factors were also collected
- From the results, after adjustment for time waiting to be seen from GP referral and age at referral, four main significant factors emerged for persistence of glue ear. These were:
  - Referral between July and December
  - Having a mother who smokes 10 or more cigarettes per day
  - Multiple upper airway symptoms
  - Siblings with a history of glue ear
- They concluded that for a child who is referred between July and December with two or more upper airway symptoms, with a sibling who has had glue ear and a mother who smokes 10 or more cigarettes per day, the odds of having persistent glue ear are over 10 times that of a child without these adverse factors

SYPHILIS

📖 **Education and debate, Syphilis: old problem, new strategy**
(L. Doherty, et al., BMJ 2002;325:153–6)

This article outlines recent changes in the epidemiology of infectious syphilis in England.

- Syphilis is on the increase again
- Syphilis is most infectious through sexual contact during the primary or secondary stages, but transmission can also occur during the early latent stage
- Syphilis is preventable, and treatable with effective and inexpensive antibiotics
- Recently, there has been an upward trend in incidence, partly due to several localised outbreaks affecting homosexual men and heterosexual men and women
- Between the 1960s and the late 1970s homosexually acquired syphilitic infection increased, in keeping with the liberalisation of attitudes towards homosexual behaviour
- Changes in behaviour in response to HIV/AIDS, particularly among homosexual men, may have contributed to dramatic reductions in syphilis in the 1980s
- During the 1990s, until 1998, the number of cases of infectious syphilis diagnosed remained stable among both sexes in England
- But it more than doubled between 1998 and 2000 (from 172 to 372) in men and rose by 53% (102 to 156) in women
- In 2000, 48% of syphilis infections in men were homosexually acquired, rates being highest in London and NW England
- Investigations into the outbreaks showed a number of common features:
  - Infection from unprotected intercourse
  - Cases linked to high-risk social and sexual networks
  - High rates of change of partners and of anonymous contacts
  - Unprotected oral sex reported as the sole high-risk sexual practice
  - Illicit drug use during sexual intercourse
  - Concomitant HIV infection
- One-third of cases presented with primary syphilis. More than one-third presented with symptoms of secondary syphilis, such as fever, malaise and pharyngitis, and with skin rashes and lymphadenopathy as well as less common problems such as iritis and uveitis

- The remainder were diagnosed as early latent syphilis on the basis of positive serology in the absence of clinical signs
- The mainstay of diagnosis is serological testing

KEY MESSAGES FOR HEALTH PROFESSIONALS

Explain that:
❖ 'Safer sex' messages need continual reinforcement among the sexually active population
❖ Unprotected oral sex is a risk factor for the transmission of sexually transmitted infections, including syphilis
❖ Healthcare professionals, particularly GPs, should refer patients suspected of having syphilis to specialist genitourinary medicine services for investigation and treatment

---

Clinical presentation and recommended treatment regimens for syphilis

- Primary syphilis:
  - Presents 9–90 days after exposure
  - One or more chancres (ulcers): 'any anogenital ulcer is syphilis until proven otherwise'
  - Regional lymphadenopathy

- Secondary syphilis:
  - Presents 6 weeks to 6 months after exposure
  - Localised or diffuse mucocutaneous ulcers
  - Generalised lymphadenopathy
  - Rash may affect palms and soles, and may be itchy
  - Condylomata lata
  - Less commonly: alopecia, iritis, uveitis, meningitis, hepatitis, cranial nerve palsies, splenomegaly

- Early latent syphilis:
  - Presents no more than 2 years after exposure
  - Positive serology
  - By definition, there should be no clinical signs

Treatment for infectious syphilis (primary, secondary, or early latent)
- Jenacillin A 3 ml = 750,000 U (Jenacillin A is a German proprietary combination of benzylpenicillin and procaine

penicillin. Note that procaine penicillin is the same as procain benzylpenicillin and is available on a named-patient basis from IDIS.)
- or benzylpenicillin benzathine 2.4 MU intramuscularly weekly for 2 weeks
- Penicillin allergy: doxycycline 200 mg twice daily for 14 days
- Parenteral treatment refused: amoxicillin 500 mg four times a day plus probenecid 500 mg four times a day for 14 days

Treatment for infectious syphilis in those who are HIV-positive
- 8 ml Jenacillin A (2 MU) intramuscularly for 17 days plus probenecid 500 mg four times a day by mouth for 17 days
- or penicillin G 4,000,000 U intravenously every 4 hours for 17 days
- or penicillin G 5,000,000 U intramuscularly every 6 hours plus probenecid 500 mg four times a day by mouth for 17 days
- or second line doxycycline 200 mg twice a day by mouth for 28 days

 USEFUL WEBSITE

www.phls.org.uk/topics_az/hiv_and_sti/guidelines/managing_outbreaks_of_sti.htm – Communicable Disease Surveillance Centre. Draft for consultation. Guidelines for managing local outbreaks of sexually transmitted infections. July 2001

CHAPTER 10: CLINICAL GOVERNANCE

Definition: 'a system through which NHS organisations are accountable for continuously improving the quality of their services and safeguarding high standards of care and creating an environment in which excellence in clinical care will flourish.'

From 'A first class service – Quality in the New NHS' www.doh.gov.uk/newnhs/quality.htm

What are the components of clinical quality?
- Professional performance (technical quality)
- Resource use (efficiency)
- Risk management (risk of injury or illness associated with the service)
- Patient satisfaction

What can we do to improve?
- Audit
- Review complaints
- Critical incident reporting
- Routine surveillance

Why is it needed?
- GP quality is too variable
- Patients have a right to expect greater consistency in access to, and quality of, primary care services
- Patients need to be assured that their treatment is up to date and effective, and is provided by 'up to date' doctors

In reality
- Doctors must take part in audit
- Leadership skills must be developed within clinical teams
- Evidence-based medicine must be practised
- Good practice must be disseminated
- Risk management procedures must be in place
- Adverse events must be detected and investigated
- Lessons learnt must be applied to clinical practice
- Poor performance must be recognised early and tackled promptly

How will it translate in primary care groups (PCGs)?
- Each PCG has to nominate a senior professional to lead on clinical standards and professional development
- Each practice must have a named clinical governance lead, responsible for liaising with the rest of the primary healthcare team (PHCT), and with the PCG
- PCGs will expect peer pressure and support to improve the quality of care within the group, by eliminating unacceptable variations
- Health authorities will expect PCGs and individual practices to implement the clinical governance agenda, but they seem to have no sanctions they can apply to recalcitrant GPs
- Within PCGs, joint clinical responsibility is now added to individual clinical responsibility
- By 2002, PCGs should be delivering measurable improvements against locally agreed milestones and targets
- Information on quality (audits) may become public and identifiable as lay members of the PCG may demand it and other doctors may want it

Conclusions
- The advent of clinical governance is a watershed in the history of general practice
- Each GP is responsible for providing high-quality care, auditing care, auditing their own standards and those of their colleagues in the PCG
- Clinical governance is a powerful tool for improving quality of care in general practice
- Clinical governance is a means of maintaining quality assurance and accountability to the public
- It may be our last chance for self-regulation

National Institute for Clinical Excellence (NICE)
NICE gives guidance by:
- Appraisal of evidence
- Development and dissemination of audit methods
- Development and dissemination of guidelines
- Effectiveness bulletins

Commission for Health Improvement (CHI)
- Government watchdog of quality
- Consists of GPs, community nurses and lay people and will visit each PCG every 4 years

- Looks at clinical governance at PCG level
- Visits a random selection of practices
- A collaborative approach with poorly performing PCGs
- Can report underperforming health bodies to the Health Secretary
- Tells us whether we are following guidance by:
  - Provider and service reviews
  - Performance indicators
  - Troubleshooting problem areas

PAPERS

The following papers, although not essential to the exam, would provide you with a more in-depth understanding of the practical problems facing general practice in the current political climate. They were part of a series of five papers written to encompass clinical governance in practice. A few key points are summarised for those who, understandably, would find it tedious to venture further.

1. Clinical governance in primary care – knowledge and information for clinical governance
(A. McColl and M. Roland, BMJ 2000;321:871–4)

This paper discussed the additional knowledge that will be needed by all staff working in primary care and the challenges faced by leaders of primary care groups and trusts. They suggested where relevant information could be found. Everyone in primary care needs to be familiar with these sources if clinical governance is to succeed as a way to improving the quality of healthcare.

SUMMARY POINTS

❖ Everyone in primary care needs to be familiar with the requirements of clinical governance if it is to succeed as a way to improving the quality of care

❖ Producing, collecting and analysing primary care information is difficult, but some practices have already overcome these barriers

❖ Individuals and primary care group and trust leaders can do much to promote clinical governance, but problems remain

❖ The version of this paper on the BMJ's website includes numerous URLs to show what information is available

---

📚 2. Clinical governance in primary care: participating in clinical governance
(M. Pringle, BMJ 2000;321:737–40)

Emphasised the need for clinicians to find information that will improve their own practice and aid learning in the primary care team as a whole. Such work is likely to go a long way towards fulfilling the General Medical Council's requirements for revalidation.

- NeLH (The National electronic Library for Health) will eventually help to improve access to information in the practice. In one English region only 20% of general practitioners had access to bibliographic databases in their surgeries and 17% to the World Wide Web
- Primary care groups and trusts will need to invest in adequate information technology hardware, software and training
- To avoid duplication of effort, relevant information should be coordinated at a national level and facilitated locally through postgraduate libraries.
- Computerised clinical-decision support systems used during consultations can help to improve performance and patient outcomes
- In England and Wales, Prodigy software is available free of charge on 85% of computer systems; it can offer advice during consultations on what to do in over 150 conditions commonly seen in primary care
- The MIQUEST project is one of the national facilitating projects within the NHS information management and technology strategy. It aims to help practices standardise their data entry and provides software to help with data extraction, including data required for national performance indicators

📚 3. Accountability for clinical governance: developing collective responsibility for quality in primary care
(A. Allen, BMJ 2000;321:608–11)

This paper discussed how the notion of accountability in clinical governance could be understood and used within primary care.

- It will use the clinical governance work of a London PCG as a case study to illustrate mechanisms and different forms of accountability between health professionals
- Clinical governance will extend primary healthcare professionals

accountability beyond current forms of legal and professional
accountability
- Clinical governance in primary care is aimed at enhancing the
collective responsibility and accountability of professionals in
primary care groups or trusts
- It is mainly concerned with increasing the accountability of
primary health professionals to local communities (downwards
accountability), the NHS hierarchy (upwards accountability) and
their peers (horizontal accountability)
- Primary care groups and trusts may find that, in addition to
encouraging a culture of accountability, financial incentives are
useful for achieving greater accountability

 4. Using clinical evidence
(S. Barton, editor for 'Clinical Evidence', BMJ 2001;322:503–4)

Points raised:
- Most health carers want to base their practice on evidence and
feel that this will improve patient care
- It has proved too difficult, alongside the competing demands of
clinical practice, to implement the original idea that each health
professional should: formulate questions themselves; search, appraise
and summarise the literature; and apply the evidence to patients
- Over 90% of British GPs believe that learning evidence-handling
skills is not a priority, and even when resources are available,
doctors rarely search for evidence
- However, 72% do often use evidence-based summaries generated
by others, which can be accessed by busy clinicians in seconds
- The NHS will now be providing many of its clinicians with one of
those sources – Clinical Evidence
- Clinical Evidence is a compendium of summaries of the best
available evidence about what works and what doesn't work in
healthcare
- It is constructed by transparent methods and updated regularly (so
earlier issues should be discarded)
- In addition NHS professionals in England, Scotland and Wales can
access Clinical Evidence through the National electronic Library
for Health (NeLH) or through one of the 14,000 paper copies
being distributed to NHS institutions
- Will the distribution of Clinical Evidence improve patient care?
Sadly, there are no large studies of the results of distributing similar
printed materials

- One systematic review (nine studies) found that the passive distribution of printed educational materials compared with no distribution produced only small effects of uncertain clinical importance
- Printed materials may be necessary to transmit knowledge, but they are probably insufficient to change practice
- No study explored why printed materials were ineffective
- It is not surprising that passive distribution of printed materials does not automatically change behaviour:
  - Information may have been difficult to access when it was needed
  - May have been difficult to understand or be irrelevant
  - May have lacked credibility without a method of checking that the information is rigorous and complete
  - Too much paper information tends to get 'filed' as circulars – better to have one person allocated to distribute the information verbally during a meeting of all practice members once every two weeks or once a month.

Clinical Evidence presents the evidence, but does not tell doctors or patients what to do because evidence is only part of making a clinical decision. Clinical expertise to evaluate each patient's circumstances and personal preferences is also important. Even the best available evidence may need adapting for individual patients. Thus a valid, relevant, and accessible source of detailed clinical evidence is a necessary, but not sufficient, precursor of innovation to achieve evidence-based healthcare. Additional professional, educational and operational support for clinical innovation will probably accelerate the use of clinical evidence. Clinical Evidence will provide access to evidence in the way the BNF provides access to prescribing information, and earn as welcome a place in the consulting room

CHAPTER 11: REVALIDATION

Self-regulation
- Self-regulation is whereby a profession determines its own training, qualifications and codes of ethics and behaviour
- Threatened by recent events causing:
  - Loss of confidence by public
  - Perception that the profession closes ranks to protect own interests
  - Demands for greater transparency and accountability
  - Undermined by less deferential and better informed public

Arguments for self-regulation
- A doctor's performance can be judged adequately only by someone doing the same job
- Self-regulation engenders self-respect and motivation to perform well
- Self-regulation helps maintain professionalism and gives doctors a direct interest in maintaining standards
- Without self-regulation, doctors would cease to be a profession

Organisation of self-regulation
- GMC currently consulting with the profession, the public and the Government
- Specialists' place on the Specialist Register may be made dependent on revalidation
- GMC may create a 'Generalists Register' for GPs with inclusion dependent on revalidation
- Mechanism of revalidation to be supportive, not punitive, and largely by peer review, not examination
- Poor performance must be recognised early, and intervention must be sympathetic but decisive
- Support/retraining for any underperforming doctor must be available
- Removal from Register to be used as last resort, only for those beyond help
- Overall, self-regulation must be robust and open to scrutiny, to avoid accusations of professional protectionism

Revalidation – latest arrangements
- Revalidation will mean that all doctors will have to demonstrate regularly to the GMC that they are up to date and fit to practise medicine

- It will also enable doctors to identify and correct any weaknesses they may have
- Doctors who are successful will be granted a licence to practise
- Doctors who choose not to participate in revalidation will be able to stay on the register without the entitlement to exercise the privileges currently associated with registration
- If concerns are raised about a doctor's Fitness to Practise during the revalidation process, they will be referred to the GMC's Fitness to Practise procedures

There will be three stages to revalidation: collection of information; 5-year assessment; GMC decision.

Collecting information and yearly appraisal
Doctors will have to collect evidence, which will be considered against the seven headings set out in the GMC guidance 'Good Medical Practice':
1. Good clinical care
2. Maintaining good medical practice
3. Teaching and training, appraising and assessing
4. Relationships with patients
5. Working with colleagues
6. Probity
7. Health

- These headings have also been used to structure the annual appraisal
- Sufficient information for headings 1–5 should be available from the documentation summaries of the appraisals
- Doctors will be asked to sign declarations about their health and their probity (including past criminal convictions)
- During the appraisal, evidence being collected should help to identify any shortcomings in the doctor's performance, which can be addressed
- However, if there is serious concern that the doctor poses a risk to themselves or to patients they should be referred to the GMC immediately

5-year assessment
- This is the second stage
- Both doctors and members of the public will be used to help to consider the evidence

- It is expected that the majority of doctors will be recommended for revalidation
- But if necessary the GMC will invoke the Fitness to Practise procedures

The GMC decision
- The third and final stage is the GMC decision
- Expected that most doctors will be granted a licence to practise
- If, as a result of the revalidation process a doctor is considered under the Fitness to Practise procedures, a number of outcomes are possible, including conditions on their practice or suspension
- Effective action will be taken to protect patients

Implementation
- In May 2001, the GMC agreed to take the next steps towards implementing revalidation
- This included working with the BMA/Academy of Medical Royal Colleges and the Council for the Heads of Medical Schools to ensure the mechanisms are in place
- The GMC is now in the process of working with the Government to obtain the legislation
- The aim is to revalidate the first group of doctors no sooner than 2 years from the introduction of the legislation, which should be in 2002

The above information and latest developments on appraisal and revalidation can be found at:

www.revalidationuk.info – this is a joint website by the Department of Health and the GMC.

Risks
- Further controls lead to reduced morale
- Maintaining standards becomes following fashion
- Possible deterioration into an empty chore, so diverting doctors' time and energy from care of patients

PAPER

📕 **Assuring the Quality of Medical Practice, Implementing 'Supporting doctors, protecting patients', January 2001.**

This report from the DoH discusses revalidation.

KEY RECOMMENDATIONS

❖ A new National Clinical Assessment Authority to assess poorly performing doctors by practice visits
❖ Annual appraisals for all GPs to started in 2001
❖ First decisions on GP revalidation in 2003
❖ A revised national disciplinary procedure for GPs
❖ Pre-employment checks introduced in 2001
❖ Guidance for a new occupational health service in 2001
❖ A new independent patient advocacy service to help patients with complaints against doctors

---

Patient power
• New national network of patient forums to monitor health organisations, supported by a Patient Advocacy and Liaison Service (PALS)
• Separate independent patient advocacy service to help with complaints
• NHS organisations to produce patient prospectuses to report action on patients comments
• Local authority scrutiny committees to monitor health authorities (HAs)
• A more patient-friendly complaint system expected after DoH review (due at the end of January)

Discipline and the GMC
• Revised disciplinary action
• Revised suspension action
• Alert letters to warn about bad doctors
• GMC future rests with Government
• GMC civil burden of proof to make it easier to strike off doctors
• Council to become part of UK Council of Health Regulators

Performance
- Annual appraisal for all doctors including locums to begin in 2002
- All doctors to carry out medical audits
- New systems to report adverse incidents, feeding into a national register
- National Clinical Assessment Authority to deal with poor and underperforming doctors

Other key points
- National Clinical Governance Support Team set up in 1999 to become part of the Modernisation Agency
- Information technology implications of NHS plan due August 2002
- New pre-employment checks for primary care to be introduced later in 2002
- New guidance on occupational health service in 2001

Statutory changes
- GPs to declare criminal convictions
- Mandatory exclusion from HA lists for murder. Other convictions at HA discretion
- HAs to keep list of locums, deputies and assistants
- Immediate suspension from HA list if there are fears for patient safety
- Only GPs on the HA list can practise
- Deaths in surgery to be reported
- GPs to declare all gifts

National Clinical Assessment Authority (NCAA)
- From April 2002, the NCAA will offer a rapid performance, assessment and support service for doctors
- To recommend monitoring, education, retraining, medical treatment or referral to the GMC
- Has special HA status
- Health authority can refer doctors for advice and assessment
- Assessment carried out via practice visits
- Health authority will still be able to refer to GMC or deal with a doctor itself
- Assessors will be lay and medical
- GPs will be able to self-refer
- NHS pays for assessment
- GPs will have input
- Links with postgraduate deans and tutors
- Disciplinary action if GPs refuse to cooperate

PRACTICE AND PERSONAL DEVELOPMENT PLANS (PPDPs)

Aims

- Combine personal self-directed learning with organisational development framework
- To predispose to, enable and reinforce change, i.e. deliver information, rehearse behaviours, provide reminders and feedback
- Require learning portfolios for all members of practice team (doctors, nurses, managers), taking into account development needs of both individuals and the working unit
- Involve shift away from individual performance to organisational performance as measure of quality
- Patient involvement should ensure local responsiveness and prevent loss of personal care

Ask yourself

- What do we need to do to improve our own practice?
- How have we identified what we need to do?:
  - Discussions
  - Surveys
  - Audits
  - Significant event analysis
- Are these needs specific to our own practice, or do they reflect priorities in our PCG, Health Authority, or the wider NHS?
- How are we going to address these needs?
- How will we judge our success?
- What do I need to improve the quality of care I provide? ('Reflection')
- How can I achieve these aims? ('Education')
- You choose your education on the basis of what you need to learn. (Continuous professional development (CPD))

A personal development plan (PDP) is part of the PPDP, as the team (practice) may require an individual to learn new skills in order to develop services.
Thus:
- There is a lot in common between Clinical Governance (CG) and PPDPs/PDPs
- Education should help you maintain and improve the quality of your care

The learning portfolio

Contains:
- All past significant sources and experiences of learning
- May include a description of your work and practice
- A summary of all your learning experiences
- A description of how you would like to develop professionally in the future
- Personal development plan would be at the heart of the learning portfolio
- Portfolio would act as a more long-term record of past experience and future aspirations

Could include:
- Workload logs
- Case descriptions
- Videos
- Audits
- Patient surveys
- Research projects
- Accounts of change or innovations
- Reflective diaries on study and ongoing education

CHAPTER 12: THE FUTURE OF GENERAL PRACTICE

Current problems
- Job satisfaction
- Morale
- Autonomy
- Workload
- Bureaucracy
- Recruitment
- Retention

GP numbers threatened by:
- More early retirement
- More part-time principals, women principals (career breaks)
- More doctors needed in secondary care
- Reduced immigration from outside the European Union (EU)

Possible solutions
- Increased medical school intake
- Increased resources for: staff premises and technology
- Increased delegation to practice nurses (nurse practitioners)
- Limiting expansion of GP workload, especially from secondary to primary care
- Core contract changed to ensure GPs retain control of workload (variable, flexible, minimal, practice- rather than individual-based)
- Appropriate funding for care transferred from secondary to primary care
- Easier re-entry arrangements after a career break
- Flexible working arrangements
- Increased linking of practices through PCGs, PCTs and cooperatives
- Other healthcare professionals working in surgeries; e.g.: pharmacists, physiotherapists, chiropractors, osteopaths, social workers, optometrists
- GPs employed by Community Trusts
- Initial triage by nurse practitioners – GP becomes specialist in family medicine (i.e. team leader) to be called upon only when needed
- Split contract – day and night elements

THE NHS PLAN

Investment
- 7,000 extra beds in hospitals and intermediate care
- Over 100 new hospitals by 2010 and 500 new one-stop primary care centres
- Over 3,000 GP premises modernised and 250 new scanners
- Clean wards – overseen by 'modern matrons' – and better hospital food
- Modern IT systems in every hospital and GP surgery
- 7,500 more consultants and 2,000 more GPs
- 20,000 extra nurses and 6,500 extra therapists
- 1,000 more medical school places
- Childcare support for NHS staff with 100 on-site nurseries

Reform
- New relationship between the DoH and the NHS to enshrine the trust that patients have in front-line staff
- A new system of earned autonomy will devolve power from the Government to the local health service as modernisation takes hold
- DoH will set national standards, matched by regular inspection of all local health bodies by an independent inspectorate, the Commission for Health Improvement (CHI)
- NICE will ensure that the availability of cost-effective drugs, like those for cancer, is not dependent on where you live
- The Modernisation Agency will be set up to spread best practice
- Local NHS organisations that perform well for patients will have more freedom to run their own affairs
- There will also be a £500m performance fund
- But the Government will intervene more rapidly in those parts of the NHS that fail their patients

Integration
- Social services and the NHS will come together with new agreements to pool resources
- New Care Trusts to commission health and social care in a single organisation
- Modern contracts for both GPs and hospital doctors
- Extension of quality-based contracts for GPs in general, and for single-handed practices in particular
- Consultants entitled to additional discretionary payments will rise

from half to two-thirds, but in return they will be expected to increase their productivity while working for the NHS
- Newly qualified consultants will be unable to do private work for perhaps 7 years?

Extended roles
- By 2004 over 50% of nurses will be able to supply medicines. £280m is being set aside over the next 3 years to develop the skills of staff
- All support staff will have an Individual Learning Account worth £150 per year
- The number of nurse consultants will increase to 1,000 and a new role of consultant therapist will be introduced
- A Leadership Centre will be set up to develop a new generation of managerial and clinical leaders, including modern matrons with authority to get the basics right on the ward

Patient power
- Letters about an individual patient's care will be copied to the patient
- Patients' views on local health services will help to decide how much cash they get
- Patient advocates will be set up in every hospital
- If operations are cancelled on the day they are due to take place the patient will be able to choose another date within 28 days, or the hospital will pay for it to be carried out at another hospital of the patient's choosing
- Patients' surveys and forums will be set up to help services become more patient-centred

Recruitment
- By 2004, patients will be able to have a GP appointment within 48 hours
- Up to 1,000 specialist GPs taking referrals from fellow GPs
- Long waits in A&E departments will be ended
- By the end of 2005, the maximum waiting time for an outpatient appointment will be 3 months and for inpatients, 6 months

Chronic diseases
- A big expansion in cancer screening programmes
- End to the 'postcode lottery' in the prescribing of cancer drugs
- Rapid-access chest pain clinics across the country by 2003

- Shorter waits for heart operations
- Hundreds of mental health teams to provide an immediate response to crises

Elderly
- Nursing care in nursing homes will be free
- By 2004, a £900m package of new intermediate care services to allow older people to live more independent lives
- National standards for caring for older people to ensure that ageism is not tolerated
- Breast screening to cover all women aged 65 to 70 years
- Personal care plans for elderly people and their carers

National inequalities target
- Increase and improve primary care in deprived areas
- Introduce screening programmes for women and children
- Step up smoking cessation services
- Improve the diet of young children by making fruit freely available in schools for 4–6-year-olds

 USEFUL WEBSITE

www.nhs.uk/nhsplan – Summary of the NHS Plan and full document

☙ SHAPING TOMORROW: ISSUES FACING GENERAL PRACTICE IN THE NEW MILLENNIUM, GPC 2000

This was a discussion document issued by the General Practitioners Committee (GPC) of the BMA; it gathered views from the profession, politicians and patients. Each subheading below is an area discussed by the three parties, the salient points of which are summarised. (This was an 80 page document – you're welcome to read all of it.)

My doctor or any doctor quickly
- Two apparent patient groups exist. The first group are essentially well and value easy access to healthcare with staff able to deal with their problem. The other comprises the chronically ill (elderly, poor) who place a high value on seeing their doctor
- Divisions exist between GPs:
  - Some feel GPs overinvest in the notion of personal doctoring, like some psychological comfort blanket
  - But the personal relationship is something that many patients do rate very highly
  - Many GPs see the personal relationship as central to what they do
  - Others see it as a fading asset in a world of portfolio careers and part-time working
  - A small minority think the concept is dead and the profession should be honest that the future is increasingly likely to be about 'one hit' consultations
  - Advocates of personal lists point out that knowledge of the patient reduces expenditure (lees investigation, etc.)

Mike Pringle, RCGP Chairman admits that in reality doctors are unable to provide continuity of care in their practice. GPs are increasingly being asked to do things that the Government (and some doctors) think is valuable, such as sit on PCG boards, organise education and do research, all of which means they are not seeing patients. Other doctors (and the Government) feel that continuity of care is not as an important issue as the continuity of patient record.

Some consensus exists that a core group of chronically ill patients benefit from having their own doctor and that this should always be a priority.

The demands of the well population must not be allowed to overshadow the demands and needs of the chronically unwell.

The consultation is all? Or letting go to gain a richer day?
- Tensions exist between the call to reduce workload and to free up more time for longer consultations
- Some fear that giving up seeing some patients will reduce the quality of care, status or even pay
- Studies show that most patients are happy to see a nurse for triage/treatment of minor illnesses
- Opposing view is that there is no such thing as a minor illness or a trivial consultation
- Each consultation is an opportunity for identifying the hidden agenda and that only someone sufficiently trained (GPs) will be able to uncover it
- Evidence is scanty that an enormous increase in nurse care will reduce the utilisation of doctors (as in the USA)
- Further research into the cost-effectiveness of nurse practitioners is needed to see if they do indeed reduce the doctor's workload

Independent contractor (IC) status versus salaried service: phoney war or real debate?
The arguments for and against overlap, but essentially could be summed up as philosophical, clinical and financial – a heady enough mix to fuel any debate.

Pros to IC status:
- Allows GPs greater control of their jobs, i.e. ways of working, hours, staff, etc.
- Allows GPs to believe themselves to be other than 'mere employees of the state'
- Allows us to be independent advocates on behalf of our patients
- Allows innovation, promotes entrepreneurial spirit, encourages change and efficiency
- Lead to the development of vocational training, primary care teams, out-of-hours care and models of commissioning
- It is a cheap service
- If all GPs were salaried and employed and therefore clocked on at 9 a.m. and off 36 hours later we would need far more GPs

Cons:
- Young doctors don't want to buy into partnerships
- Young doctors want a more flexible way of working
- Perverse financial incentives, whereby a high list size and lack of investment in facilities and staff produces a better income than services provided by more conscientious GPs
- Researchers and academics complain of a data 'black hole' in general practice
- Much of the independence is illusory, and will become more so in the future in a world of clinical governance, CHI, NSF, PCTs
- A salaried system might stop GPs worrying about money and allow them to get on with doctoring
- At its heart, independent contractor status has a lack of revalidation and supervision

A job for life or portfolio careers
It isn't just changing patient expectations that will affect the shape of tomorrow's primary care – it's changing expectations among tomorrow's GPs. If young doctors want part-time working, flexible careers, the chance to move practices every few years and the opportunity to mix general practice with other kinds of employment, then ultimately these desires need to be accommodated. It's undoubtedly tempting for an older generation of GPs to complain about 'Generation X slackers'. There is a growing feminisation of the workforce, which raises issues around career breaks for motherhood and part-time working, and perhaps leads to wider questions about public and political perceptions of general practice in the future.

Failure to recognise and to respond to these issues risks underusing a considerable resource – female doctors, ethnic minority doctors and, in particular, non-principals.
This way of working will be better accommodated under a salaried rather than premises-owning, IC partnerships. Personal medical services (PSM) pilot schemes explore different ways of providing primary care – and are heavily supported in the NHS Plan/Government.

NHS Direct and walk-ins: will they change the game?
More access points now exist – NHS Direct, walk-in centres.

Direct access to specialist care is expensive (but specialist GPs may be cheaper?)

Those supporting NHS Direct and walk-ins believe they will work to reduce trivial demands on the time of GPs. Replacing phone calls to a surgery with a more systematic service, with quality-assurance protocols, doesn't seem to pose a threat to general practice. It seems to be potentially of considerable benefit. This Government is encouraging self-care, and this potentially benefits GPs.

There's an unreasonable fear and paranoia about walk-in centres. Something like 38 are being established. Even if there were 60 or 70 or 400, you have to think of the numbers. If 100 centres treated 100,000 people a year that would be 10 million consultations. But there are 300 million patient contacts a year in general practice. Nurses are also convinced that the service can help reduce unnecessary work for GPs, without undermining their position in primary care.

Clinical autonomy, does it have any place anymore?
In a world of NICE, NSF, guidelines and protocols, Prodigy and Evidence-based Medicine (EBM) clinical governance as well as CHI, does the concept of clinical autonomy still have any real meaning? Does this mean that GP will lose the ability to mould care and treatment to individual patients? Many GPs take the view that guidelines and protocols are counsels of perfection, which are unobtainable under current resources. Yet doctors, rather than politicians, will be held to account, when it is not possible to deliver services to such standards.

Revalidation, poor performance, Bristol, are all saying to doctors 'you had better conform to the written standards otherwise you are out'. But if they do this it will produce huge cost pressures on the NHS. It's only because we use our generally excellent clinical judgement to flout almost every guideline going that this hasn't happened. Politicians are getting away with the rhetoric of perfection, and doctors are being held to account for not delivering it.

Primary care groups: working together or professional straitjacket?
Will primary care groups, or trusts as they will eventually become, encourage GPs to work together in a more collective and cooperative way, or will they emerge as a new bureaucracy imposing a deadening uniformity and extinguishing innovation and diversity?

Alongside new structures, a new public mood is emerging, which is demanding greater accountability from doctors, and a more transparent understanding of how they arrive at the judgements they do, and what yardsticks are used in these decisions. In a narrow sense, it isn't immediately clear to whom PCGs or PCTs will be accountable. The health authority? The NHS Executive? Ultimately to the Secretary of State, of course, but what will that mean for democracy on the ground?

In the wider sense of accountability, how will family doctors make it clear they want a genuine partnership with patients, and are prepared to explain, and justify, what they do?

One of the hypotheses on which PCGs are based is that if you get doctors working in a more collaborative way you will then institute more peer comparison, peer review and ultimately more peer pressure to improve performance. On the other hand, it is also a very clever political ploy to give clinicians an essentially inadequate unified budget and leave to them the impossible decisions regarding the monetary distribution. GPs will need to decide how much they feel that they are acting in the patients' best interests by using their local and medical knowledge to distribute resources, or whether they are compromising their role as the patients' advocate by becoming responsible for effectively rationing resources.

Accountability
Mike Pringle believes the profession is drinking in 'the last chance saloon' when it comes to self-regulation, and unless accountability is improved this will increasingly be imposed from outside by the Government.

If we don't do it ourselves soon, we are going to end up with a system of external regulation. We have to put in place a system of self-regulation, which is there on the streets for everybody. Most doctors want to be good doctors. We all have a strong internal need to feel good about work (hopefully). Nobody wants to do a bad job, although some people get themselves trapped. We have to value that professional drive.

Promoting quality – what makes a good GP?
Is it possible that doctors, patients and politicians have different visions of what constitutes a quality service and, if so, how can these be reconciled? Among the mechanisms due to be launched to shore up quality, revalidation is the profession's own answer to charges that self-regulation is no longer up to the job of protecting the public. But will it work, or just be another burden GPs have to attend to every 5 years then forget about? If it's not to be too onerous and time-consuming, diverting

resources from patient care, revalidation must judge with a fairly light hand, but will the public believe it has any validity?

Amongst many questions about how general practice develops in the future is the issue of the generalist versus the subspecialist. The generalist role is very dear to the heart of most GPs, and is perhaps gaining increasing importance with the demise of the generalist hospital physician.

But many GPs also have special interests, and many would argue such interests increase intellectual stimulation and allow GPs to better serve their patients. Should such interests and expertise be further formalised, and made available not just within a practice but also between practices or even across a PCG?

What do patients want?
It's an old joke, but it still raises a smile at every medical retirement party. When asked what was the best part of the job, the GP always says 'the patients'. Asked next what was the worst thing about the job, the GP always replies 'the patients'.

If GPs obtain intellectual stimulation from solving medical jigsaw puzzles, or boost their inner psyche by feeling they are contributing to a kinder world or making a difference, or even saving life, that's fine. But the patient just wants to get better. So what should the relationship of the future be between GPs and patients? Everyone talks of partnership and the end of benign paternalism, and patient autonomy and shared care, but sometimes it's not hard to feel that the profession looks over its shoulder and rather wishes that 'doctor knows best' was still a politically correct option.

If we are moving into a more honest and sharing relationship with patients, when doctors are advisers and guides and not gurus and wizards, there still seem few clear mechanisms to listen to what patients actually want, as opposed to doctors assuming they know what patients want.

If patients become clients, or even customers, does that make doctors into therapists and shopkeepers? And if it does, is that any bad thing? What do patients want?

Claire Rayner, of the Patients' Association, believes firmly that the way forward is for the profession to see that patients are part of the health team and are as much involved with the provision, design, delivery and cost of healthcare as anyone else. She also recognises that because patients are recipients it doesn't alter the fact they have responsibilities to the service. But better ways of listening are needed. Patients' liaison groups, citizens' juries and patient advisory panels – this is the road we are going down. We do need much better mechanisms to hear the voice of the patient. GPs can't carry on being paternalistic. The days of a submissive, subdued, semiliterate, lumpen proletariat, people who were underfed, had rotten lives of quiet desperation, are over. Controlling people like that when you were better fed, better educated and had a better life was a doddle.

Funding and rationing – how is it all going to be paid for?
Most GPs would welcome a system that takes them out of the rationing front-line, be it a national rationing council, the Department of Health or NICE. At the very least, many would welcome a little more political honesty about the current situation. Proponents of the co-payment system argue that it would not only boost income for the health service, but also reduce workload. The counter-argument, of course, is that if people pay they become more demanding.

'THE NEW NHS' (1997 GOVERNMENT WHITE PAPER)

- 10-year programme of evolution rather than revolution
- Competitive internal markets to be replaced by cooperative integrated care, i.e. partnership driven by performance
- Purchaser–provider split for hospital care to continue
- Local doctors, nurses and health authorities to have new powers to commission services according to needs of patients
- NHS overhead costs to be cut, saving £1b in next 5 years
- Health authorities to have greater supervisory roles, but will devolve responsibility for commissioning for services to PCGs
- NHS trusts to remain in present role as providers, but accountable to NHS regional offices, and required to publish costs of treatment to expose inefficiency
- Fundholding schemes were abolished from 1999 and replaced by PCGs
- PCGs, comprising all GPs and community nurses in an area, will commission healthcare for about 100,000 patients each
- CHI will oversee quality of clinical services in NHS
- NICE will promote cost-effectiveness
- Telephone help line – NHS Direct – will advise patients on self-treatment 24 hours per day
- Local Health Improvement Programmes will monitor, plan and improve healthcare locally
- Advisory Committee on Resource Allocation will distribute NHS funds more fairly
- Annual survey of patients' and users' experience will compare performance
- Task force will involve NHS staff in planning the service

PRIMARY CARE GROUPS

- Serve a population of about 100,000
- Accountable to health authority
- Resourced out of current fundholding allowances
- Involve all GPs and community nurses
- Primary care budget to be fully cash-limited
- Services commissioned by PCGs must meet national standards to ensure fair access and uniform quality
- PCTs to be managed by a Trust Board comprising GPs, nurses, managers, social services, representatives and lay people
- PCGs will eventually purchase 90% of hospital and community care
- Health authorities will monitor standards, allocate resources, control progress to (or from) complete autonomy
- Four grades with increasing independence:
  1. Provide advice on commissioning to health authority
  2. Manage devolved budget
  3. Independent PCTs responsible for some commissioning
  4. Independent PCTs responsible for commissioning all primary and secondary care, with a fully integrated budget

Concerns
- Is there enough public health/management/commissioning expertise to support 500 PCGs?
- Will they be big enough/powerful enough to effect more than minor changes and improvements by providers?
- Will PCGs or Whitehall have ultimate control with regard to priorities, quality and equity?
- Will health authorities have the power of veto?
- Will devolving healthcare rationing to PCGs render them liable to litigation?
- What happens if they run out of money?
- Will devolving budgetary control to PCGs merely be a smokescreen to conceal NHS underfunding?

PERSONAL MEDICAL SERVICES' (PMS) PILOTS

As a result of the NHS (Primary Care) Act 1997, PMS schemes were designed to allow experimental schemes to test alternative models for delivering primary and community care.

British GPs have traditionally been self-employed, the contract under which they perform work for the NHS is elaborate and is perceived as being inflexible and bureaucratic. This is termed 'General Medical Services' (GMS), arrangements of which are set out in the 'Red Book'.

Although the PMS scheme has sometimes been called the 'salaried doctors' scheme (to contrast with the normal self-employment arrangements), this has not been its defining characteristic.

The PMS scheme has been well received, and a third wave of successful applicants is due to be announced towards the end of this year. The reasons for its popularity are several.

The scheme has generally succeeded in giving those taking part a perception of self-determination and relative freedom from the constraints of NHS bureaucracy. How much this perception is based on the active attitudes of the health authorities who hold the personal medical services contracts and how much on the fact that these authorities have often not had the capacity to manage the scheme at all remains a moot point. Schemes in deprived areas were more likely to attract extra resources that were not generally available to practices working under the old regime, since GMS allocations are not usually linked to population needs.

These resources have been used to create new services, liberate practitioners for professional development and improve facilities, especially for disadvantaged groups such as homeless and mentally ill people.

Aims
- Attract GPs to areas with recruitment problems
- Get GPs and community nurses to work more closely together
- Tackle inequalities and health problems of deprivation

From 94 begun in April 1998, approximately one-third of all primary care is now PMS. Different models exist:

- Salaried GPs and nurses providing primary care to homeless people
- Partnership of GP and nurse with joint responsibility for running a single practice
- Nurse practitioners act as team leaders in a practice and/or employ their own salaried GPs
- Local practice to run a cottage hospital as a primary care and minor injuries unit
- NHS trusts to employ salaried GPs to provide primary care under same roof as other community health services

Significance and implications

- All have an individual contract negotiated directly with their health authority, dispensing with the 'Red Book' and all its restrictions and limitations
- Break the monopoly of the single national contract
- Allow GPs to switch to salaried status, pass management responsibilities to others and concentrate on clinical work
- Give Primary Care Groups and Trusts a new tool for discharging their local responsibilities to provide primary care
- Offer great potential for innovation and service development

THE NEW CONTRACT

The proposals for the new national contract were announced on 19th April, 2002, jointly by the NHS confederation and the British Medical Association.

Following a ballot to see if, in principle, GPs accepted the framework, the contract would then be costed and a further ballot would take place. On the 16th July, 2002, the initial phase was accepted by the profession following the result of the primary ballot.

Some 75.8% of GPs voted 'Yes' to the question: 'Do you believe that the new GMS contractual framework is an acceptable basis on which to proceed to the next stage of detailed negotiations and the preparation of a priced contract on which the profession will be balloted?' 24.2% voted 'No'.

A total of 43,075 ballot forms were sent out to GPs/GP registrars all over the UK. 28,085 valid forms were returned by the ballot deadline of 12 noon on Monday 8th July, a turnout of 65.2%.

Much has been said about the new contract in the GP and medical press. Despite the array of concerns voiced, most GPs appeared to accept the proposals as a step in the right direction.

Whether or not it will be implemented is currently unknown, but appears rather likely.

Current problems
- The 'Red Book' as discussed previously has long been criticised as bureaucratic and inflexible
- The PMS pilots in 1998 were an acknowledgement by the Government for a need for change
- Currently, resource allocation poorly reflects patient need
- The GMS contract is focused on the individual practitioner and fails to recognise the role of the practice team
- The perverse incentive for GPs to manage large lists with a limited range of services, for high income
- Quality measures are poor and crudely implemented
- A recent BMA survey of the profession showed:
  - Devastatingly and unacceptably low morale – a profession in poor heart

- Consequential intentions to retire early or to leave general practice
- Excessive workload, and the need to control that workload in the future
- The need to negotiate a radically modernised new GP contract
- The need to secure national negotiating rights on behalf of all GPs
- The perception that the role of general practice within the NHS is undervalued
- A commitment to quality and to better services for patients, delivered in part through lower average list sizes and through longer consultations, which the research evidence shows are the best available markers for high-quality care

USEFUL WEBSITE

www.bma.org.uk/ap.nsf/Content/annrep2002%5Cannrep2002+-+survey –You will need to be a BMA member to access this site.

Aims of the new contract
- Weighted capitation formula will replace the work of the recently abolished medical practices committee
- National pricing of the contract will take into account the changing demands on primary care through an annual assessment of workload
- If workload rises, new resources will be made available
- Contract will be between a primary care organisation and a practice (rather than an individual GP)
- Services will be categorised as either essential, additional or enhanced
- Services, such as cervical cytology, contraception services and immunisation, need not be provided by every practice in a primary care organisation
- GPs must provide core essential services, but can reduce some of their current commitments
- Opting out of 'out-of-hours' care will be introduced for some, as yet to be decided, financial loss/payment
- Out-of-hours care in the future will be managed through NHS Direct
- Primary care organisations will have new responsibilities to commission alternative providers to fill any gaps created (other healthcare professionals will be involved, not just GPs)

- Doctors who wish to offer enhanced services will get extra pay
- Some enhanced services will be nationally specified and priced; others will be locally agreed
- A new quality and outcomes framework will cover standards to measure clinical and organisational quality as well as patients' experiences
- GPs will be able to trade workload for leisure, at a price
- GPs will be encouraged to hand over about one-third of their duties, including managing chronically ill patients and those with minor ailments, to nurses and pharmacists
- Quality of care is likely to be a more powerful motivator
- Shifting the contract to practices allows new incentives to make greater use of non-medical staff (currently many payments are linked to the existence of a GP)
- Practices may become larger, with subspecialisation amongst GPs
- The new capitation formula should be welcome for deprived areas because funding will be delivered regardless of whether GPs are already in post

The Risks
- All incentive systems encourage competition, but it is unclear if that is good for health
- GPs will inevitably concentrate on those specified quality targets at the expense of others
- The standards of the new quality and outcomes framework will be constantly disputed, and how will they be universally agreed?
- The Government's bill for clearly specifying tasks, which currently are undertaken for free and which will attract payment under the new contract, may be excessive, some say it will break the camel's back
- Can primary care organizations cope with the complexities and managerial responsibilities that active commissioning will have? Many argue that they are organisationally immature
- Patients may receive services from a number of providers that may or may not be linked, this will fragment continuity
- Link between daytime and out-of-hours services seems set to split permanently
- Domiciliary general practice visiting may be contracted out to a separate organisation
- The GP will no longer be the pivot of services, but is that important?

Sources

- NHS Confederation. *The new GMS contract – delivering the benefits for GPs and their patients.* London: NHS Confederation, 2002
- General Practice Committee. *Your contract your future.* London: British Medical Association, 2002
- Editorial: *A fresh new contract for general practitioners.* BMJ 2002 (4 May)

RATIONING

Know examples of scenarios of where rationing may affect your practice, moral obligations, duty of care, postcode prescribing, etc. For example, Sildenafil (Viagra) and Donepezil (Aricept).

- What in your practice do you not prescribe to certain patients because of cost and not doubt over clinical efficacy?
- Rationing is regarded by many as the only method open if the NHS is to survive whilst delivering an apparently high standard of publicly funded quality care to the masses
- Can we continue to offer 'gold standard' publicly funded care as well as comprehensive care, or are the two subject to financial forces?
- With rationing you could either deliver the 'best to most' or the 'average to all'; what choice would you make?
- The general consensus is that the 'best to most' strategy is the best solution, whilst maintaining a honesty and transparency to the public
- Politicians are unlikely to make this a public issue whilst trying to win elections, the stark reality that widespread rationing exists has rarely been admitted to and hence would ruffle many a feather

This problem has been actively explored in other countries. In 1993, 'The Oregon Experiment' took place in the USA; discussed in detail in an Education and Debate article in the BMJ (*1998;316:1965*). A decade ago, the state of Oregon attracted worldwide interest when it began an ambitious attempt to set priorities for healthcare on a systematic basis.

Stimulated by the death of a 7-year-old boy who had been waiting for a bone marrow transplant operation, and led by John Kitzhaber, a doctor turned politician, Oregon passed legislation in 1989 designed to provide access to health insurance for all residents. This was a huge market research exercise, which gathered opinions from a broad public base, treatments were explained and justified and a list was compiled according to priority. Compilation of the list included a weighting to clinical effectiveness, social values and emphasis on primary/preventive care. The difference was that the information gathered was used; a cut-off line for conditions to be funded was decided according to available resources, but it remained dynamic with regular review.

In New Zealand, a Government-appointed committee made a broad assessment of treatment priorities, as in the USA involving the public. It initiated a programme to devise guidelines for the provision of services. Criteria were written to determine access to publicly funded elective surgery. Treatment is given on the ability of patients to benefit (clinical and social), those with highest need would go first and those with little need may be refused.

The obvious disadvantage of either system is that the wealthy could by-pass it altogether and hence a two-tier system would (and has) be created. The poor do not have that option. Means testing may be an alternative to 'all care'.

Would a modest charge, say, to see a GP help: the answer is 'Yes'. Evidence shows this leads to a reduction in help-seeking behaviour.

The alternative is to raise income tax.

Hopefully, evidence-based practice and guidelines from NICE will help avoid implicit rationing.

OUT-OF-HOURS CARE and 24-HOUR RESPONSIBILITY

Risks of split contract (day and night)
- Rolling, renewable contract could result in insecurity
- Other primary care providers may bid for out-of-hours work, e.g. community trusts, A&E departments and BUPA
- Further threatens integrity of GPs' role, already at risk from hospital outreach, community paediatricians, community psychiatric teams, midwives, etc.
- Dilution and fragmentation of GPs' work
- Loss of control of care outside hospitals

Advantages
- Satisfaction from personal service
- Educational benefits
- Financial reward
- Prevention of erosion of GPs' role by other providers

Disadvantages
- Heavy workload – demand increased fivefold in last 25 years
- Stress – may result in: impaired quality of care at the time; impaired quality of care the next day; burn out
- Risk of violence

Deputising services
- Surveys show high degree of patient satisfaction
- Quality must be maintained
- Deputies must be well paid and well supported

PAPER

A qualitative study of older people's views of out-of-hours services
(J. Foster, et al., BJGP 2001 51(470):719–23)

- This study looked to ascertain the views of the elderly in relation to their use of various models of out-of-hours care
- While older people are more likely to have increased needs for such services, evidence suggests they are reluctant users of GP out-of-hours services
- A total of 30 people aged between 65 and 81 years from

community groups based in SE London attended focus-group sessions of 90 minutes and comprising between 5 and 12 participants
- The study was conducted in Lambeth, Southwark and Lewisham, a socially deprived, multi-ethnic area of south London
- The session was audiotape-recorded with consent and then transcribed verbatim
- Two related themes were identified:
  1. Attitudes to health and healthcare professionals with reference to the use of health services prior to the establishment of the NHS, a stoical attitude towards health, and not wanting to make excessive demands on health services
  2. The experience of out-of-hours care and the perceived barriers to its use, including the use of the telephone and travelling at night. Participants preferred contact with a familiar doctor and were distrustful of telephone advice, particularly from nurses
- They concluded that older people appear reluctant to make use of out-of-hours services and are critical of the trend away from out-of-hours care being delivered by a familiar GP
- With increasing numbers of older people in the population it is important to consider steps to address their reluctance to use out-of-hours and telephone-advice services, particularly those based around less personal models of care

NHS DIRECT

Nurse-led, 24-hour telephone help line has been available throughout England and Wales since the end of 2000.

In response to:
- Growth of the 24-h society
- Increasing demand for primary and emergency care
- Problems in recruiting and retaining nurses and general practitioners

Aims to:
- Reduce workload
- Provide easy access to an appropriate level of expertise
- Empower patients with knowledge and thus foster self-care

Long-term aims
- Health promotion, information centres, health guides, Internet services

Concerns
- It will uncover unmet demand, so fuelling workload
- Will threaten continuity of care
- Telephone contact by nurses rather than a consultation with a GP may mean that important diagnoses are missed
- It will not be integrated with the rest of gateway services such as GP cooperatives
- Would result in waste of resources and patient confusion

Criticisms
- Service needs to be equally accessible to those without English as a first language, mentally ill people and elderly – they are less likely to use a telephone service
- Money for NHS Direct was not offered to existing primary care services to update the existing service arrangements
- Not enough liaison with GPs
- Lack of consistent advise in clinically identical cases

PAPERS

📖 **1. Evaluation of NHS direct first wave sites: First interim report to the Department of Health, J. Munro, 1998**

Looked at three aspects of the service in the first three pilot sites:
- Descriptive account of the organisation and users of NHS Direct
- Caller satisfaction
- 'Before and after' assessment of its effects on other services

Showed that in the first 8 months:
- Demand was only one-third of that expected (expected to rise)
- Essentially used as an out-of-hours service, with 72% of calls being out-of-hours
- Demographics reflected patterns for GP services, except that the elderly were underrepresented
- Caller satisfaction rates were high
- Significant differences in the percentage of callers advised to attend A&E and/or their GP between the three sites
- Significantly different advice given to 120 dummy cases (clinically identical) between the three sites

A follow-up study by J. Munro et al. (*BMJ 2000;321:150–3*) showed:

Same three pilot sites studied over 24 months, in summary:
- No significant changes in uses of ambulance services and A&E departments
- Changes in use of GP out-of-hours cooperatives were small but significant (increase of 2% per month to a decrease of 0.8%)
- May have restrained increasing demand
- Overall, in the first year did not reduce pressure on the NHS
- No evidence that it had uncovered extra demand
- Apparently is still popular with the public

📖 **2. National Audit Office Report published January 2002**

- Stated – NHS Direct is used less by ethnic minorities, people aged over 65 years and disadvantaged groups than by the general population
- Report stated that these groups had 'as much need as others and perhaps an even greater one'
- Service is nevertheless operating safely and effectively

- Details only 29 cases of adverse events between its inception in 1998 and 2001 (less than one in every 220,000 calls)
- Service has also reduced demand on healthcare services that are provided outside normal working hours, e.g. GPs
- One GP cooperative providing out-of-hours services saw an 18% fall in the number of calls received when callers were transferred to NHS Direct first
- However, NHS Direct is underperforming in some areas
- Only 64% of callers managed to speak to a nurse within 5 minutes
- Target set by the Government was 90%
- One in five callers had to wait more than 30 minutes for a nurse to call them back

WALK-IN CENTRES

- Announced in April 1999
- Offer people the opportunity to see a healthcare professional face to face on a walk-in basis
- Open from 0700 h to 2200 h weekdays and weekends to provide information and treatment for minor conditions
- With or without appointments
- Sited in convenient locations, mainly in large towns
- Consultations mainly provided by nurses, using clinical assessment software
- These nurse-led centres provide advice and treatment for minor illnesses and also direct people to the most appropriate healthcare provider for their needs
- Centres will be funded initially for 3 years, but concerns have been voiced about subsequent funding
- Same concerns voiced over NHS Direct have been discussed with regard to walk-in centres
- Run by PCGs, cooperatives, GPs and NHS Trusts

Objections
- Diversion of funds from other parts of primary care
- May generate additional demands
- Cause fragmentation of primary care and erosion of Family Doctor Service which has:
  - Comprehensive medical record
  - Continuity of care at its core
  - Gatekeeper role

Benefits
- May reduce workload of GPs (especially trivial)
- Responds to demand for wider access
- NHS Direct may help public make more appropriate use of health and social services

PAPERS

📖 **1. An observational study comparing quality of care in walk-in centres with general practice and NHS Direct using standardised patients**
(C. Grant, et al., BMJ 2002;324:1556)

The UK Government, as part of a bid to modernise health services and to make them more convenient to use, has introduced NHS walk-in centres and commissioned their evaluation by an independent team. This study forms one component of that evaluation.

- They directly compared the quality of clinical care in walk-in centres with that provided in general practice and by NHS Direct
- It was an observational study involving assessment of clinicians by standardised patients
- It involved 20 walk-in centres, 20 general practices, and 11 NHS Direct sites
- 297 consultations with standardised patients were analysed, 99 in each setting, carried out by professional role players trained to play five clinical scenarios (postcoital contraception, chest pain, sinusitis, headache and asthma)
- Outcome measures were mean scores on consensus-derived checklists of essential items for the management of the clinical scenarios
- Data were also collected on access to and referral by walk-in centres, general practices and NHS Direct
- Walk-in centres achieved a significantly greater mean score for all scenarios combined than general practices (difference between groups = 8.2) and NHS Direct (10.8)
- Walk-in centres performed particularly well on postcoital contraception and asthma scenarios. In contrast to general practices, walk-in centres and NHS Direct referred a higher proportion of patients (26% and 82%, respectively)
- They performed significantly less well than general practice in examination of chest pain and the diagnosis, advice and treatment of sinusitis
- The authors state that these inadequacies do not necessarily provide evidence of poor quality care:
  - Examination may be of secondary importance in the overall management of musculoskeletal chest pain
  - Significantly lower antibiotic use by walk-in centres for sinusitis may reflect acknowledged difficulties identifying patients who

will benefit from antibiotics
- Walk-in centres' better performance was particularly noticeable for history taking, perhaps owing to the longer consultations undertaken in this setting
- The authors concluded that walk-in centres perform adequately and safely compared with general practices and NHS Direct for the range of conditions under study, but the impact of referrals on workload of other healthcare providers requires further research
- Although walk-in centres may provide a comparable quality of care, both the centres and NHS Direct referred a proportion of standardised patients elsewhere. Some of the referrals were to emergency departments, which may not be appropriate for the conditions studied and raises questions about the impact on workload of other providers

Problems
- Non-random sampling of participating sites
- Use of a limited number of scenarios, some more discriminating than others
- Participating sites, particularly general practices, were likely to be more interested in the research question and may have provided a higher quality of care, possibly attenuating the study findings
- Scenarios were chosen as typical of those seen in walk-in centres and because they were appropriate for portrayal by standardised patients
- Scenarios necessitating the presence of abnormal findings or potentially involving certain types of physical examination or referral to third parties could not be included

2. Questionnaire survey of users of NHS walk-in centres: observational study
(C. Salisbury, et al., BJGP 2002 52(480):554–61)

- The principal aim of NHS walk-in centres is to improve access to primary healthcare
- This study attempted to ascertain the client group that attended and their satisfaction through a questionnaire
- The survey was also conducted among people who attended general practices close to a walk-in centre on a 'same-day' basis; that is, by attending without an appointment booked before the day of their consultation
- For this group of people, attending a nearby walk-in centre would

be a realistic alternative source of care
- The survey was conducted at all walk-in centres that were open by March 2001
- The general practice nearest to each walk-in centre was approached to act as a control site; if this practice declined the invitation, they approached the next nearest practice and so on
- The questionnaire was divided into two sections. The first was designed to be completed before the consultation and included questions about sociodemographic characteristics, convenience of location and opening hours, reasons for consulting, expectations, recent use of health services and attitudes to continuity of care. The second section, completed after the consultation, included questions about waiting times, satisfaction, treatment, referrals and enablement
- 38 walk-in centres and 34 neighbouring general practices took part
- The results showed that walk-in centre visitors were more likely to be:
  - Owner-occupiers (55% vs. 49%)
  - To have further education (25% vs. 19%) and
  - To be Caucasian (88% vs. 84%) than GP visitors
- Therefore the authors stated that visitors to walk-in centres in the UK were younger, better educated and more affluent than those attending general practice
- Main reasons for attending a walk-in centre were speed of access and convenience
- Walk-in centre visitors were more likely to attend on the first day of illness (28% vs. 10%)
- Walk-in centre visitors were less likely to expect a prescription (38% vs. 70%) and placed less importance on continuity
- People were more satisfied with walk-in centres
- Enablement scores were slightly higher in general practice
- Following the consultation, 13% of walk-in centre visitors were re-referred to their GP, but 32% intended to make an appointment
- They concluded that NHS walk-in centres improve access to care, but not necessarily for those people with greatest health needs
- It then has to be argued whether they are a justified use of scarce resources for a patient group, in least need

3. Editorial: NHS Direct audited. Customer satisfaction, but at what price?
(BMJ 2002;324:558–9)

This editorial was written by a board member of an NHS Direct site and gives a surprisingly unbiased view as to the evaluation of the service. In summary:

- Three NHS Direct pilot sites were launched in March 1998 and sites now cover whole of England and Wales
- While not the first telephone health service in the world, it promised something more than triage of emergency calls
- It is now set to become the hub of out-of-hours care
- In January 2002, the National Audit Office, an independent body that scrutinises public spending on behalf of Parliament, published its report on NHS Direct in England and Wales
- Generally, the report is positive but there are problems
- In addition to difficulty with meeting call-handling targets, there has been no visible effect on demand for NHS services overall
- The hoped for reduction in demand for other services might be achieved by the proposed integration of NHS Direct with existing out-of-hours general practice cooperatives and ambulance services
- Where such integration has taken place, demand for general practice consultation has fallen, especially for telephone consultation
- Despite its shortcomings, customer satisfaction with NHS Direct is high, that is, among those who use it
- Evidence indicates they are the same people who use existing health services
- It is underused by older people, ethnic minorities and other disadvantaged groups
- Rather than reach people who are currently failed by the health system, NHS Direct may have discovered previously unexpressed demand among the worried well of the middle classes
- The Internet version of the telephone service makes only a brief appearance in the report, but its use is clearly limited to those with access to the Internet and money to pay for it
- When callers reach a nurse the advice they get may vary, usually on the side of caution
- This is predictable, but has inevitable consequences. For every caller with a serious condition detected by NHS Direct, many more with self-limiting conditions will be directed into the health system

- Consistently to err on the side of safety might seem logical, but the effect of doing so is to fill a health system with people who do not need to be there
- Is it worth the money? The report suggests that half of the £90m annual cost of NHS Direct has been offset by encouraging more appropriate use of NHS services
- Is £45m, the theoretical additional cost of NHS Direct, worth it for a system that eventually might work as a coordinator of access to healthcare? It seems unlikely that NHS Direct will do anything to address health inequality, and it may even serve to widen existing differences
- If you had £45m a year to spend on improving health, empowering the socially disadvantaged and reducing health inequality what would you spend it on?

Key sources

Department of Health. *Raising standards for patients: new partnerships in out-of-hours care.* London: Stationery Office, 2000.

The Comptroller and Auditor General. *NHS Direct in England.* London: Stationery Office, 2002.

SPECIALIST GPs

Over the last year much has been quoted in the GP press about the introduction of new 'specialist GPs'. As such there has also been the inevitable barrage of criticisms about such a grade. Key points regarding the benefits and threats of the new grade were raised in a joint report by the RCGP and RCP in May 2001.

Potential benefits:
- Getting high quality care more rapidly and closer to home offers patients considerable advantages
- Increased communication between local GPs may enhance team working and continuity
- Clinical care outside general practice also offers interest, personal development, and heightened self-esteem for GPs
- For GPs advantages may include enhanced retention, delayed burn out, and increased job satisfaction
- Increased working with consultants will also help to break down barriers

Potential threats:
- The creation of GPs with special interests may degrade the discipline of general practice and the value of generalism
- Fragmentation of general practice with the devaluing and eventual loss of generalism to the detriment of patient care as occurred to the general physicians
- Adverse effects on resources: "For every session done by a GP with a clinical special interest, there will be one session less of clinical care in other environments. Many of these sessions will come from clinical general practice. Some may be a direct transfer of a general practitioner from a clinical assistantship in the hospital setting. Whatever the source, the new sessions will remove capacity from elsewhere in the NHS"
- Specialist GP's may become a second-class service designed to ease the pressure on hospital outpatient clinics, reducing clinical standards while denying patient access

General Practitioners With Special Interests is accessible at www.rcgp.org.uk

NURSE PRACTITIONERS

What work might they do?
- Prevention, immunisation, smears, contraception, review, BP, asthma, diabetes, etc.
- Medical triage, independent management of minor illness with limited prescribing rights, referring on to GP only when necessary
- Social triage – guiding patients needing social or financial help

How would GPs benefit?
- Overtrained for much of what we do – less time on trivia would mean more time available for patients with more serious problems
- Skills learnt in training need no longer atrophy through disuse
- Potential for GPs to specialise in aspects of primary care
- Increased job satisfaction
- Improved morale
- Increased income through larger lists, e.g. 4,000 patients per doctor

What are the possible problems?
- Dilution of continuity of care and of personal care
- GPs may feel themselves redundant
- Nurses may fail to diagnose rare but life-threatening conditions, or to spot unusual presentations
- More specialisation by GPs may lead to loss of 'generalist role'
- Cost of training programmes and salaries to be borne by health authorities
- Legal responsibility – nurses are responsible for own actions but GPs still have 'vicarious liability'
- Need to protect themselves by writing evidence-based protocols for delegated tasks
- Patients must be informed that they are not seeing a doctor so they don't consent to procedures believing a doctor – not a nurse – will do them

What do the studies show?
Nurse practitioners are:
- Safe
- Effective
- Popular with patients
- Good at listening, understanding and explaining
- Good at following protocols

- Less likely to prescribe
- More likely to use non-prescription approaches
- Likely to advise on prevention
- Good at using drug formularies

How can they act as point of first contact?
- Triage
- Telephone advice
- Same-day appointments
- Home visits

Effect on GPs
GPs report:
- Reduced workload
- Increased satisfaction
- Improved standards of care
- More patients seen

What are the pitfalls? (This is food for thought, not necessarily the authors' views)
- 'Nurse Practitioner' title not regulated, the courses they go on are neither externally assessed nor regulated
- Are we in fact allowing non-medically trained people to practise as doctors?
- Having to access a GP only via a nurse, is it acceptable that patients do not have a choice to see a doctor first
- Introduction of a two-tier service with nurses providing much of the care in areas where it is difficult to recruit GPs, whereas leafy suburbs where GPs want to work are well staffed but patients have the least need
- What effect would it have on the nature of general practice?
- Ability to distinguish self-limiting from serious disease and the opportunity to develop a close rapport with patients are key skills of GPs, would these be compromised?

What does a practice need before appointing a nurse practitioner?
- Job description to clarify role, responsibilities, accountability and liability
- Protocols and guidelines
- Formulary
- Education of staff on role of nurse practitioner
- Education of patients on role of nurse practitioner

What will the nurse practitioner need?
- Mechanisms of support, supervision, professional development, i.e. a mentor
- Mechanisms of problem resolution
- Training in protected time
- Accreditation scheme in addition to the Nurse Practitioner Degree
- Education funded by health authority
- Fewer prescribing restrictions

PAPERS

📖 1. Nurse management of patients with minor illnesses in general practice: a multicentre RCT
(C. Shum, et al., BMJ 2000;320:1038)

From a themed issue, explored the changing roles of nurses in the NHS. Four trials of nurse impact on primary care were published.
- Practice nurses attended a degree-level course on managing minor illness for half a day a week for 3 months, also observed GPs in surgeries twice a week. Two sessions equates to one day or two surgery lists. Two-month pilot period after the nurses were recruited
- Patients asking for same-day appointments with minor illness were randomly distributed between a GP and practice nurse

Outcomes
- High satisfaction for both doctor and nurse consultations (but significantly higher for nurses)
- Consultations with nurses took and average of 10 minutes, with doctors 8 minutes
- Similar prescription rates for a similar number of patients
- 73% of patients seen by nurses required no input from doctors
- Conclusion – practice nurses offer an effective service for people with minor illness

📖 2. Randomised controlled trial comparing cost effectiveness of general practitioners and nurse practitioners in primary care
(P. Venning et al., BMJ 2000;320:1048–53)

This further RCT in the same issue as Paper 2 looked at cost-effectiveness. It showed that:
- Nurse consultations were significantly longer than those of doctors

- They carried out more tests and asked patients to return more often
- There was no significant difference in patterns of prescribing or outcome
- Patients were more satisfied with nurse consultations (allowing for time difference)
- No significant difference in health service costs between the two groups
- Conclusions were that costs were similar, but that if nurses could maintain the benefits whilst reducing their return consultation rates or shortening consultation times then they could be more cost-effective than general practitioners

3. Systematic review of whether nurse practitioners working in primary care can provide equivalent care to doctors
(S. Horrocks, et al., BMJ 2002;324:819–23)

- This study asked the question 'can nurse practitioners provide care at first point of contact equivalent to doctors in a primary care'
- Nurse practitioners have existed in North America for many years
- An increasing number are being employed in the UK in general practice, emergency departments and other primary care settings
- It was a systematic review of RCTs and prospective observational studies comparing nurse practitioners and doctors providing care of undifferentiated health problems in primary care
- Outcome measures were patient satisfaction, health status, costs and process of care
- 11 trials and 23 observational studies met all the inclusion criteria
- They found that patients were more satisfied with care by a nurse practitioner
- No differences in health status were found
- Nurse practitioners had longer consultations and made more investigations than did doctors
- No differences were found in prescriptions, return consultations or referrals
- Quality of care was in some ways better for nurse practitioner consultations
- They concluded:
  - Increasing availability of nurse practitioners in primary care is likely to lead to high levels of patient satisfaction and high-quality care

- Patients are more satisfied with care from a nurse practitioner than from a doctor, with no difference in health outcomes
- Nurse practitioners provide longer consultations and carry out more investigations than doctors
- Most recent research has related to patients requesting same-day appointments for minor illness, which is only a limited part of a doctor's role
- Further research is needed to confirm that nurse practitioner care is safe in terms of detecting rare but important health problems

OUTREACH CLINICS

Advantages
- Improved communication between GP and consultant
- Increased range of services in general practice
- Fewer non-attending patients
- Reduced and more appropriate referral to hospital
- Patient convenience
- Better management
- GP education

Disadvantages
- Widens divide between progressive and inert practices
- Inefficient use of consultant time
- Inadequate facilities
- No hospital records available
- No diagnostic services available
- Reduced consultant cover, teaching and research at hospital
- Increased referral waiting time for patients of non-participating practices
- Unnecessary referrals

The above are theoretical points as no evidence is available. As such, more evaluation is needed.

Q. What are the costs to patient, GP and the hospital?
Q. How would they impact on referral, prescribing and effect on junior training (lack of consultant cover)?

PRACTICE FORMULARY

Aim
- Improved quality of care through rational, cost-effective prescribing

Criteria for inclusion
- Drugs must be: necessary, safe, effective and economic

Method
- Develop own formulary
- Participate in development of district formulary
- Take over and amend established formulary

Benefits
- Education
- Generic prescribing increased
- Prescribing costs reduced
- Influence of drug companies reduced
- Prescribing policies/management policies agreed
- Self-audit
- Peer review

Problems
- Patients reluctant to change
- Doctors feel restricted
- Hospital-initiated therapy with non-formulary drug

Q. How would you instigate a practice formulary?

COMPUTER-GENERATED REPEAT PRESCRIPTIONS

- The GMC have issued guidelines
- Must take full account of your obligation to prescribe responsibly and safely
- Satisfy yourself it is safe to sign every repeat prescription
- Ensure provision is made for monitoring each patient's condition
- Ensure patients needing examination or assessment do not get repeat prescriptions without seeing a doctor, especially for drugs with potentially serious side-effects

Q. What is your responsibility for repeat prescriptions?

POST 'SHIPMAN', WHAT ARE THE LONG-TERM EFFECTS?

Alan Milburn ordered a wide-ranging inquiry into the issues raised by the case.

Following the publication of the inquiry into the Shipman case it appears that Harold Shipman murdered at least 215 of his patients (171 women and 44 men). 45 other cases are possibly suspicious.

The head of the inquiry, High Court Judge, Dame Janet Smith, also speculated that Shipman may have been hoping to get caught when he altered the will of his last victim, Kathleen Grundy, aged 81 years. The forgery was described as 'crude' and 'made detection inevitable'.

The report 'Death Disguised' examined a total of 888 cases in its 2,000 pages.

As to whether his motive will ever be identified, the Judge said, 'The short answer, I think, is no. Only he could answer that question and at the moment it seems very unlikely he will.' At the time of writing, Harold Shipman continues to proclaim his innocence and has refused to consent to a psychiatric examination.

The inquiry also identified addictive personality traits in Shipman: first, to pethidine but also perhaps to killing itself.

However, the inquiry continues into its second phase, which examines how he evaded detection for so long and how the corroborating signatures form other doctors appeared on so many cremation certificates.

 USEFUL WEBSITE

www.the-shipman-inquiry.org.uk/reports.asp – Shipman inquiry report

Possible effects of the case on single-handed/small practices
- NHS plan has given special consideration to small practices.
- Additional requirements of revalidation
- Imposition of additional contractual quality requirements?
- Forced into PMS?
- Repeated patient surveys show patient satisfaction is higher in single-handed practices than in group practices

- GPs can also be professionally and individually isolated in group practices

An editorial in the BJGP by Mike Pringle (May 2000) looked at the implications of the Shipman case:
- Profession should be defending single-handed practices
- Professional isolation should be the focus
- Restore patient confidence by professional development, revalidation and appraisal
- Death certification will be investigated by the inquiry, and it is likely that the second signatory on the cremation form will be a doctor who is appointed, trained and paid for the task, and who will make appropriate inquiries into circumstances surrounding the death
- Death rates, although crude, may become part of any clinical governance monitoring system
- Stricter control of use and storage of controlled drugs

PAPERS

1. Do single-handed practices offer poorer care? Cross sectional survey of processes and outcomes
(J. Hippisley-Cox, et al., BMJ 2001;323:320–3)

This study, published at the height of the Shipman fallout in general practice, looked at whether there are important differences in performance between group practices and single-handed GPs, and the extent to which any differences are explained by practice characteristics such as deprivation.

We already know that:
- 10% of all GPs are single-handed
- Single-handed general practitioners tend to work in areas of high deprivation and need
- Patients like single-handed practices because they are offer good communication, rapport and continuity
- Concerns have been expressed about professional isolation and quality of single-handers, on the basis of little evidence
- NHS Plan will have an impact on single-handed GPs, through either a negotiated change to the 'Red Book' or the new national contract into which all single-handed GPs will be transferred by 2004

The study
- Cross-sectional survey design
- 206 single-handed practices and 606 partnerships in the Trent region were analysed
- Routinely collected data on hospital admissions and target payments for single-handed practices and partnerships were studied, as well as confounding effects of general practice characteristics such as deprivation, percentage of Asian residents, percentage of Black residents, proportion of men over 75 years, proportion of women over 75 years, rurality, presence of a female general practitioner and vocational training status
- They found no difference in achievement of immunisation and cytology targets after adjustment for other general practice characteristics
- There were no significant differences for three types of hospital admission seen on initial observation after adjustment for other practice characteristics
- They concluded that there was, 'no evidence that single handed general practitioners are under performing clinically. Our results offer insight into the structural difference between the two types of practice and underline the importance of the effect of other practice characteristics on process and outcome measures'

Limitations
- Largely based on routinely collected data on hospital admissions and target payments (small selective part of general practice)
- They were unable to adjust for more subtle population characteristics, such as smoking habits
- Private referrals were excluded

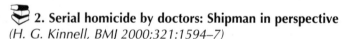 **2. Serial homicide by doctors: Shipman in perspective**
(H. G. Kinnell, BMJ 2000;321:1594–7)

A somewhat stranger perspective on the whole tragic affair appears in this next article.
The author, Kinnell who is a retired psychiatrist, discussed serial homicide in the medical profession.

Kinnell discussed that, as a profession, worldwide we account for more notorious murderers than any other profession. He gives a historical perspective over the decades of other such cases in rather too much detail (for a medical journal?).

Needless to say this will not be a 'Hot Topic', a snip-it from the article has been included. This is partly because I was surprised to find it was published at all, in such volatile times.

For those of you who are interested please feel free to read the full article, otherwise I have quoted a few points:

- The previous BMA chairman, among others, is on record as saying that Harold Shipman is unique, yet medicine has arguably thrown up more serial killers than all the other professions put together
- Nursing comes a close second
- Dentistry too has had its notorious characters
- Among veterinarians, homicide seems to be almost unknown
- The medical profession seems to attract some people with a pathological interest in the power of life and death
- Doctors have been responsible for killing not only patients and strangers but members of their own family
- The political killers par excellence were the Nazi doctors and the Japanese doctors engaged in biological warfare

CHAPTER 13: MEDICINE AND THE INTERNET

Typing the word 'health' into a well-known search engine will throw up almost 54 million relevant websites!

Increasingly, patients are using the Internet to search for detailed information about their medical condition; they can obtain a second opinion from a 'cyberdoc' and can also check with various patient support groups about their best treatment options. The knowledge gained can then be used to challenge their doctor during subsequent consultations, which may then affect the doctor–patient relationship.

What makes the Internet attractive?
Doctors and other healthcare professionals want information as part of their everyday work. The Internet accelerates and broadens such provision. Patients often want more information and they can search for remedies on the Internet.

It has been estimated that more than 25 million people use the Internet to search for health information. Medical information is thought to be one of the most retrieved types of information on the web. More Internet users have sought medical information on the web than have shopped online, looked up share prices or checked sports scores (*BMJ 2002;324:567*)! Recent surveys have shown that 40–54% of patients access medical information via the Internet and that this information affects their choice of treatment.

Through the Internet, patients not only have access to almost as much information as clinicians, but they are also starting to provide advice to other patients through websites that they host and manage. Even children can provide information to their peers, their parents and clinicians.

Is there any regulation of the information available on the Internet?
A major concern is the reliability of the information accessed, opinions offered, claims made and materials supplied by the Internet. The NHS Plan does set out its intention for patients to have 'greater access to authoritative information about how they can care for themselves', which includes the quality of information of governmental related websites. In addition, the European Commission is aiming to publish a code of good practice for health websites. This is going to contain a set of criteria for quality, and is part of a wider programme to clarify the legal aspects of online information and promote best practice.

Along with the rapid growth of healthcare websites came a number of initiatives, both academic and commercial, that generated criteria by which to ensure or judge the quality of websites offering health information. Some of these rating instruments took the form of logos resembling 'awards' or 'seals of approval' and appeared prominently on some websites. A recent paper reviewed the instruments used to assess the quality of information available on the Internet (*BMJ 2002;324:569–73*). This is interesting because it found that, although 51 rating instruments had been developed in the past 5 years, only five actually provided some information by which they could be evaluated! It also showed that many incompletely developed rating instruments continue to appear on websites providing health information, even when the organisations that gave rise to them no longer exist.

However, the exact purpose of controlling the quality of information on the Internet remains unclear and debatable. Health information in other media has received nowhere near the amount of attention, even though the public is exposed to misleading and inaccurate information from a variety of sources (TV, radio, magazines, etc.).

What is the Health on the Net Foundation?
Health on the Net Foundation (see website) is an international, non-profit-making organisation based in Geneva. It provides a database of evaluated health materials, and also promotes the use of the HON code as a self-governance initiative to help unify the quality of medical and health information available. Users of website health information displaying the HON logo can be assured that the material has been developed in accordance with these guidelines. This is the oldest, and probably best known, quality label and is currently used by over 3,000 websites.

What problems may the Internet pose to healthcare professionals?
The biggest problem with obtaining health information from the Internet is that it is not always easy to decide what is reliable. As an example, one website has apparently reported the mortality from a certain type of bone cancer as 5%, while in reality it is closer to 75%! Only about half of medical sites are estimated to have their content reviewed by doctors. In addition, many sites are American where the investigations and treatments for diseases are very different to those in UK, which often adds confusion to patients.

Although data are not yet available, it is evident that clinicians can find themselves upstaged by and ill prepared to cope with patients who bring along information downloaded from the Internet.

More resources are needed to study the implications of the Internet for the role of patients and clinicians and also to ensure that the clinician–patient relationship is strengthened rather than undermined.

What is the NHS net?
All GP practices should now be connected to the NHS net. It has been proposed that Networked Electronic Health Records will be developed which will be available to all healthcare professionals 24 hours a day. All appointments and laboratory requests will be booked via the NHS net and community prescribing will also go electronic, with pharmacists accepting prescriptions via the net. An electronic library with health information for both the public and professionals will be available on the NHS net.

The main concern of all this is confidentiality. It is, however, likely to take far longer to be running smoothly than the time proposed by the Government!

What are the problems with e-mail consultations?
The GPs' Committee has recently produced a guide to online consulting ('Consulting in the Modern World'). This warns practices that electronic communications systems could seriously damage the consultation process, may increase workload and also leave GPs open to legal action. It states that e-mail exchanges are best suited to arranging repeat prescriptions or booking appointments. In addition, GPs are warned to always be wary of responding to patients who are abroad as this could potentially cause conflicts between overseas regulatory bodies and the General Medical Council.

The GMC recently found two doctors guilty of serious professional misconduct through their provision of services over the Internet. The first involved a private doctor who recommended weekly testosterone injections through an e-mail consultation without seeing the patient or any medical records.

The GMC's 'Good Medical Practice' clearly states that doctors who provide advice to patients who are not registered with them should endeavour to provide the patient's GP with any information necessary for the continuing care of that patient. Doctors who do not tell the patient's GP, before or after providing treatment, will be responsible for providing or arranging all necessary aftercare until another doctor agrees to take over.

Are there any problems with writing for medical websites?
Doctors are less likely to face criticism for placing medical information on a website, providing it does not refer to specific cases. It is recommended that a statement should be added stating that the medical advice provided is as accurate as possible, but should not be used as a substitute for advice patients can obtain from their own doctors.

Technology is increasingly becoming integrated into modern clinical practice, so it is important therefore that all users are fully aware of any of its potential pitfalls.

 USEFUL WEBSITE

www.hon.ch/ – Health on the Net Foundation

📝 **SUMMARY POINTS ON MEDICINE AND THE INTERNET**

❖ Medical information is very commonly searched for over the Internet
❖ Downloaded information is often very challenging to doctors
❖ Information is often inaccurate
❖ HON code is a self-governance initiative for health sites
❖ Confidentiality is still a concern
❖ e-mail consultations are not encouraged by the GPs Committee

---

CHAPTER 14: ALTERNATIVE MEDICINE

Many more people are using alternative and complementary medicine; up to 10% of NHS physiotherapists currently use acupuncture. It has been estimated that alternative medicine is used by about 30% of the population in the UK, which is actually much less than in Germany and the USA. Currently, it is legal for anyone in the UK to practise alternative medicine without any training (except chiropractic and osteopathy).

The House of Lords Select Committee on Science and Technology have recommended that in the interests of public safety the complementary medicine sector should be properly regulated and more research carried out into its effectiveness (*BMJ 2000;321:1365*). Many complementary practitioners claim that their treatments are more cost-effective and safer than conventional medicine; however, the evidence for this is still very scanty and weak.

Why is alternative medicine so popular?
Positive motivations:
- Perceived effectiveness and safety
- Control over treatment
- 'High touch, low tech'
- Pleasant therapeutic experience
- Affluence
- Gives support in chronic illness – and optimism to patients

Negative motivations:
- Dissatisfaction with (some aspect of) conventional care
- Poor doctor–patient relationship
- Insufficient time with doctor
- Long waiting lists
- Desperation

Why are herbal remedies so popular?
- False belief that natural plant products are harmless
- Conventional treatments are perceived as being ineffective or dangerous
- Trend towards ecological 'natural' living

With rationing looming in virtually all healthcare systems, the question of whether herbal medicines can save money is important. Not all herbal medicines are cheap. A standard daily dose of St John's wort, for instance, will cost more than that of a tricyclic antidepressant.

What have been some of the problems with herbal remedies?
There is a huge variation in the quality of different herbal medicinal preparations. Herbal remedies are sold as food supplements in the UK and so evade any regulation of their quality and safety.

Practitioners of traditional Chinese medicine have agreed to cooperate with the Department of Health to improve the safety of traditional medicines, after concerns that they may contain potentially toxic or carcinogenic ingredients. Over 1 million people in the United Kingdom use traditional Chinese medicines every year.

The Committee on Safety of Medicines have found banned substances such as mercury and arsenic in traditional Chinese medicines sold in the United Kingdom, despite previous warnings. Some medicines also contained steroids, even though there was no declaration on the label. Banned products containing the herb aristolochia, which has been associated with two cases of kidney disease in the UK, are also still being offered for sale.

What is St John's wort?
St John's wort (*Hypericum perforatum*) is an increasingly popular choice in the treatment of depression, and there is plenty of evidence which shows that hypericum is as effective as imipramine in the treatment of mild to moderate depression (*BMJ 2000;321:536–9*). In addition, the side-effects are less when compared with imipramine, but as yet there have been no randomised controlled trials comparing SSRIs with St John's wort. The use of St John's wort is more limited than initially thought as it is a liver inducer and therefore reduces levels of digoxin, carbamazepine, warfarin and the oral contraceptive pill. It has numerous interactions with other drugs, which patients should be warned of before starting it.

However, a randomised controlled trial involving 200 adults has actually shown St John's wort is ineffective against major depression (*JAMA 2001;285:1978–86*). This obviously highlights the need for further RCTs before St John's wort can confidently be recommended for patients with depression.

What is ginkgo biloba?
The published evidence suggests that ginkgo is of questionable use for memory loss and tinitis but has some effect on both dementia and intermittent claudication (*Ann Int Med 2002;136(1):42–53*). It is, however, also a potent inhibitor of platelet-activating factor, so

increasing the risk of intracerebral haemorrhage in those people taking aspirin and warfarin.

Is there any good evidence available to support homoeopathy?
There is currently insufficient evidence that homoeopathy is clearly efficacious for any single clinical condition. For many of the conditions treated in homoeopathic practice, such as depression, fatigue and eczema, randomised trials have not been undertaken. In addition, few of the existing studies of homoeopathy have been independently replicated. However, many people have reported numerous benefits from homoeopathy.

A recent study carried out by the NHS Centre for Reviews and Dissemination (based at York University) reviewed data from over 200 randomised clinical trials of homoeopathy in a variety of conditions. It concluded that not only was there little evidence to support the efficacy of homoeopathy, but the data that did exist were of poor quality and came from often deeply flawed trials. Common problems included underpowered studies, failure to analyse by intention to treat and failure to use allocation concealment. Some of the published systematic reviews are criticised for pooling clinically heterogeneous data.

Despite many longstanding doubts, homoeopathic remedies remain widely used in the NHS.

There are five homoeopathic hospitals and it has been estimated that 20% of GP practices provide access to homoeopathy (*BMJ 2002;324:565*). A BBC telephone survey in 1999 suggested that 470,000 people take homoeopathic remedies in the United Kingdom each year.

What are the problems with RCTs of homoeopathic treatments?
Most trials of homoeopathic medicines do not individualise treatment, which is obviously the hallmark of homoeopathic practice. Moreover, randomisation and blinding of participants substantially distorts the context of homoeopathic prescribing, potentially weakening its effect. There is much debate that a lack of supporting evidence does not mean these treatments are ineffective.

What are the implications to the doctor of patients receiving alternative therapy?
- Doctor may feel threatened or angry
- May need to review doctor–patient relationship
- May need to review consultation times and techniques

- Lack of information about patient's treatment from alternative practitioner
- Need to consider drug interactions with conventional medicine
- May even lead to misdiagnosis or mistreatment of patient

The Medicines Control Agency has launched the website 'Herbal Safety News', which provides a convenient reference source by bringing together the latest issues about complementary medicine. This website also includes information on possible interactions with herbal remedies.

It is likely that complementary therapies will become more available on the NHS as further studies are undertaken and the therapies evaluated properly.

 USEFUL WEBSITES

www.parliament.uk - full report from House of Lords select committee
www.medical-acupuncture.co.uk - British Medical Acupuncture Society
www.acupuncture.org.uk - British Acupuncture Council
www.bsmdh.org - British Society of Medical and Dental Hypnosis
www.osteopathy.org.uk - Osteopathic Information Service
www.mca.gov.uk/ourwork/licensingmeds/herbalmeds/herbalsafety.htm
– Medicines Control Agency website
www.york.ac.uk/inst/crd – homoeopathy report

SUMMARY POINTS FOR ALTERNATIVE MEDICINE

- ❖ 30% of UK population use alternative medicine
- ❖ Lack of good supportive RCTs
- ❖ Contents of herbal remedies vary widely
- ❖ Need to consider implications on doctor/patient relationship

---

CHAPTER 15: MEDICOLEGAL ISSUES AND GUIDELINES

GENERAL MEDICAL COUNCIL

The General Medical Council (GMC) was established in 1858, and licenses doctors to practise in the UK under the provisions of the Medical Act 1983.

The GMC's core functions are:
- Maintaining an up-to-date register of qualified doctors
- Fostering good medical practice
- Promoting high standards of medical education
- Protecting the public from doctors whose fitness to practise is in doubt.

The GMC produces a number of booklets setting out the standards which the Council expects individual doctors to follow. Of particular interest and relevance to general practice (and especially the MRCGP) are:
- Good Medical Practice
- Confidentiality
- Consent: the ethical and legal issues

What is 'Good Medical Practice'?
In 1995 the GMC published a comprehensive statement (or code) setting out the principles of Good Medical Practice, at the core of which it listed the Duties of a Doctor – which should be read carefully, for the exam as well as for good clinical practice! Good Medical Practice now sets the framework of professional standards within which doctors must practise in this country. Doctors accepting GMC registration are therefore making a commitment to their patients and to their profession to practise accordingly.

The GMC has recently set out a proposed 3rd edition of 'Good Medical Practice' with the intention of preparing doctors for revalidation checks.

What are the 'Duties of a Doctor'?
Doctors as a profession have a duty to maintain a good standard of practice and care and also show respect for human life. The guidelines emphasise what is expected of a doctor in practice today; they state a doctor must, among other things:
- Make the patients their first concern

- Treat patients politely and considerately and respect their dignity and privacy
- Listen to patients and respect their views
- Give patients information in a way they can understand
- Respect the rights of patients to be fully involved in decisions about their care
- Keep their professional knowledge and skills up to date
- Recognise the limits of their professional competence
- Be honest and trustworthy
- Respect and protect confidential information
- Make sure their personal beliefs do not prejudice their patient's care
- Act quickly to protect patients from risk if they have good reason to believe himself or herself or a colleague may not be fit to practise
- Avoid abusing their position as a doctor
- Work with colleagues in the ways that best serve patients' interests

In all these matters, doctors must never discriminate unfairly against their patients or colleagues and they must always be prepared to justify their actions to them.

 USEFUL WEBSITE
www.gmc-uk.org – General Medical Council

 SUMMARY POINTS FOR GENERAL MEDICAL COUNCIL

- ❖ GMC gives doctors licences to practise
- ❖ 'Good Medical Practice' provides framework of professional standards
- ❖ 'Duties of a Doctor' are very important

COMPLAINTS

Complaints are a fact of life; the best approach is to manage them quickly and efficiently. Failure to satisfy a complainant at an early stage often results in entrenchment of positions, and ultimately demands a much greater investment of time in resolving the conflict. Complaints in general practice are increasing; and have been estimated to increase threefold over the past 10 years. It is difficult to obtain exact figures because the majority of complaints are dealt with 'in-house' so are only recorded in the practice records.

The GMC guidance regarding complaints states that: 'Patients who complain about the care or treatment they have received have a right to expect a prompt, open, constructive and honest response. This will include an explanation of what has happened, and where appropriate, an apology. You must not allow a patient's complaint to prejudice the care or treatment you provide or arrange for that patient.'

What are common complaints in primary care?
The majority of complaints in primary care are dealt with promptly and efficiently, with minimal repercussions.

Common complaints include:
* Complications of requests for visits
* Prescribing errors
* Delay or missed diagnosis
* Delay in referral
* Failure to explain investigation or treatment plans
* Breach of confidentiality
* Failure to seek consent
* Unacceptable attitude on the part of professionals

What is the complaints procedure?
The new NHS patient complaints procedures were introduced in April 1996 and have certain key objectives:
* Ease of access for patients and complainants
* A thorough and local resolution phase
* Fairness for both complainants and staff
* Investigation of complaints entirely separately from any subsequent disciplinary proceedings

The process for dealing with complaints is relatively simple:
- The first stage is local resolution, to resolve the issue within the practice
- The second stage is an independent review
- The third stage is review by the Health Service Commissioner (Ombudsman) if requested by either the complainant or the doctor

How are complaints dealt with in primary care?

All GPs are now required under the terms of service to operate a practice-based complaints procedure. A complaints manager should be appointed within each practice (usually the practice manager). The in-house procedure must be:
- Practice-owned and supported by all staff
- Adequately publicised with detailed written information

When are complaints dealt with?

All complaints must:
- Be dealt with at the time, if a verbal complaint
- Be acknowledged within 2 working days
- Have a full written response and explanation within 10 working days

Complainants should always be invited to discuss the matter in an attempt to resolve it at an early stage.

 USEFUL WEBSITE
www.doh.gov.uk/NHScomplaintsreform

SUMMARY POINTS FOR COMPLAINTS

- ❖ Complaints are common
- ❖ They should be resolved promptly
- ❖ Complaints procedure is simple to follow
- ❖ Most complaints are dealt with 'in-house'

CONFIDENTIALITY

Confidentiality is both a legal and ethical principle and is the cornerstone of medical practice. Confidentiality is, in theory, a very straightforward issue; however, translating it into practice often proves problematic. Confidentiality issues are far the commonest reason for doctors to contact medicolegal advisers for independent expert advice.

Practitioners have a professional obligation to protect confidentiality and the presumption should always be made that all information is confidential. It is only under extreme circumstances (e.g. legal or moral duty) that confidentiality can be breached.

When can doctors disclose information without consent?
This question often crops up in the oral examination.

Disclosure of personal information without consent, or against a patient's wishes, should only occur in the most exceptional circumstances; it may be justified when failure to do so may expose the patient or others to a risk of death or serious harm. Consent should be sought prior to disclosure where third parties are exposed to a risk so serious that it outweighs the patient's privacy interest. However, if this is not practicable, the information should be disclosed promptly to an appropriate person or authority.

This can occur in the following circumstances:
* Patient with an illness that is placing others at substantial risk (e.g. HIV infection)
* Patients continuing to drive against medical advice (see later)
* Where disclosure may assist in prevention, detection or prosecution of a serious crime
* Death certificates
* Statutory requirement (e.g. notification of communicable diseases)
* Following an order by a judge or presiding officer of a court
* When the patient is unable to give consent and it is in the patient's best interests (e.g. to relatives)

The GMC clearly states: 'Doctors who decide to disclose confidential information must be prepared to explain and justify their decision to the patient, if appropriate, and to the GMC and the courts, if called on to do so.'

Under which circumstances can doctors disclose information to the DVLA?

The Driver and Vehicle Licencing Agency (DVLA) is legally responsible for deciding if a person if medically unfit to drive, and patients have a legal duty to inform the DVLA of any medical condition that affects their ability to drive. The patient's doctor must make sure the patient understands that their medical condition may impair their ability to drive.

If patients are incapable of understanding the advice (e.g. dementia) the DVLA must be informed immediately.

If a patient refuses to inform the DVLA the doctor should make every reasonable effort to persuade the person to stop driving, which may even include telling the next of kin. If the patient cannot be persuaded to stop driving the doctor should then disclose the relevant medical information immediately, in confidence, to the medical advisor of the DVLA. Before giving the information to the DVLA, the patient should be informed of the doctor's decision to do so. Once the DVLA has been informed, a letter should be written to the patient confirming that the disclosure has been made.

What is the Data Protection Act 1998?

This came into force in March 2000 and has significant implications to all healthcare professionals, and it is important to be aware of the main provisions of this Act.

The Act means that:
- Patients are entitled to see all manual and computer medical records
- All health records are now disclosable (previous deadline of 1 November 1991 under the Access to Health Records Act no longer applies)
- Application to do this should be made by written request
- Applicants can inspect his/her own record or request a readable copy
- The data must be disclosed within 40 days of receipt of the request
- A data controller can exclude information which breaches the confidentiality of, or relates to, a third party who has not consented to disclosure
- Disclosure may be withheld if it would be likely to 'cause serious

harm to the physical or mental health or condition of the subject or any other person'.

⬜ SUMMARY POINTS FOR CONFIDENTIALITY

❖ Confidentiality must always be respected
❖ Should only be breached in extreme circumstances
❖ Data Protection Act has many implications

CONSENT

Consent is a fundamental principle of medical law. Most doctors are aware of the importance of obtaining consent from their patients, but many are uncertain about what consent actually means and also fear that their instincts about what is right may not be enough to protect them from a legal challenge.

Case law on consent has evolved significantly over the past decade and the Department of Health has recently published an important and exceptionally useful guide on English law concerning consent for examination or treatment (see website).

The GMC has issued guidance on seeking patients' consent which all registered practitioners in the UK should be aware of when counselling patients. For consent to be valid, three conditions must be satisfied. First, the patient must be competent. Second, he or she must have sufficient information to make an informed choice and lastly, the consent must be given voluntarily.

Doctors must respect the right of their patients to be fully involved in decisions about their care. Wherever possible, they must be satisfied, before providing treatment or investigating a patient's condition, that: the patient has understood what is proposed and why; any significant risks or side-effects associated with it; and has given consent.

Any competent adult has the right to give or withhold consent to examination, investigation or treatment. Consent may be implied, oral or written. Consent should be based on information patients want to know and ought to know about their condition and treatment. This information should include:
- Details of the diagnosis and prognosis
- Results of undergoing treatment or refusing treatment
- Risks of uncertainties of treatment
- Possible complications of treatment

Patients may change their mind and withdraw their consent at any time. It should also be noted that no person can give consent for another adult; this is often not realised by many healthcare professionals.

What is meant by a 'competent adult'?

A competent adult must be able to:

- Understand the nature and purpose of treatment
- Understand the benefits, risks and alternatives
- Understand the consequences of refusal
- Retain the information long enough to make an effective decision
- Make a free choice

Any mentally competent adult can refuse treatment for any reason (rational or irrational) or for no reason at all, even if doing so may result in his or her own death. In addition, a competent pregnant woman may refuse any treatment, even if it would be detrimental to the fetus.

What about consent for incompetent adults?

For an incompetent adult, the doctor should:

- Act in the patient's best interests
- Attempt to ascertain the patient's past wishes
- Review the medical and social knowledge of the patient's background, culture and religion
- Consult relatives, friends and carers
- Consider the option which least restricts the patient's future choices

What is the Human Rights Act?

A recent important development is the Human Rights Act 1998 which came into force in October 2000. It is a momentous development in the constitutional history of the UK, and doctors need to take it seriously.

Issues about consent and confidentiality are likely to be affected. Teenagers should get greater autonomy in making decisions about whether to accept or refuse treatment. Parents of children who do not want certain types of treatment on religious or other grounds should have more power to determine what happens to their infant children. The Act should give patients greater opportunities to obtain information.

Patients will be able to challenge lengthy delays in treatment on the NHS. Elderly people can no longer be subjected to arbitrary 'do not resuscitate' orders in hospital or to degrading treatment in nursing homes. Drug companies too will be vigilant in protecting their rights to property and freedom of speech: bans on direct-to-consumer advertising will almost certainly be challenged. Health professionals will also be able to claim protection under the Act. Junior doctors forced to work long shifts may claim the benefit of Article 4,

Can children give their own consent?

Young people aged 16 and 17 are presumed to have the competence to give consent for themselves. The Fraser (previously Gillick) ruling clarifies the legal position of treating children under 16 years of age without parental consent – children under 16 years may give their consent if they are mature enough to understand the nature, purpose and possible consequences, risks and benefits of their decision and are not making the decision under duress.

Ideally, the parents will be involved. If a competent child consents to treatment, a parent cannot override that consent. Legally, a parent can consent if a competent child refuses, but it is likely that taking such a serious step will be rare.

What about consent for children who lack capacity to consent?

Consent can be given on a child's behalf by any one person with parental responsibility or by the court. The Children's Act 1989 describes who may have parental responsibility. These people include:

- The child's parents if they are married to each other at the time of conception or birth
- The child's mother (but not father) if they were not so married, unless the father has acquired parental responsibility via a court order or a parental responsibility order or the couple subsequently marry
- The child's legally appointed guardian
- A person in whose favour the court has made a residence order
- A local authority designated in a care order of the child

Failure to obtain a suitable consent may open a doctor to a GMC complaint, a civil claim or even criminal charges.

 USEFUL WEBSITES

www.dvla.gov.uk – Medical standard of fitness to drive
www.gmc-uk.org – GMC website
www.doh.gov.uk/consent – Reference Guide to Consent for Examination or Treatment, Department of Health

---

SUMMARY POINTS FOR CONSENT

- ❖ Valid consent must always be obtained
- ❖ Competent adults can change their mind about consent
- ❖ Children are able to give their consent
- ❖ The Human Rights Act may affect consent and confidentiality issues

---

MEDICAL NEGLIGENCE

It is widely known that the tide of medical litigation continues to rise. The Medical Defence Union's (MDU's) recent figures indicate an annual increase in litigation of 15%.

To pursue a medical negligence claim a patient has to prove, on the balance of probability (i.e. meaning more likely than not), three things:
* The doctor owed a duty of care
* There was a breach of that duty
* Harm followed as a result

What is the Bolam standard?
Independent medical doctors use the 'Bolam' standard to assess the doctor's clinical management. This means that the doctor has acted in a way that would be in agreement with a responsible body of doctors practising in the same field, and does not have to be the standard of the majority.

The Bolam test is another tenet of medical law which may be reviewed. This test defines the standard of care which doctors must meet, if they are not to be negligent. Patients' lawyers are keen to argue that it should not be a sufficient defence to a medical accident (especially when life is lost) to say that other responsible professionals would have done the same thing.

However, in cases such as Bolitho and Pearce, the courts have said they will depart from the professional practice approach if they see fit, the ultimate tests being what the court itself thinks was a reasonable amount of information to give the patient. This obviously leaves an element of doubt, as doctors cannot obviously guess what the courts are going to say.

What is the commonest reason for a medical negligence claim?
A recent review of all claims involving GPs by the MDU found that almost half (45.5%) of all settled claims were related to a delay in a patient's diagnosis. A delay in diagnosis per se is not necessarily negligent, provided that the clinical management can be shown to be competent and reasonable.

However, the main problems are usually:
- Failure to examine properly
- Inadequate follow-up arrangements
- Lack of appropriate investigations
- Reports misfiled in the notes
- Poor communication with colleagues and patients
- Poor medical record keeping

The increase in litigation in the UK does not reflect changing standards of clinical practice, which remains very high, but rather an increase in patient's expectations and their tendency to resort to litigation. The majority of claims do not go beyond disclosure of medical records, and less than 5% get as far as a court hearing.

SUMMARY POINTS FOR NEGLIGENCE

❖ Bolam standard often still used
❖ Most claims are due to delayed diagnosis
❖ Harm must result for a negligence claim

GUIDELINES

Clinical guidelines have increasingly become a familiar part of clinical practice. They have been defined as 'systematically developed statements to assist practitioner and patient decisions about appropriate health care for specific clinical circumstances.' The BMJ has published a series of four articles on issues in the development and use of clinical guidelines which are still useful to read (*BMJ 1999;318:527–30, 593–6, 661–4, 728–30*). Clinical guidelines are only one option for improving the quality of care. They do, however, have both potential risks and harms.

Guidelines should be practical, realistic and based on valid up-to-date evidence. They should also be easily accessible to practitioners, and should ideally be adapted to suit the local target population. They should always be practical and take into consideration the available resources needed for them to be successfully implemented. A poor example of this are the BTS guidelines for COAD where routine spirometry is recommended.

The successful introduction of guidelines is dependent on many factors, including their clinical context and the methods used for developing, disseminating and implementing them. One survey revealed that although 45% of GPs have seen the National Osteoporosis Guidelines, only 22% had ever used them in their clinical practice (*Osteoporos Rev 1999;7.2:1–3*). This reflects the major difference between dissemination and implementation of guideline recommendation.

What are NICE guidelines?
The National Institute for Clinical Excellence was introduced to provide national guidance, especially on interventions of uncertain value, and also to provide clinical guidelines and clinical audit packages. NICE therefore has an important role in providing the NHS with consistent and timely guidance on what is best for our patients. A recent 'Education and Debate' article in the BMJ considers what NICE needs to succeed (*BMJ 2002;324:842–5*). This article states that NICE can only fulfil its promise if its guidance is implemented by a health service that supports the changes NICE promotes – which is not the case currently.

There has been no published information to date on the implementation by the NHS of NICE's guidance, so it is still not possible to conclude how successful (or unsuccessful) NICE has been in the overall cost-effectiveness and appropriateness of the interventions it discusses.

What are the problems with NICE?
The Consumer's Association has strongly criticised the work of NICE to a House of Commons inquiry. It said they had found 'serious flaws' in all nine of the documents it had reviewed.

The analysis was carried out by the Drug and Therapeutics Bulletin, which found the various guidelines, including those for influenza, type 2 diabetes, motor neurone disease and obesity, unreliable. In some cases there were weaknesses in the way evidence about treatments had been collated, interpreted and extrapolated. In others, NICE had looked at treatments in isolation to alternative options or previous advice.

The deputy editor of the Drug and Therapeutics Bulletin said, 'The NICE guidance issued so far appears to raise as many problems as it seeks to solve'.

Another concern is that because all health authorities (or PCTs) are now compelled to implement NICE recommendations, the use of other effective treatments that had not yet been reviewed by the body would be cut to contain costs. The NHS at a local level will probably have to dent other services' funding in order to fund NICE's recommendations. This will apply both to specific interventions for which there is no NICE guidance and to whole services for which guidance is never likely (such as those for people with learning disabilities).

What are the benefits of guidelines?
- Improve consistency of care
- Empower patients to make more informed choices
- Improve quality of clinical decisions
- Can improve efficacy (save money)
- Reduce inappropriate practice

What are the problems with guidelines?
- Recommendations may be wrong
- May be biased
- May be inflexible and not relate to individual patient
- Evidence used to write the guidelines is not always from appropriate, well-designed studies
- Can be time-consuming to use
- Need to be updated regularly
- Do not address all the uncertainties of clinical practice

What is the role of guidelines in court?
Guidelines could be introduced to a court by an expert witness as evidence of accepted and customary standards of care, but they cannot be introduced as a substitute for expert testimony. Courts are unlikely to adopt standards of care advocated in clinical guidelines as legal 'gold standards' because the mere fact that a guideline exists does not of itself establish that compliance with it is reasonable in the circumstances, or that non-compliance is negligent.

How easy is it to comply with guidelines?
A study published in the BJGP has highlighted that it is not always easy to comply with guidelines, even if they are well-accepted guidelines. It showed that GPs targeted their actions regarding treatment for their patients with hypertension at a diastolic BP of 100 mmHg rather than the recommended guideline of 90 mmHg, despite being aware of the guidelines (*BJGP 2001;51:9–14*).

Conversely, an evaluation of clinical guidelines on the management of infertile couples has demonstrated that guidelines can lead to an improvement in GPs' performance (*BMJ 2001;322:1282–4*).

Difficulties with always adhering to guidelines can be appreciated when considering the following clinical scenario:
A 68-year-old patient with type 2 diabetes presents at the end of a busy Friday afternoon surgery with a sore throat. You notice her blood pressure has not been taken for the past 2 years. You take it and find her BP to be 146/92 mmHg! There are probably certain questions you might ask yourself when faced with a similar patient:
* What shall I tell the patient about their blood pressure?
* Is it likely that this patient's BP is consistently raised?
* Shall I arrange for her to have blood tests/ECG?
* Shall I start medication now with all its potential risks/side-effects?
* How will she react to taking another medication when she is already taking other regular medication?
* Will this patient realistically respond to advice re weight loss/lifestyle/smoking when she never has before?
* What is her compliance with medication really like?

Although you know the BHS guidelines it is not always that easy to stick to them!

Guidelines are essentially written for the management of patient populations rather than for individuals. They will not address all the uncertainties of current clinical practice and should be seen as only one strategy that can help improve the quality of care that patients receive. Although guidelines are meant to tackle variations in practice there is always a risk of standardising practice around the average, which is not necessarily always the best for every clinical situation (*BMJ 1993;43:146–51*).

SUMMARY POINTS FOR GUIDELINES

❖ Only one option for improving care
❖ Should ideally suit the local target population
❖ Numerous benefits and drawbacks
❖ Do not address all the uncertainties of clinical practice

CHAPTER 16: ADVANCE DIRECTIVES AND END-OF-LIFE DECISIONS

ADVANCE DIRECTIVES

Definition: **An advance directive gives patients the legal right to give or withhold consent to specific medical treatments in advance of becoming incompetent.**

(Advance Statements about Medical Treatment – Code of Practice Report of the British Medical Association, April 1995)

- From October 1999, people in England and Wales have been able to appoint a friend or relative to take health care decisions if they lose the ability to make their own decisions.
- This is termed a 'Continuing Power of Attorney' and would allow the named person, called the 'proxy decision maker' to make decisions regarding the health and welfare of that person.
- Competence is best confirmed by having a person's signature witnessed by 2 people one of whom should be a doctor capable of attesting to the person's state of mind.

Advance statements about medical treatment - Code of Practice Report of the British Medical Association, April 1995

Current legal position
- In 1997, the Government for England and Wales announced that it believed there to be a clear need for reform of the law to improve and clarify decision-making processes for people unable to make decisions for themselves, or people who cannot communicate their decisions.
- It based this view on the extensive work the English Law Commission had undertaken in the preceding six years.
- The Law Commission had investigated and proposed improvements to the law in this area, including a proposal to introduce legislation to put advance directives on a statutory footing. This was one of the issues on which the Government consulted in 1997.

The BMA's code of practice is a response to the House of Lords Select Committee on Medical Ethics, which in 1994 called for a Code of Practice on advance directives for health professionals.

- Published two years before the Government's consultation, it describes the common law and the BMA's views on advance decisions.

- Following its consultation, the Government in October 1999 published detailed proposals for law reform.
- The Lord Chancellor's Department stated its intention to legislate to give statutory recognition to the definitions of capacity and best interests, and to clarify the basis on which decisions may be made on behalf of incapacitated adults.
- It also proposed to make provision for the appointment of proxies entitled to take medical treatment decisions.
- Advance directives, however, are not part of the legislative plans. Instead, the Government published clear statements of the present legal position:

"The current law and medical practice is as follows. It is a general principle of law and medical practice that all adults have the right to consent to or refuse medical treatment. Advance statements are a means for patients to exercise that right by anticipating a time when they may lose the capacity to make or communicate a decision.

"Adults with capacity have the right to refuse or withdraw their consent to medical treatment. We do not accept that the decision has either to be reasonable or has to be justified to anyone apart from the individual who is making the decision. It follows that the Government respects the right of people with capacity to be able to define, in advance, which medical procedures they will and will not consent to at a time when that individual has become incapable of making or communicating that decision."

BMA Summary
- Although not binding on health professionals, advance statements deserve thorough consideration and respect.
- Where valid and applicable, advance directives (refusals) must be followed.

Health professionals consulted by people wishing to formulate an advance statement or directive should take all reasonable steps to provide accurate factual information about the treatment options and their implications.
- Where an unknown and incapacitated patient presents for treatment some checks should be made concerning the validity of any directive refusing life-prolonging treatment. In all cases, it is vital to check that the statement or refusal presented is that of the patient being treated and has not been withdrawn.

- If the situation is not identical to that described in the advance statement or refusal, treatment providers may still be guided by the general spirit of the statement if this is evident. It is advisable to contact any person nominated by the patient as well as the GP to clarify the patient's wishes. If there is doubt as to what the patient intended, the law requires the exercise of a best interests judgement.
- If an incapacitated person is known to have had sustained and informed objections to all or some treatment, even though these have not been formally recorded, health professionals may not be justified in proceeding. This applies even in an emergency.
- If witnessed and made at a time when the patient was competent and informed, such objections may constitute an oral advance directive. Health professionals will need to consider how much evidence is available about the patient's decisions and how convincing it seems. All members of the health care team can make a useful contribution to this process.
- In the absence of any indication of the patient's wishes, there is a common law duty to give appropriate treatment to incapacitated patients when the treatment is clearly in their best interests.

BMA Checklist for Writing an Advance Statement

In drawing up an advance statement you must ensure, as a minimum, that the following information is included:

- Full name
- Address
- Name and address of general practitioner
- Whether advice was sought from health professionals
- Signature
- Date drafted and reviewed
- Witness signature
- A clear statement of your wishes, either general or specific
- The name, address and telephone number of your nominated person, if you have one

Other sources:
Lord Chancellor's Department. 'Making decisions' The Government's proposals for making decisions on behalf of mentally incapacitated adults. London: HMSO, October 1999.

END-OF-LIFE DECISIONS

- The Dutch have done most of the work in this field
- Doctors make end-of-life decisions in about 40% of deaths
- 75% involve withdrawal or withholding treatment
- Doses of opiates likely to end life in 25% of cases

📖 **Guidelines by BMA 1999 – Withholding and withdrawing life-prolonging treatment**

The key principles are:
- Life cannot be preserved at all costs – treatment must be more of a benefit than a burden
- Artificial nutrition and hydration constitutes medical treatment
- Competent patients have the legal right to refuse treatment
- Where patients cannot express their view, doctors must take account of previously expressed wishes, the likelihood of any improvement and the likelihood of the patient experiencing severe pain or suffering
- Close cooperation with the other professionals in the team is vital in decision-making
- All proposals to withdraw or withhold artificial nutrition and hydration should be formally reviewed by a senior clinician who is not part of the team

📖 **General Medical Council. Withholding and withdrawing life-prolonging treatments: good practice in decision-making. London: GMC, 2002.**

- Following the BMA guidelines above, the GMC laid out their directives in 2002
- New guidelines on end-of-life decisions
- The guidelines were prompted by concerns about the withdrawal of treatment from elderly patients and by inappropriate 'do not attempt resuscitation' orders
- Sets out the legal and ethical framework for taking decisions
- The guidelines remind doctors that patients who are mentally competent have a legal right to refuse treatment even if the outcome is certain death
- Patients must not be assumed to lack mental capacity just because their decision might seem irrational or seems to doctors not to be in their best interests

- Doctors with a conscientious objection to a decision not to start or continue with life-prolonging treatment may withdraw from the patient's care, but must hand the care over without delay to another suitably qualified colleague so that patient care does not suffer
- Guidance takes account of differences among the UK jurisdictions of England and Wales, Scotland, and Northern Ireland
- In Scotland, proxy decision-makers may be appointed for patients without the capacity to decide for themselves
- In England and Wales, doctors must take decisions for patients who are mentally incompetent, acting in the patient's best interests and weighing up the benefits and burdens of the proposed treatment
- Doctors are reminded that they must not allow factors such as the patient's age, disability or lifestyle to prejudice the choice of treatment

'Doctrine of Double Effect'

States that if measures taken to relieve physical or mental suffering cause the death of a patient, then it is morally and legally acceptable provided the doctor's intent is to relieve distress and not to kill the patient.

In general, the doctor must make a full assessment of the patient's condition, consult with relatives, carers and other healthcare professions involved in the case, and ask for a second medical opinion either from a specialist or from another GP.

PAPERS

1. Physician assisted suicide, euthanasia or withdrawal of treatment – Editorial

(L. R. Churchill and N. M. King, BMJ 1997;315:137–8)

The Oregon Death with Dignity Act was passed in 1994. It allows primary care physicians to comply with a request for lethal drugs from a competent patient with less than 6 months to live.

Holland has become the testing ground for the world, as although assisting with requested euthanasia remains a criminal act, Dutch doctors have not been prosecuted when they follow strict guidelines.

2. Why active euthanasia and physician assisted suicide should be legalised
(L. Doyal and L. Doyal, BMJ 2001;323:1079–80)

- Focused around the Dianne Pretty trial (suffered from motor neurone disease (MND)); the Court denied her the request of allowing her husband to aid her in ending her life
- A professor in ethics at Barts wrote this editorial
- Argued that moral and legal status of not saving a life through failing to treat can be the same as actively taking that life
- Provided the circumstances are clinically warranted, doctors should be able to withdraw life-sustaining treatment when they intend to accelerate death as well as to relieve suffering

Editorials in BMJ

Do not resuscitate (DNR) decisions
In 2000, the British Medical Association, the Resuscitation Council (UK) and the Royal College of Nursing jointly said that do not resuscitate orders could be considered only after discussion with the patient or others close to the patient. Age Concern's dossier is evidence that this guideline is being flouted (they have 50 case histories of inappropriate DNR decisions).

Resuscitation after a cardiopulmonary arrest is effective in only one in five patients. Although it may be appropriate to withhold resuscitation when a patient is dying, failure to involve patients in decisions on DNR orders negates their autonomy. It is most unfair for age to be used as a criterion for withholding cardiopulmonary resuscitation. Most patients and relatives consider that discussions about death and DNR orders are essential aspects of planning their care. It is doctors and nurses who find such discussions painful.

Do not resuscitate orders are increasingly used and have greater implications than merely not calling the resuscitation team.

Over two-thirds of patients with DNR orders are not involved in making these decisions. After adjustment for disease severity, prognostic factors, age and other covariates, patients given these orders are more than 30 times more likely to die, suggesting that DNR orders may reduce quality of care.

Do not resuscitate orders are more commonly used in the United States, for Black people, alcohol misusers, non-English speakers and people infected with HIV, suggesting that doctors have stereotypes of who is not worth saving.

The courts' role in decisions about medical treatment
- Circumstances occur in which it is necessary or wise to obtain authority from a court as to the lawfulness of proposed medical treatments when patients are not capable of consenting or have refused consent to such interventions
- In cases of permanent vegetative states, the courts' authority must be obtained before artificial nutrition and hydration is withdrawn
- In other cases, the courts can protect doctors from criticism and claims that they have acted unlawfully
- In the case of adults, the legal criteria are whether patients lack the capacity to give or refuse consent, and, if so, what is in their best interests; in the case of children, welfare is the paramount consideration

Dealing with children
- Those having parental responsibility – usually the parents, can give consent to medical treatment. If the parents refuse to give consent to treatment recommended by the doctors, it will be necessary (and possible) for the consent to be supplied instead through an order of the court
- There is a starting point that the united view of both parents is correct in identifying where their child's welfare lies
- Cancelled out where the court finds on the evidence that their view is contrary to the welfare of the child
- It is well established that, for example, although Jehovah's Witnesses may in accordance with their religious beliefs withhold consent to blood transfusions for themselves as adults, if their children's lives are endangered the courts will provide the missing consent for the administration of blood
- When a child is able to express his or her own view, this becomes a factor in the decision about treatment. The courts have described a category of child as 'Gillick Competent' (of sufficient understanding and intelligence to understand fully the specific treatment proposed)
- A court may use its inherent jurisdiction to override the refusal of consent if satisfied that is what the welfare of the child requires

The Special Position of 16–18-year-olds
- Section 8 of the Family Law Reform Act 1969
- Able to give consent to medical treatment as if they were adult
- It does not, however, follow that if they refuse to give their consent and are on the face of it capable of making that decision, their refusal will be determinative in the same way as it would be if they were adult
- No minor of any age has power by refusing treatment to override a consent given by the court or by a person having parental responsibility. The child's level of competence is relevant in assessing the weight to be given to his or her views, but these views will not determine the issue
- The paramount consideration is the welfare of the child

PAPERS

 1. The separating of conjoined twins – Editorial
(A. M. Smith, BMJ 2000;321:782)

Summary of points raised:
- This controversial case of conjoined twins was recently decided by the Court of Appeal in England.
- What is the legal significance of this case?
- The parents did not want Jodie to be saved at the cost of Mary's life. They took the view that this would be to end a life, a position in which their Roman Catholic Church supported them. In these circumstances the first issue that the court had to address was whether parents could refuse to allow treatment.
- Here, the court applied a well-established principle of English law, which is that judges can overrule parental opposition to treatment if it is in the best interest of the child to do so. This is the so called 'welfare principle'.
- In a normal case that would have been enough, but this was no ordinary case. The judges were at pains to hold that Mary's life had intrinsic value, even if she was dependent on her sister and had no hope of a reasonable quality of life.
- Then there was the issue of 'criminal law'. The judges might decide to favour one child over another, but they could not authorise a procedure that could amount to homicide. At this point the principle of 'necessity' entered the courtroom
- 'Necessity' is a broad criminal law defence, that may authorise an otherwise criminal act provided that the act is the lesser of two evils.

- The judges have made it abundantly clear that the value of every human life must be upheld, and it is only when there is absolutely no alternative but to make a choice between lives that this will be permitted. This decision acknowledges that the making of a hard choice in favour of one life over another may be defensible in legal terms. Critics of this decision will say that it represents a further step towards the legal recognition of euthanasia. This is not so. What it does is to endorse the position that, although human life is of the greatest value, no good end is necessarily served by taking an absolutist position.

CHAPTER 17: MISCELLANEOUS TOPICS

REFUGEES

The issues regarding refugees, asylum seekers and immigration have all been visible in the media for the last few years. Whatever your views are on the subject, it is abundantly clear that there are group of people in our society who, in most cases, have been uprooted from their homes because of fear, famine and war. We have a responsibility to provide them with a quality healthcare service that we would afford our own population. Hypothetically, if the tables could be turned, I am fairly sure we would want the same. The refugee issue can provide a fruitful number of ethical questions, especially when the healthcare element is introduced.

The issues of refugees are discussed in the summary below:

📖 Refugees and primary care: tackling the inequalities
(D. Jones and P. S. Gill, BMJ 1998;317:1444–6)

This interesting article appeared in the BMJ when a large number of refugees were arriving in England from the troubles in the Balkans. As the twentieth century drew to a close, outbreaks of hatred between human population groups showed no sign of abating and conflicts continued to erupt. Families across the world found themselves forced to leave their homes and seek refuge where it could be found. Globally, there are 18 million refugees, with 230,000 living in the United Kingdom. Almost half of these live in London, where 100,000 people are refugees or awaiting confirmation of refugee status. Many refugees have health problems but experience difficulty having their needs met by the NHS. This article explores the challenges that refugees pose for primary care and suggests alternative strategies to address inequalities in the care of refugees.

* The refugee population in Britain is highly diverse and is likely to remain large as conflicts continue to occur throughout the world
* Refugees, unlike other migrants, have had to flee to escape oppression
* The refugee population is concentrated in the Greater London area, but new legislation will result in dispersal throughout the United Kingdom
* Refugees may be vulnerable to mental health problems, yet have

difficulty communicating their needs because of language barriers
- All refugees are entitled to the full range of NHS services free of charge, including registration with a general practitioner
- A strategic approach is needed to address the inequalities in primary care

Definition of refugees
- Those applying for asylum (refugee) status in the UK
- Those who have been given temporary admission by the immigration service while their applications are considered
- Those who have been given exceptional leave to remain in or enter the country
- Those who are required to renew their status at the Home Office at regular intervals
- Those given refugee status
- Those who gain the right to stay in this country indefinitely
- Those who have had their application refused and are going through the Appeals process
- Dependants of the above groups
- Other individuals or groups who may fall outside the legal definition but who face similar problems: such as those entering the country under family reunion rules, policy or discretion

What happens to refugees?
- Refugee population is not evenly spread
- Concentrated in areas where local authorities have given refugee housing a higher priority
- Legislation will result in greater dispersal of refugees, which will make the provision of specialist services more difficult
- 'Cultural bereavement' and coping with 'deeply disruptive change' are widely shared experiences of migration
- Refugees are distinguished from other migrants by their lack of choice
- Refugees have had to leave their countries of origin to escape persecution, imprisonment, torture or even death
- Families may have been physically separated, causing much grief
- Refugees are often preoccupied by worry about relatives left behind in their country of origin
- Many refugees, including children, have no other relatives in the UK
- Poverty and dissatisfaction with housing is widespread

Health problems
- A recent UK study of Iraqi refugees found that all had been separated involuntarily from some close family members
- 65% had a history of systematic torture during detention
- 29% were unable to speak any English
- Over 50% had significant psychological morbidity
- Evidence that refugees who have not yet been granted the right to remain are under particular stress

Deficiencies of primary care
- All refugees are entitled to the full range of NHS treatment free of charge
- Have the right to register with a GP
- There is evidence that some GPs are confused about this
- Some patients are asked for passports when trying to register, which raises a number of questions:
  - What happens to patients unable to produce a valid passport?
  - Are they sent away?
  - Who makes these decisions?
- Some practices are, perhaps reluctantly, open for refugees, whereas others are effectively closed, creating neighbouring general practices with very different demographic profiles and unequal needs
- When refugees join a GP's list they are often registered on a temporary rather than a permanent basis
- This removes financial incentives to undertake immunisation and cervical smear tests
- Why do general practitioners avoid giving refugees permanent registration status?
- High mobility of refugees is a myth – 70% of refugees had been living in their current home for more than a year (Home Office Survey 1995)
- Language barriers at the reception desk and in the consultation are common
- Health authorities lack interpreter services, generally not available outside working hours
- Telephone interpreting using 'hands free' technology may offer a solution
- Lack of adequate professional interpreting services presents a barrier for all non-English-speaking patients, but this barrier is larger for those with psychological and emotional difficulties

Q. If tragic mistakes are made as a result of communication failure, does the moral responsibility rest with the doctor or with a medical system which expects doctors to communicate well but fails to provide adequate resources?

Increasing spending on refugee primary care
- Is fully justifiable on clinical and ethical grounds
- Recognise that it requires considerable political courage to prioritise refugees at a time when other groups in the population, such as elderly people and the mentally ill, have been identified as in need of more resources
- It is important to remember that many refugees who settle in Britain have made valuable contributions to society

What can be done to improve primary care for refugees?
- A strategic approach is required
- Intensive courses in spoken English
- The DoH needs to commission an information pack that includes a certificate of entitlement to NHS treatment and to develop patient-held medical records
- The development of a national telephone interpreting service in a range of languages is a priority
- A separate capitation payment for refugee patients, together with a new item of service payment linked to the duration of each professionally interpreted consultation, should be introduced
- Healthcare facilitators should be recruited from each specific refugee population and could help to provide patient-held records with an accurate and detailed medical history and to support health promotion and screening

Conclusions
- The refugee population is likely to remain large
- High needs, especially psychological distress, combined with language barriers require a great deal of additional time in consultations
- GPs in inner cities need adequate resources, especially interpreting services, and should be properly rewarded
- A truly effective solution requires the political will to develop a comprehensive strategy at national level

PAPER

 Asylum seekers and health: A BMA and Medical Foundation for the care of the victims of torture dossier

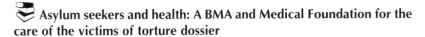 www.bma.org.uk/ap.nsf/Content/Asylum+seekers+and+health

In the joint dossier they state:
- The Government should 'develop a more humane system'
- 'The Government's system for the handling of asylum-seekers is not focused on helping but on deterring them. Present procedures are not compassionate but punitive.'
- 'Health care for asylum seekers in Britain is patchy, belated and often inappropriate'
- It contains 22 case histories, reported by doctors, that show how Britain is 'failing' in its obligations to provide healthcare for asylum seekers
- The dossier states that the cases document 'the personal cost of this failure, measured in the suffering of refugees'
- The Government should 'abolish vouchers and forced dispersal'. They claim that these policies put the health of asylum seekers at risk
- It calls for the scrapping of the voucher system in favour of cash benefits for asylum seekers
- It cites cases of mothers who water down baby milk to make their vouchers go further

RECENT ADVANCES IN ETHICS

Clinical review - Recent advances in medical ethics
(P. A. Singer, BMJ 2000,321:282)

This interesting review focused on the continuing evolution of medical ethics through new technology, some of which could be envisaged making good viva material. The goal of medical ethics is to improve the quality of patient care by identifying, analysing and attempting to resolve the ethical problems that arise in practice.

Review advances in five areas:
1. End of life care
2. Medical error
3. Priority setting
4. Biotechnology
5. Medical ethics education
+ two future issues: 'eHealth' and 'global bioethics'

1. End of life care
See Chapter 16

2. Medical error
The main recent advance is the development of the Tavistock principles, which serve as an ethical foundation for those working to reduce medical error.

All the Tavistock principles are relevant to the problem of medical error, but the most important are:
- Cooperation with each other and those served is the imperative for those working within the healthcare delivery system
- All individuals and groups involved in healthcare, whether providing access or services, have the continuing responsibility to help improve its quality
- In developing a culture of safety, clinicians will need to act as role models for their students by applying these principles themselves the next time they encounter a medical error
- Healthcare leaders will need to 'feel personally responsible for error' and 'declare error reduction to be an explicit organisational goal and [devote] a significant proportion of the board and management agenda...to achieving this goal'

3. Priority setting
Development of an ethics framework – 'Accountability for Reasonableness' – for legitimate and fair decisions on setting priorities.

Priority setting = 'rationing' 20 years ago = 'resource allocation' 10 years ago and will be called 'sustainability' 10 years from now.

The four conditions of Accountability for Reasonableness
*   Publicity – Decisions regarding coverage for new technologies (and other limit-setting decisions) and their rationales must be publicly accessible

*   Relevance – These rationales must rest on evidence, reasons and principles that fair-minded parties (managers, clinicians, patients and consumers in general) can agree are relevant to deciding how to meet the diverse needs of a covered population under necessary resource constraints

*   Appeals – There must be a mechanism for challenge and dispute resolution regarding limit-setting decisions, including the opportunity to revise decisions in the light of further evidence or arguments

*   Enforcement – There must be either voluntary or public regulation of the process to ensure that the first three conditions are met

4. Biotechnology
*   Emerging consensus on the acceptability of stem-cell research
*   The UK Nuffield Council on Bioethics have issued a report supporting stem-cell research
*   Latest in a series of important consensus documents on biotechnology, such as the 'WHO's guiding principles on medical genetics and biotechnology' and the 'Human Genome Organization's' statement on benefit sharing
*   Stem cells are 'cells with the capacity for unlimited or prolonged self-renewal that can produce at least one type of highly differentiated descendant'
*   The clinical potential of stem cells is enormous, including neuronal repair, haematological reconstitution and organ transplantation
*   The problem with embryonic stem cells is that they are derived from human embryos

- Opponents of embryonic stem-cell research are concerned with the moral and legal status of the embryo and advocate a moratorium
- Proponents, however, focus on the potential benefits to patients
- Recent reports suggest that adult stem cells can differentiate into developmentally cell types – this would mitigate the ethical tensions related to embryonic, unrelated stem cells

5. Medical ethics education
- The revolution in information technology will dramatically change medical practice
- Many ethical issues, including confidentiality of electronic medical records and the relation of clinical records to research and management of health systems
- Dramatic changes in the way doctors learn and access medical literature

Global bioethics
- In this era of advanced globalisation the problems of medical ethics can no longer be viewed only from the perspective of wealthy countries
- Global bioethics seeks to identify key ethical problems faced by the world's six billion inhabitants and envisages solutions that transcend national borders and cultures
- An International Association of Bioethics has been formed and a discussion board on global bioethics has been launched

'eHealth'
- The revolution in information technology will dramatically change medical practice
- This raises many ethical issues, including how we can keep electronic medical records confidential and how we use our patient data to research and manage health systems
- Doctors will also dramatically change the way they learn and access medical literature
- A code of ethics for 'eHealth' has been developed by the Internet Healthcare Coalition, who are an organisation with representatives from industry, academic groups, government, patient and consumer organisations
- A draft of the code can be found at:

 www.ihealthcoalition.org/ethics/draftcode.html

CHAPTER 18: THE CONSULTATION

The next group of studies covers many areas of the consultation, at the end of which we will also look at recent studies of telephone consultations and non-attendance.

📖 1. Deprivation, psychological distress, and consultation length in general practice
(A. M. Stirling, et al., BJGP 2001;51(467):456–60)

- Up to 40% of patients presenting to GPs are psychologically distressed as measured by screening tools, such as the General Health Questionnaire (GHQ)
- Of these distressed patients, doctors correctly identify about half (see previous studies)
- Poor mental health is a major predictor of future poor physical health
- Failure to diagnose and treat appropriately may promote chronicity and the inappropriate and unnecessary referral and medical treatment characteristic of somatic fixation
- Correct identification of the patient's psychological problem may reduce somatisation
- This study aimed to examine factors associated with the presentation and recognition of psychological distress in GPs' surgeries and the interaction of these factors with consultation length
- It was a cross-sectional study carried out in the West of Scotland, between November 1997 and May 1998
- 1,075 consultations of 21 full-time GPs were assessed
- The main outcome measures were patient psychological distress (measured by the GHQ), doctors' identification of psychological distress, consultation length and Carstairs Deprivation Category Scores
- They showed the mean consultation length was 8.71 minutes and the prevalence of positive GHQ scores was 44.7%. Increasing GHQ (greater psychological distress) and Lower Deprivation Category Scores (greater affluence) were associated with longer consultations
- Positive GHQ scoring increased with greater socioeconomic deprivation and also peaked in the 30–39 years age group
- Recognition of psychological distress was greater in longer consultations (50% increase in consultation length associated with

32% increase in recognition)
- They concluded that increasing socioeconomic deprivation is associated with a higher prevalence of psychological distress and shorter consultations
- This provides further evidence to support Tudor Harts' 'inverse care law' (the availability of good-quality medical care is inversely proportional to its need) and has implications for the resourcing of primary care in deprived areas

Problems
- Because recruitment was by invitation, this group of doctors is not representative
- All the practices used were in some way involved in teaching and were therefore potentially more motivated than average
- It is likely that these doctors have an interest in psychological medicine
- This is borne out in the results, with 59% of distressed patients correctly identified as such by the doctor (which is far higher that previous studies)
- Bias may also have resulted from participating GPs knowing that their 'performance' was being observed

2. Preferences of patients for patient centred approach to consultation in primary care: observational study
(P. Little, et al., BMJ 2001;322:468–72)

- Consecutive patients in the waiting room of three doctors' surgeries took part
- One in a deprived area of a large provincial city, the second a training practice serving an urban population of a cathedral city and the third a training practice in a market town serving a mixed urban and rural population; characteristics of the sample were similar to the attending sample from the National Morbidity Survey
- 865 patients participated: 95% returned the questionnaire and were similar in demographic characteristic to national samples
- Patients were given questionnaires prior to seeing the GP asking them to agree or disagree on questions about what they wanted the doctor to do in the consultation
- It focused on communication (agreed with by 88–99% of patients), partnership (77–87%) and health promotion (85–89%)
- Fewer wanted an examination (63%), and only one-quarter

wanted a prescription
- Patients who strongly wanted good communication were more likely to feel unwell, be high attenders and have no paid work
- Strongly wanting a partnership was also related to feeling unwell, worrying about the problem, high attendance and no paid work
- Those strongly wanting health promotion were high attenders and those worried about their problem
- Patients who wanted a prescription were more likely to want good communication, partnership and health promotion
- Patients wanting a prescription were more likely to be unmarried, have a partner with no paid work, no education beyond GCSE and be aged over 60
- Those wanting an examination were more likely to have no education beyond GCSE and feel worried about their problem
- Patients required about 3–5 minutes to complete the questionnaire before seeing the doctor, so those seeing doctors running on time (a small minority) could not be approached
- Time limitation meant fewer questions asked

KEY POINTS

- ❖ They concluded patients in primary care strongly want a patient-centred approach, with communication, partnership and health promotion
- ❖ Improved communication can improve satisfaction and biomedical outcomes
- ❖ Involving patients in partnership can have benefits without increasing their anxiety, and with the potential to reduce side-effects of prescribing
- ❖ Patients with a very strong preference for patient centredness are those who are vulnerable either socioeconomically or because they are feeling particularly unwell or worried

---

3. Patients unvoiced agendas in general practice consultations: qualitative study
(C. A. Barry, et al., BMJ 2000;320:1246–50)

- 20 general practices in SE England and the West Midlands
- 35 patients consulting 20 general practitioners in appointment and emergency surgeries
- Patient agendas was confirmed prior to the consultation

- Consultation was recorded and the GP interviewed the following day
- Patients interviewed a week later

Results:
- Average of five points per patient agenda
- Voiced agenda items were: most commonly symptoms, requests for diagnoses and prescriptions
- Unvoiced agenda items were: worries about possible diagnosis, what the future holds, patients' ideas about what is wrong, side-effects, not wanting a prescription and information relating to social context
- 4/35 patients voiced their full agendas
- 24 patients voiced all their symptoms, but psychosocial issues were more likely not to be mentioned
- Active steps should be taken in daily practice to encourage voicing of patients' agendas

4. Quality at general practice consultations: cross sectional survey
(J. G. Howie, et al., BMJ 1999;319:738–43)

- Questionnaire study
- 25,000 participants
- Average length of consultations was 8 minutes
- Enablement score was linked to small practices, familiarity with GP and length of the consultation
- Advocated longer consultations to promote continuity of care

5. Evolving general practice consultation in Britain: issues of length and context
(G. K. Freeman, et al., BMJ 2002;324:880–2)

Is there any justification for a further increase in mean time allocated per consultation in general practice?

This commissioned, systematic review involving 14 relevant papers attempts to answer the question.
In summary:
- Longer consultations are associated with a range of better patient outcomes
- Modern consultations in general practice deal with patients with more serious and chronic conditions

- Increasing patient participation means more complex interaction, which demands extra time
- Difficulties with access and with loss of continuity add to perceived stress and poor performance and lead to further pressure on time
- Longer consultations should be a professional priority, combined with increased use of technology and more flexible practice management to maximise interpersonal continuity
- Consistently showed that doctors with longer consultation times prescribe less and offer more advice on lifestyle and other health-promoting activities
- Longer consultations have been significantly associated with better recognition and handling of psychosocial problems and with better patient enablement
- Clinical care for some chronic illnesses is better in practices with longer booked intervals between one appointment and the next
- The most effective consultations are those in which doctors most directly acknowledge and perhaps respond to patients' problems and concerns
- Research on implementation is needed

6. Observational study of effect of patient centredness and positive approach on outcomes of general practice consultations
(P. Little, et al., BMJ 2001;323:908–11)

- This paper attempted to measure patients' perceptions of patient centredness and its relation to outcomes
- It was a observational study using questionnaires
- Three general practices in SE Hampshire took part
- 865 consecutive patients attending the practices were recruited
- Participants completed a short questionnaire before their consultation, in which they were asked to agree or disagree on a seven-point Likert scale (very strongly agree to very strongly disagree) with statements about what they wanted the doctor to do. A questionnaire after the consultation asked patients about their perception of the doctor's approach. Both questionnaires were based on the five main domains of the patient-centred model: exploring the disease and illness experience; understanding the whole person; finding common ground; health promotion; and enhancing the doctor–patient relationship.
- Patients were followed up after 1 month and the notes were reviewed after 2 months for re-attendance, investigation and referral

- Main outcome measures were patients' enablement, satisfaction and burden of symptoms
- Analysis identified five components:
  1. Communication and partnership (a sympathetic doctor interested in a patient's worries and expectations and who discusses and agrees the problem and treatment)
  2. Personal relationship (a doctor who knows the patient and their emotional needs)
  3. Health promotion
  4. Positive approach (being definite about the problem and when it would settle)
  5. Interest in effect on patient's life
- Satisfaction was related to communication and partnership and a positive approach
- Enablement was greater with interest in the effect on life, health promotion and a positive approach
- A positive approach was also associated with reduced symptom burden at 1 month
- Referrals were fewer if patients felt they had a personal relationship with their doctor
- The author concluded that 'if doctors don't provide a positive, patient centred approach patients will be less satisfied, less enabled, and may have greater symptom burden and higher rates of referral.'

7. An exploration of the value of the personal doctor–patient relationship in general practice
(K. E. Kearley, et al., BJGP 2001;51(470):712–18)

- Within the context of general practice, the opportunity exists for a personal relationship to develop between the patient and GP
- This has benefits for both patients and GPs:
  - Patient enablement is improved
  - Compliance with medication is increased
  - Clinical decision-making process and disclosure of psychosocial problems are facilitated
  - The doctor–patient interaction itself can be therapeutic, enhanced by feelings of trust and understanding
- The aims of this paper were to determine how many patients report having a personal doctor and when this is most valued, to compare the value of a personal doctor–patient relationship with

that of convenience and to relate these findings to a range of patient, GP and practice variables

- It was a cross-sectional postal questionnaire study
- 960 randomly selected adult patients from a stratified random sample of 18 practices and 284 GP principals in Oxfordshire took part
- Qualitative interviews with patients and GPs were conducted and used to derive a parallel patient and GP questionnaire
- Each patient (100 from each practice) was invited to complete a questionnaire to evaluate his or her experience and views concerning personal care
- All GP principals currently practising in Oxfordshire were sent a similar questionnaire, which also included demographic variables
- The results showed that 75% of patients reported having at least one personal GP
- The number of patients reporting a personal GP in each practice varied from 53% to 92%
- Having a personal doctor–patient relationship was highly valued by patients and GPs, in particular for more serious psychological and family issues
- 77–88% of patients and 80–98% of GPs valued a personal relationship more than a convenient appointment
- For minor illness it had much less value
- They concluded patients and GPs particularly value a personal doctor–patient relationship for more serious or for psychological problems. Whether a patient has a personal GP is associated with their perception of its importance and with factors that create an opportunity for a relationship to evolve

8. Long to short consultation ratio: a proxy measure of quality of care for general practice

(J. G. Howie, et al., BJGP 1991;41(343):48–54)

- Howie in 1991 showed that longer consultations were linked to higher patient satisfaction
- This was probably due to the fact that the longer consultations dealt with more psychological and social issues

9. Editorial: Engaging patients in medical decision-making
(BMJ 2001;323:584–5)

- There is a consensus that patients ought to be more involved in their own care.
- Ethicists generally accept that the principle that autonomy (what the competent, informed patient wants) trumps beneficence (what the doctor thinks best for the patient) in all but the most extreme circumstances
- Quality in Health Care (Sept. 2001) focused on engaging patients in medical decisions
- 12 articles from a MRC conference
- The proceedings gave a clear impression that although respecting patients' preferences is a fundamental goal of medicine, these preferences are vulnerable to manipulation and bias
- But they are too important to be abandoned by professional frustration
- Three questions dominated the debate:
  - Can patients take a leading role in making decisions?
  - Do they want to?
  - What if doctors and public health professionals don't like their choices?

In discussion of these:
- Decisions are complicated, and depend on patients' attitudes to risk
- Some patients prefer a very bad outcome put off into the future to a moderately bad outcome occurring now
- This is one of several reasons why patients' decisions are sometimes at odds with recommendations
- Cultural beliefs can have a profound influence on decisions regarding treatment, e.g. some SE Asian cultures consider that surgery results in perpetual imbalance, causing the person to be physically incomplete in the next incarnation
- May go some way to explain why fully informed, shared decision-making is so difficult to conduct in practice
- Yet communication with patients can be improved, including evidence-based approaches such as training doctors, coaching patients and using aids to decision-making.
- However, not all patients want to make their own decisions. In a study of 1,012 women with breast cancer, 22% wanted to select

their own treatment, 44% wanted to collaborate with their doctors in the decision and 34% wanted to delegate this responsibility to their doctors (*JAMA 1997;277:1485–92*)
- Yet there is a desire for information that is nearly universal
- Concluded, 'Most patients want to see the road map, including alternative routes, even if they don't want to take over the wheel'

NON-ATTENDANCE

📖 **Non-attendance at general practices and outpatient clinics. Local systems are needed to address local problem**
(D. J. Sharp and W. Hamilton, BMJ 2001;323:1081–2)

- This editorial looked at the problem of non-attendance, the ramifications and thoughts regarding solutions
- At times of increasing debate on rationing of resources, this topic tends to be increasingly mentioned in the medical press

In summary:
- Non-attendance at NHS outpatient clinics and at general practices is more common in deprived populations
- The national figure of 12% for non-attendance at outpatient clinics in the United Kingdom hides large variations between specialties and between regions
- Studies report figures that range from 5% to 34%
- Much less research has been done on non-attendance in general practices, though figures of 3% and 6.5% have been reported
- The first figure comes from an unpublished doctor–patient partnership survey in 1998 and an unpublished survey of 500 non-attenders in Exeter. The higher figure is from a study of 221,000 appointments in practices in Sheffield
- The main associations with hospital non-attendance are reported as being male sex, youth, the length of waiting time for the appointment and deprivation
- Non-attendance in general practices are associated with youth and deprivation, but not sex
- Non-attenders are less likely to own a car or a telephone and are more likely to be unemployed
- Some non-attendance arises from an inability to cancel the appointment, either because the hospital's system for cancelling or changing appointments is poor or because the patient has no access to a telephone
- Non-attendance is not thought to be related to the severity of the patient's condition, except in the case of psychiatric illness, where non-attendance may be a marker of severity of illness
- The commonest reasons cited for missing an appointment, after forgetting it, are family or work commitments
- Patients with lower paid jobs may have difficulty in getting time off work or arranging childcare

- These reasons also partly explain the peak age range of 20–30 years in non-attenders, as this is the usual age for raising a family
- The key seems to be to allow the patient to select a suitable time and date; indeed, such flexibility may largely explain the lower non-attendance rate in general practices, although evening surgeries and shorter time intervals to the appointment probably also contribute
- The strongest predictor of non-attendance is the time interval to the appointment; reducing non-attendance reduces waiting times, which further reduces non-attendance, creating a virtuous circle
- Increased consumerism in the NHS means that current systems are stale, at best
- No single solution will work across the NHS and in outpatient clinics as well as general practices
- Local trusts in primary and secondary care should be able to devise local systems to allow convenient access for their patients
- New systems should be the subject of research and development
- Non-attendance should fall if some of these measures are adopted, though it will never disappear – we are all human

TELEPHONE CONSULTATIONS

PAPER

📖 **Telephone consultations to manage requests for same-day appointments: a randomised controlled trial in two practices**
(B. A. McKinstry, et al., BJGP 2002;52(477):306–10)

- GPs in the UK have recently begun to adopt the use of telephone consultation during daytime surgery as a means of managing demand, particularly requests for same-day appointments
- However it is not known whether the strategy actually reduces GP workload
- The aim of the study was to investigate how the use of telephone consultations impacts on the management of requests for same-day appointments, on resource use, indicators of clinical care and patient perceptions of consultations
- It was an RCT of all patients (n = 388) seeking same-day appointments in each surgery in two urban practices (total population 10,420) over a 4-week period
- The primary outcome measure was use of doctor time for the index telephone or face-to-face consultation
- Secondary outcomes were subsequent use of investigations and of services in the 2-week period following consultation, frequency of blood pressure measurement and antibiotic prescriptions and number of problems considered at consultation
- Patient perceptions were measured by the Patient Enablement Instrument (PEI) and reported willingness to use telephone consultations in the future
- The results showed telephone consultations took less time (8.2 vs. 6.7 minutes)
- Patients consulting by telephone re-consulted the GP more frequently in the 2 weeks that followed.
- Blood pressure was measured more often in the group of patients managed face-to-face (13.3% vs. 6.6%)
- There was no significant difference in patient perceptions or other secondary outcomes
- They concluded that the use of telephone consultations for same-day appointments was associated with time-saving, and did not result in lower PEI scores
- Possibly, however, this short-term saving was offset by a higher re-consultation rate and less use of opportunistic health promotion

CONSULTATION MODELS

During my registrar year, it seemed a trivial task to learn consultation models in order to pass the exam and show some knowledge when asked. However, I have come to realise that learning these models is one step closer to an increased awareness of how your consultations work, they are of benefit in predicting outcome and as times passes, they become second nature.

My argument is that, despite the endless debate of increased paperwork taking time away from patient contact and increased managerial responsibilities, the core of your daily routine remains a one-to-one patient interaction. If this can be achieved more efficiently, with greater satisfaction for the patient and leads to less re-attendance you would expect there to be an endless line of takers. However, that is not the case. The techniques are often forgotten shortly after the registrar year has ended, and rarely does one look back. As food for thought for those of you who remain free of too much cynicism, these models and their various facets do work in allowing less stressful and more fruitful consultations. They can help you with your stress levels and ultimately keep you going. Use them and experiment during the trainee year, and after if you are so inclined; everybody's style is different and you may find some facets too difficult or unproductive. Obviously you will concentrate on getting your video done, but this still allows tuning of your consultation. For those of you lucky few who were genuinely inspired by your trainer, remember it takes years of practice to make slick consultations look easy, but it is attainable – just enjoy getting there.

For those taking the exam it is advisable for you to learn the models and some working clinical case models to illustrate certain points. This may be a question in your viva and certainly there is always an odd MCQ or two.

BIOMEDICAL MODEL

The classic medical diagnostic process
- Observation: history and examination
- Hypothesis: provisional diagnosis
- Hypothesis testing: investigations
- Deduction: definitive diagnosis

In essence, this is a hypothetico-deductive model but:
Reductionist: Patient regarded as collection of signs, symptoms

and diagnosis
Doctor-centred: Patient's ideas, concerns and expectations
Sharing information
Agreeing management plan

- No progress can be made if no objective physical disorder is unearthed
- Omits use of doctor–patient relationship

Other models have been developed which are more holistic:
- Not competing, but complementary
- Several are often needed to give a broad understanding of something as complex as human interaction

ALTERNATIVE MODELS

Byrne and Long
Phase I   The doctor establishes a relationship with the patient
Phase II   The doctor either attempts to discover or actually discovers the reason for the patient's attendance
Phase III   The doctor conducts a verbal or physical examination, or both
Phase IV   The doctor, or the doctor and the patient, or the patient (in that order of probability) consider the condition
Phase V   The doctor, and occasionally the patient, detail further treatment or further investigation
Phase VI   The consultation is terminated, usually by the doctor

Used the terms 'Doctor-centred' and 'Patient-centred'. This model was produced after analysing over 2,000 tape recordings of consultations.

Pendleton, Schofield, Tate and Havelock
Seven tasks:
1. To define the reason for the patient's attendance, including: the nature and history of the problems; their aetiology; the patients' ideas, concerns and expectations; the effects of the problems
2. To consider other problems: continuing problems and risk factors
3. With the patient, to choose an appropriate action for each problem
4. To achieve a shared understanding of the problems with the patient
5. To involve the patient in the management and encourage him to accept responsibility
6. To use time and resources appropriately: in the consultation and in the long term

7. To establish or maintain a relationship with the patient which helps to achieve the other tasks

Emphasises the importance of the patient's view and understanding of the problem. Includes the term 'Consultation mapping.'

Stott and Davis

Management of presenting problems	Modification of help-seeking behaviour
Management of continuing problems	Opportunistic health promotion

Neighbour
The inner consultation

Connecting:	needs rapport-building skills
Summarising:	needs listening and eliciting skills to facilitate effective assessment
Hand over:	needs communicating skills to hand over responsibility for management
Safety netting:	needs predicting skills to suggest contingency plan for worst scenario
Housekeeping:	needs self-awareness to clear your mind of the psychological remains of one consultation so that it has no detrimental effect on the next (clearing your head)

Rosenstock, Becker and Maiman
Health beliefs model
It shows that the patient is more likely to accept advice, diagnosis or treatment if the doctor is aware of their ideas, concerns and expectations.

Patient's behaviour is determined by:
- Alarming symptoms
- Trigger factors such as advice from family and friends, messages from media
- Health motivation (interest in health)
- Perceived vulnerability to the condition
- Perceived seriousness of the condition
- Perceived balance of benefits of treatment against costs
- Belief that the doctor has/has not understood patient's concerns

Heron

Six-category intervention model
Doctor can use any of six types of intervention.

1. Prescriptive: instructions; advice
2. Informative: explanations; interpretations; new knowledge
3. Confronting: feedback on behaviour; challenging but caring attitude
4. Cathartic: aiding release of emotions in form of anger, laughter, crying
5. Catalytic: encouraging patient to explore feelings, thoughts and behaviour
6. Supportive: bolstering self-worth

Berne

Transactional analysis ('games people play')
- Explores behaviour within relationships
- Identifies three 'ego-states':
  - Parent: critical or caring
  - Adult: logical
  - Child: spontaneous or dependent
- Examines implications of, and reasons for, the different states
- Explores 'games' – useful for analysing why consultations repeatedly go wrong and encouraging doctors to break out of these unproductive cycles of behaviour

Balint

The doctor, his patient and the illness (1957)
The doctor–patient relationship is fundamental. Patients are more than broken machines, and doctors have feelings, which have a function in the consultation.

Proposed:
- Psychological problems are often manifested physically and even physical disease has its own psychological consequences which need particular attention
- Doctors have feelings and those feelings have a function in the consultation
- There needs to be specific training to produce limited but considerable change in the doctor's personality so that he can become more sensitive to the patient's thoughts during the consultation

The doctor must:
- Discover the patient's beliefs, concerns and expectations about the problem or problems presented
- Share his own understanding of the problems with the patient in terms that are understood by the patient
- Share the decision-making with the patient
- Encourage the patient to take appropriate responsibility for his own health

Key concepts and phrases:
1. The doctor as a drug

2. The child as the presenting complaint
   - Patient may offer another person (e.g. child) as the problem when there are underlying psychosocial problems

3. Elimination by appropriate physical examination
   - May reinforce the patient's belief that neurotic symptoms are in fact due to physical illness

4. Collusion of anonymity
   - Mistaken beliefs in the origin of symptoms are reinforced by examination
   - Responsibility of uncovering underlying problems becomes increasingly diluted by repeated referral
   - No-one takes responsibility

5. The mutual investment company
   - Formed and managed by the doctor and the patient
   - 'Clinical illnesses' equal 'Offers' in a long relationship
   - 'Offers' of problems (physical and psychosocial) are presented to the doctor for his 'Acceptance'

6. The flash
   - When the real reason of the 'Offer' (underlying psychosocial and neurotic illness) is suddenly apparent to both doctor and patient
   - Acts as a central point for change
   - Consultation can now deal with the underlying basic 'Fault'

NB. For the exam, think of clinical scenarios to illustrate each of the above and understand what is meant by each term.

Triaxial model
Address patient's problem in:
1. Physical terms
2. Psychological terms
3. Social terms

Tate's tasks

 From The Doctors' Communication Handbook

Involves use of concepts featured in other models. Similar to those used to assess tasks in the summative assessment and MRCGP videos.

1. Discover the reasons for attendance
   - Listen to the patient's description of the symptom
   - Obtain relevant social and occupational information
   - Explore the patient's health understanding
   - Enquire about other problems
   - Obtain additional information about critical symptoms or other details
   - Appropriate physical examination
   - Make a working diagnosis

2. Define the clinical problem(s)
   - Address the patient's problem(s)
   - Assess the severity of the presenting problem
   - Choose an appropriate form of management
   - Involve the patient in the management plan to the appropriate extent

3. Explain the problem(s) to the patient
   - Share your findings with the patient
   - Tailor the explanation to the needs of the patient
   - Ensure that the explanation is understood and accepted by the patient

4. Make effective use of the consultation
   - Make efficient use of resources – time, investigations, other professionals, etc.
   - Establish an effective relationship with the patient

GLOSSARY

A&E	accident and emergency
ACE	angiotensin-converting enzyme; also Asthma Control and Expectations
ACEI	angiotensin-converting enzyme inhibitor
AD	Alzheimer's disease
ADAS-cog	Alzheimer's disease assessment scale – cognitive subscale
ADFAM National	National Charity for the Families and Friends of Drug Misusers
ADHD	attention deficit–hyperactive disorder
ADL	activities of daily living
AF	atrial fibrillation
AIDS	acquired immunodeficiency syndrome
AOM	acute otitis media
ARB	angiotensin-II receptor blocker
b	billion (1,000,000,000)
BHS	British Hypertension Society
BMA	British Medical Association
BMD	bone mineral density
BMI	body mass index
BP	blood pressure
BTS	Blood Transfusion Service
CAMS	Cannabis in Multiple Sclerosis [trial]
CARE	Cholesterol and Recurrent Events [study]
CBT	cognitive behaviour therapy
CFC	chlorofluorocarbon
CG	clinical governance
CHD	coronary heart disease
CHI	Commission for Health Improvement
CIBIS	Cardiac Insufficiency Bisoprolol Study
COAD	chronic obstructive airways disease
COCP	combined oral contraceptive pill
CONSENSUS	Cooperative North Scandinavian Enalapril Survival Study
COR	cardiopulmonary resuscitation
CPA	Care Programme Approach
CPD	continuous professional development
CSM	Committee on Safety of Medicines
CT	computed tomography
CVA	cardiovascular accident

CVD	cardiovascular disease
DBP	diastolic blood pressure
DCCT	Diabetes Control and Complications Trial
DEXA	dual-energy X-ray absorptiometry
DGH	district general hospital
DNR	do not resuscitate
DoH	Department of Health
DPAS	Drug Prevention Advisory Service
DSPD	dangerous and severely personality-disordered
DTI	Department of Trade and Industry
DVLA	Driver and Vehicle Licencing Agency
DVT	deep vein thrombosis
EBM	evidence-based medicine
ELITE	Evaluation of Losartan in the Elderly [study]
ERA	Estrogen Replacement and Atherosclerosis [trial]
EU	European Union
GHQ	General Health Questionnaire
GMC	General Medical Council
GMS	General Medical Services
GP	general practitioner
GPC	General Practitioners' Committee
GUM	genitourinary medicine
HA	health authority
HDL	high-density lipoprotein
HDP	Hampshire Depression Project
HERS	Heart and Estrogen/Progestin Replacement Study
HIV	human immunodeficiency virus
HMP	Her Majesty's Prisons
HOPE	Heart Outcomes Prevention Evaluation
HOT	Hypertension Optimal Treatment [trial]
HRT	hormone replacement therapy
IC	independent contractor
IHD	ischaemic heart disease
INR	international normalised ratio
ISDD	Institute for the Study of Drug Dependence
IUCD	intrauterine contraceptive device
LCR	ligase chain reaction
LDL	low-density lipoprotein
LIFE	Lorsartan Intervention For Endpoint [reduction in hypertension]

LIPID	Long-term Intervention with Pravastatin in Ischaemic Disease
LRTI	lower respiratory tract illness
LSP	local strategic partnerships
LVH	left ventricular hypertrophy
m	million
MDU	Medical Defence Union
MERIT-HF	Metoprolol CR/XL Randomised Intervention Trial in Congestive Heart Failure
MI	myocardial infarction
MMR	measles, mumps and rubella
MMSE	Mini-Mental State Examination
MND	motor neurone disease
MS	multiple sclerosis
NA	Narcotics Anonymous
NCAA	National Clinical Assessment Authority
NeLH	The National electronic Library for Health
NICE	National Institute for Clinical Excellence
NNT	number needed to treat
NRT	nicotine replacement therapy
OGTT	oral glucose tolerance test
PALS	Patient Advocacy and Liaison Service
PCG	primary care group
PCT	primary care trust
PE	pulmonary embolism
PEI	Patient Enablement Instrument
PHCT	primary healthcare team
PMS	personal medical services
PROGRESS	Peridopril pROtection aGainst REcurrent Stroke Study
ProtecT	Prostate testing for cancer and Treatment
PSA	prostate-specific antigen
RALES	Randomized Aldactone Evaluation Study
RCGP	Royal College of General Practitioners
RCN	Royal College of Nursing
RCOG	Royal College of Obstetricians and Gynaecologists
RCP	Royal College of Physicians
RCPsych	Royal College of Psychiatrists
RCT	randomised controlled trials
RESOLVD	Randomised Evaluation of Strategies for Left Ventricular Dysfunction
SBP	systolic blood pressure

SERMs	selective oestrogen-receptor modulators
SMAC	Standing Medical Advisory Committee
SMAS	Substance Misuse Advisory Service
SPAF	Stroke Prevention in Atrial Fibrillation [trial]
SSRI	selective serotonin-reuptake inhibitors
STD	sexually transmitted disease
STI	sexually transmitted infection
STOP	Swedish Trial in Old Patients
STORM	Sibutramine Trial of Obesity Reduction and Maintenance
TACADE	The Advisory Council on Alcohol and Drug Education
TCA	tricyclic antidepressant
TIA	transient ischaemic attack
tPA	tissue plasminogen activator
UKPDS	UK Prospective Diabetes Study
ValHeFT	Valsartan Heart Failure Trial
VTE	venous thromboembolism
WHI	Women's Health Initiative [study]
WHO	World Health Organisation
WISDOM	Women's International Study of long Duration Oestrogen after Menopause
WOSCOPS	West of Scotland Coronary Prevention Study

JOURNALS REFERENCED
IN THIS BOOK

Am J Cardiol	American Journal of Cardiology
Ann Int Med	Annals of Internal Medicine
Ann Rheum Dis	Annals of Rheumatic Diseases
Arch Dis Child	Archives of Disease in Childhood
Arch Neurol	Archives of Neurology
Asthma	Asthma
BJGP	British Journal of General Practice
BJU Int	BJU (British Journal of Urology) International
BMJ	British Medical Journal
Can Med Assoc J	Canadian Medical Association Journal
Circulation	Circulation
Clin Evid	Clinical Evidence
Diabet Med	Diabetes Medicine
Diabetes	Diabetes
Drug Ther Bull	Drug and Therapeutics Bulletin
Eur Heart J	European Heart Journal
Gut	Gut
Heart	Heart
Int J Clin Pract	International Journal of Clinical Practice
J Card Fail	Journal of Cardiac Failure
J Clin Epidemiol	Journal of Clinical Epidemiology
J Consult Clin Psychol	Journal of Consulting and Clinical Psychology
J Fam Pract	Journal of Family Practice
J Hum Hypertens	Journal of Human Hypertension
J Natl Cancer Inst	Journal of the National Cancer Institute
J Public Health Med	Journal of Public Health Medicine
JAMA	Journal of the American Medical Association
Lancet	Lancet
N Engl J Med	New England Journal of Medicine
Osteoporos Rev	Osteoporosis Review
Stroke	Stroke
Thorax	Thorax

INDEX

PASTEST REVISION BOOKS

MRCGP Practice Papers 3rd Edition
P Ellis and R Daniels   *1 901198 66 9*
- Contains five Practice Papers
- Content of Practice Papers reflects current MRCGP examination
- Features a mixture of Extended Matching, Single Best Answer, Multiple Best Answer and Summary Completion Questions
- Full answers and detailed teaching notes
- Expert advice on successful examination technique
- Comprehensive revision index for easy reference to specific topics

Practice Papers for the MRCGP Written Paper
R Daniels et al   *1 901198 16 2*
- Contains six Practice Papers each consisting of 12 questions for the Written Paper (Paper 1 Exam)
- Features MEQs, Current Awareness and Critical Appraisal type questions to be answered in 3.5 hours
- Each Practice Paper features all question formats and includes the journal articles relating to certain questions
- Each question is accompanied by a set of suggested answers

MRCGP Modular Approach: 2nd Edition
Louise Newson and John Sandars   *1 901198 91 X*
- Thoroughly revised and updated edition
- Written specifically for the modular exam format
- New Paper 2 section featuring EMQs, SBAs and MBAs, with answers and teaching notes
- Advice on the Consulting Skills video component
- New section on Membership by Assessment
- Written by a team of Royal College examiners and recent successful exam candidates
- Also relevant for candidates taking Summative Assessment

MRCGP: Multiple Choice Revision Book
P Ellis   *1 901198 55 3*
- Over 1500 multiple choice items in EMQ, SBA and MBA formats
- Answers and detailed teaching notes
- Subject-based book enables doctors to focus on specific subject areas
- Expert advice on successful examination technique
- Comprehensive revision index for easy reference to specific topics
- Invaluable intensive practice material for all MRCGP candidates